ALL HONEST MEN

a biographical novel by

Claude Stanush
and Michele Stanush

THE PERMANENT PRESS
SAG HARBOR, NY 11963

Library of Congress Cataloging-in-Publication Data

Stanush, Claude, 1918-
    All honest men : a biographical novel / by Claude Stanush and
Michele Stanush.
          p. cm.
    ISBN 1-57962-084-1 (alk. paper)
    1. Newton, Willis, 1889—-Fiction. 2. Children of
sharecroppers—Fiction. 3. Outlaws—Fiction. 4. Gangs—Fiction.
5.Texas—Fiction. I. Stanush, Michele. II. Title.

PS3619.T4745 A78 2003
813'.6—dc21   2003005405

Printed in The United States of America

THE PERMANENT PRESS
4170 Noyac Road
Sag Harbor, NY 11963

"All men are honest by the light of the moon."

—an old Texas sheriff to J. Willis Newton

Willis as a young man

PART ONE: THE MARK OF CAIN

ONE

In my day I gone by a lot of diff'rent names, but my rightful name, the one give me by my folks, is James Willis Newton. I sign my checks "J. Willis Newton." Most people just call me "Willis." I'm eighty-eight years old now.

Lots of people that know me say I shoulda been buried up on Boot Hill, fifty or sixty years ago. They say I shoulda rotted into dirt alongside all them old-time Wild West outlaws that died when they was young, like Billy the Kid or Dynamite Dick Clifton. Well, let 'em think whatever the hell they want. I'll give 'em this much, I never thought I was gonna live this long myself—me and my partners stole so much money in our day we made that Jesse James gang look like pickpockets. I've had prison hounds after me, big hats after me, Baptists after me. I been chewed on, hung up by my thumbs, and near blown to bits by a blast of nitroglycerin.

Some of the ones that worked with me wasn't so lucky. They ain't here. But I am. And even if I am eighty-eight, I can still piss a straight line right up the side of a wall. Straight as a arrow. And I got a mind that can call up just about ever'thing that's happened to me, from the time when I got dropped in Callahan County, Texas, in the year eighteen and eighty-nine, to this very day. Some people say that's a "camera memory." All I know is I can call up near ever' detail—dates, times, what people said to each other, what they looked like, how much cotton they could snatch in a day, all of it. If somebody was packing a big .45 thumb-buster Colt with a star of Texas cut into the pearl handle, or if they had on a pair of Mex'kin cowboy boots with flowers carved into the leather, I can tell you that exact.

Some things is so much in my mind it's like they was burned there. Like what happened on the twelfth day of September, nineteen and oh-five. That was the day Mister H.L. Pike drove out to the farm to talk to Pa. I was sixteen years old then, and cotton was ten cents a pound.

***

Back in them days, ever'body in Rising Star, Texas, tipped their hats to that sorry old bastard, Mister H.L. Pike. He was the president of the Prairie State Bank, the only brick building in that whole town.

Being that Mister Pike was who he was, he rode around in a dudey horse carriage that was pulled by two high-stepping bays and glinted in the sun like it was fresh-painted yesterday. Ever'body in our end of Eastland County knowed that carriage and feared the sight of it churning up dirt towards their farms. Wasn't more'n four or five tenant farmers around them parts that didn't owe money to Mister H.L. Pike.

We owed more'n we could ever pay back.

The sun was a-blazing down that day. Hot, hot, hot. I'll never forget how hot it was. Ten of us Newtons'd been working steady in the field since the first peek of daylight. We was humped over, our backs about to break, dragging long, heavy cotton sacks behind us down them middles. Even little Joe was out with us, he was only four, stuffing lint into a little seed sack that Ma'd sewed a strap on and hung around his neck. We was all dog-tired and smelling like polecats. And our fingers was raw and bleeding; you can't snatch that cotton without sometimes grabbing the burrs that was sharp and edgy.

Them rows went on and on.

Mister Pike's visit to us Newtons that day wasn't no surprise. We'd been expecting it for some time. And a-fearing it like the other farmers, only a lot more. What was surprising was the thing he come riding in. I spotted it first, then dropped my cotton sack and run for the fence. I couldn't run fast, my ankle'd got all shot up over some trouble out near Sweetwater, but I hit for that fence as fast as that gimpy leg'd take me. Ever'body else just straightened up and looked.

What a sight! It was a black machine, near the size of a horse buggy, and it was coming down that road lickety-split, a-shaking and a-bouncing from one side to the other. Even at a quarter mile, we could hear it a-clattering. I'd seen 'em in Rising Star, bob-tailed, funny-looking things, but there wasn't no more'n three or four of 'em in the whole county, and nobody'd ever drove one out to our place before.

Wasn't half a minute, the rest of the family was a-running for the fence too. Two sunbonnets, seven floppy straw hats. And in a little bonnet, Sister Ila too. She'd been watching Baby Brother on a stretched-out cotton sack at the edge of the field. Ma yelled, "Go back, go back," but that didn't stop her, not a'tall. She kept a-coming just like the rest of 'em. It wasn't till Ma caught up with her, and give her a good whack across the backside, that she run back to the baby, bawling.

By the time the thing pulled up in front of the field, there was ten of us lined up outside the fence like birds on a tree limb.

Mister Pike didn't slow down 'til he got right to where we was standing, and then he slammed on the brakes. That machine musta skidded ten feet 'r more before it hunched and shook and shivered to a stop. Shivers shot up my spine, too, just looking at the thing, like one of them miracles outa the Bible. That could run on its own without being pulled by a horse or a mule. That had so much power in it, it could knock down a cow.

But when I looked over at Pa, I seen his cheek was a-twitching. And Ma's jaw had set tight.

"Hoddy, Mister Newton. Missus Newton." Mister Pike climbed outa his machine, took off the slicker he was wearing over his clothes, and shook off the dust. Up front, his chest puffed out over his vest like a fighting cock. And there was a frown on his face; it musta been there when he was born. Mister Pike was the kind of man that just naturally looked important. Six feet tall at least, side whiskers that was long and black, and big dark eyes that could narrow quick as a shot and drill right through you.

"Hoddy, Mister Pike." Pa's cheek was twitching a mile a minute now. "See you bought yerself a automobile."

"That I did. Cover ten times the ground, half the time, in this machine. And in my line o' work, time's money." And then Mister Pike give my old man the damndest look you ever saw, like a banker's time was pure gold but a farmer's time wasn't worth nothing, nothing a'tall.

"What kinda automobile is it?" Pa knowed he was wasting Mister Pike's time.

"They call it a 'Curved Dash Oldsmobile.' Got seven horsepower." Mister Pike pulled his watch out of his vest pocket and flipped open the lid. "But really, Mister Newton, I don't have time right now to go on about my automobile."

Hell, that's all I wanted them to do—to go on talking about that machine. I moved around to the side of it and eyeballed it up and down, side to side. The body was painted black as pitch, except for the spokes of the wheels and the seat boxes, which was a bright, glossy red. Where the driver set, there was a long metal rod that come outa the floor to steer with, and hooked to the end of that rod was a little brass horn that honked if you squeezed a black rubber bulb. On the front end of the automobile, there was two brass lamps sticking out round and proud, like the breasts on a lady. Wasn't no engine there, though. The black metal body come up right in front of the driver's feet and then curved towards him into a roll. But the thing's hind-end was big and square, like a box, and I figured that's where the workings was.

At the same time my eyes was glued to that machine, my ear was cocked to Mister Pike and my old man.

"Mister Newton, I'm not happy over this crop o' yours," Mister Pike was saying. "How much you think you'll make?"

"Quarter bale t' the acre. Maybe not that much." Pa said it real casual-like, like he was talking to us kids. "It's the land. Wore-out. No life in it."

"The land!" Mister Pike's voice went up. "If it's the land, Mister Newton, how do you explain those crops over there?"

I peeled my eyes offa his Oldsmobile and looked at where his finger was pointing. To Gib McCutcheon's land, south of us.

"And there?" He was pointing west of us, to Tom Fonski's patch.

"And there?" He was pointing north of us, to Rob Roberts' patch.

"And there?" He was pointing east of us, to Fess Johnson's patch.

Pa hiked up his pants. "Cain't speak for them other farmers," he said. "I c'n only speak for myself. And all I know is, this land here's cottoned out. Besides which, them other farmers all got a good rain in June. I didn't get a drop."

"You telling me all of 'em got rain but you, Mister Newton?"

"That's just what I'm saying. Them summer storms can be damn queer."

"Too bad. Let me get my pad out here and figure it." Mister Pike pulled a pad and a pencil outa his coat pocket. "Quarter bale to the acre. Ten cents a pound, that's $12.50 an acre. Eighty acres at $12.50 is $1,000."

I hated the sound of that pencil scratching on that paper.

"My share's $400," Mister Pike went on, "assuming you and your family pick that cotton clean, and assuming you don't get hit by rain 'r hail before the crop's in. And those'r big 'ifs', Mister Newton. You know I already put out more'n $300 on seed and weevil dust. Add on $250 credit for food, already gone. Add to that, twenty percent interest on your loan."

Hard numbers, I remember ever' one.

Now Mister Pike was squinting his eyes at his pad and asking my old man who was gonna pay the taxes on that land if them numbers wasn't gonna add up. "I don't think I need to be doing business with you anymore, Mister Newton," Mister Pike said to Pa. "No sir. You're gonna have to move on."

"Yeah, well, I wasn't gonna stay here next year no way." Pa hiked up his pants again. "No use working yourself to death trying to make a living outa wore-out land. Already found me another place. Scurry County."

Scurry County. I knowed it. Erath County. Callahan County. Eastland County. Pa never stayed nowhere more'n one year. He was one of them cyclone farmers. Always moving, always hunting for honey ponds and fritter trees, for God's Country. Sometimes we just moved over the fence, but we always moved.

"Settle up 'fore you go," Mister Pike said. "Good-day to you. Mister Newton, Missus Newton."

He climbed back into the automobile and set hisself down on that black leather seat.

Pa didn't say nothing.

"Good-day," said Ma. Her whole body sagged. And it was a big body, 'cause Ma was tall for a woman, and she had bulk, arms that bulged outa her sleeves like hog thighs. I hated it, her being shamed this way. That's how come, when Mister Pike looked over at me and told me to give him a crank, I didn't move.

"I said, I need a crank, son." Mister Pike said it again. "You hear me?"

Ma's eyes shot over. I seen her look. I still didn't say nothing, but I did lean over and grab that black iron crank. Then I squeezed it so tight my knuckles went white. I wanted to spin that crank so hard and so rough it'd snap plumb off. I wouldn't a-minded a whit if Mister Pike had to walk all them seven and a half miles back to Rising Star.

Mister Pike moved a little stick by the steering rod.

"Watch that thing," he said. "I been having some trouble with it. It might spin on back and break your arm. When you turn it, be sure to keep it going."

"Don't you worry." I pressed my lips together and give that crank the hardest twist I could muster. WHAMMO! It give a kick and spun right on back the other way around. If I hadn't a-let go quick, it woulda broke my arm for sure. Mister Pike shook his head, moved that little stick again, and nodded at me. I stiffed up my arm muscle and spun. BANGO! This time something caught and the whole machine started a-shuddering. And when the whole machine started a-shuddering, the crank started a-shuddering, and when the crank started a-shuddering, my fingers that was still wrapped around the handle started a-shuddering too. That shudder raced right up my arm and through my chest and down my legs clear to the end of my toes.

Damn! That automobile had power!

Mister Pike pulled on another stick and the machine give a backfire like a mule farting. I quick let go of the crank and hopped outa the way. Mister Pike turned the long rod that was for steering, and that Oldsmobile made a big wide circle in front of us and headed on back the way it come, a-bouncing and a-jumping from one rut to the other. We watched until it got swallowed up in a cloud of sandy brown dust.

Nobody said a word. We just turned around and walked back to the field and went to picking.

***

Cotton cotton cotton cotton cotton, ever'where I looked, no end to it.

Right hand...left hand...

I couldn't get that automobile outa my head. That shudder...that clatter...that cloud of brown dust a-puffing out into the hot, hot air, and a-whipping around like a cyclone...and how that machine had the power of seven galloping horses...Seven of 'em! Way off, I could still see Mister Pike's cloud of dust, and it was getting longer, and longer, and longer.

Right left...left right...

I wasn't going nowhere...only down one row, up the other...my back was bent, the strap of that sack looped over my shoulder, the veins in my neck a-popping. I jerked them soft white puffs outa them sharp sticky burrs and fed 'em into the long canvas sack a-dragging ten feet behind me and getting fatter, and fatter, and heavier, and HEAVIER! Much as I hated cotton picking, it was something I was good at. Picked two rows a time, while most folks only did one. My fingers was just natural-born fast, fast as a cat's paw.

Right hand...left hand...

Godamighty it was hot! Like the whole field was the inside of one big blazing oven. I felt like a biscuit left in that oven too damn long, dry and hard and crusty, not a drop of moisture left in me. I needed to straighten up to give my shot-up foot a rest, and get the kinks outa my spine. I took the straw hat offa the back of my head to let some air in, but by then it was Pa—not that car—that was stuck in my mind like a cockleburr.

Ever'body said Pa was a good man, but nobody could figure out what he was good for... Go-day, come-day, God-give Sunday, that was Pa. Little bacon, white gravy and bread, he was satisfied. Couldn't get him outa my mind. Some people thought he was a good man 'cause if he borrowed five dollars he was apt to give you ten dollars back. Had to be good for something, but what?

All I could see of him, from the rear, was his big straw hat, faded blue shirt, drawstring pants. Picking one row at a time. One-Row Newton. One thing at a time. Wasn't never in no hurry though even if he tried, he couldna kept up with me. I moved fast as a jackrabbit, no matter where or how I was a-moving. That's why neighbors needing a extra hand wanted me, not him, to grub 'r plow 'r thin 'r pick...

Right hand...left hand...

Ever'body else—Ma, Joe, Jess, Dolly, Bill, Tull, Bud, Dock—was all humped over like they was praying. Except for Baby Brother in the washtub, at the end of the field, and Sister Ila, taking care of Baby Brother by digging in the dirt with a stick after doodlebugs. When I was five, watching Dock in the washtub, I dug in the dirt too and thought about how when I growed up...

I was gonna be a gin-stand man like Hank Tobin who kept the cotton moving through the blades where the wheels was a-whirling and the belts was a-slapping and the engine was a-rattling, sucking

12

up that cotton from them high-slatted wagons, and when one man's cotton was finished Hank'd stand in the second-story window and yell "All Out!" and another wagon'd drive up....

But I didn't know what I wanted no more.

Right left...left right...

Goddamn!

I near put my hand in the mouth of that devil!

***

It was thick as my fist, that diamondback rattler was. Curled up around the bottom of the plant, hugging it for shade. I could almost see it a-panting.

I'd just turned a row and was bending down to snatch the first cotton outa the first burr on the next row when I heard them rattles a-buzzing. Two seconds later, my hand woulda stuck plumb between his fangs.

"Jess! Dock! Joe!"

They all had their backs bent.

"Hey-a, git over here!"

They come over, and they all whistled at how big it was, and how droopy it was. I went over to the wagon to get a hoe. Jess said he wanted to beat it dead so he could make him a bronc-rider's belt outa the skin. But it was Dock that reached over and grabbed the hoe outa my hand.

"Lemme take a whack at it, lemme take a whack at it," he said. He was trembling all over.

Dock was fourteen, two years younger'n me. When he was ten, he'd got bit on the head by a mad coyote. It'd happened down in South Texas, where Pa'd took us that one spring, hunting for God's Country. We was all sleeping out on the ground, on pallets, when something licked Dock on the head, then bit him. Pa had to take him all the way to Austin to get the shots. But ever' since, when Dock got worked up, he was apt to tremble and shake his head and let fly with a little slobber. It wasn't foam that come outa his mouth. Just a little flying slobber.

"Lemme take a whack at it!" Dock said it again. "I think it's got them rabies. Look at its eyes."

I grabbed the hoe back.

"Ain't no such thing as a mad snake, Dock," I said. "It's jus' had too much sun."

I poked at the snake. It jerked its head back. Wilted as it was, it was gonna strike.

I raised up that hoe and ragged back on my heels and WHAM! I come down on that snake so hard its head popped clear offa its body and flied six feet to the south. Its tail was still a-rattling.

"Fool snake," I said. "If it'd wanted some shade, it shoulda crawled over across the fence."

"What d'ya mean by that, Willis?" Pa'd come over to see why we'd all stopped picking and now his eyes had fire in 'em. He knowed darned well what I meant. "Sure, McCutcheon's cotton has got a lotta leaves," he said, "but down at the gin they don't pay for leaves."

"Hell's fire, Pa. Ten more minutes and that snake woulda got sunstroke." I couldn't help myself. "When one outa three of your seeds don't even come up..."

Pa's cheek was twitching again. "What in damnation d'ya know about planting cotton, Willis?"

"Even Ila'd know we planted too shallow. Want me to show you some o' that rotted seed?"

Wham! I seen it coming. I didn't even have time to duck. Right across my face. It stung.

It took ever'thing in me to keep from jumping Pa and throwing him to the ground, making him eat some of that brown sandy dirt. I was strong enough to do it. And I was mad enough to do it. And I'd a-done it too if it'd been anybody else except my old man. Ma didn't say or do nothing. Only stood there, her shoulders kinda slumped, her breasts big and full as a Jersey cow's, sagging almost to her waist. She was still nursing Baby Brother. She shoulda weaned him, her nipples was sore and scabby. But the baby was gonna be her last, she told us. Ma knowed I was right about the planting, but maybe she thought I'd gone too far.

"You're too smart for your britches, Willis," Pa said. Now he was pacing back 'n fro. "When we go t' Scurry County, we'll make two bales t' the acre. You never seen such good black land. Black as a Brazos Bottom nigger. If we don't make two bales t' the acre I'll eat this hat."

He yanked the straw hat offa his head and held it up. The sweat was rolling down his cheeks.

Pa was kinda short for a man like Ma was kinda tall for a

woman. But he wasn't bad-looking when his cheek wasn't twitching. He had thick hair that was gray like iron, and a thick gray mustache and a little bush of a beard below the lip. It was only alongside somebody like Ma that he looked stumpy.

In the field he always carried a old rag in his back pocket, to wipe the sweat off his face. He pulled it out. The sweat kept a-rolling.

***

That night, while I was soaping my face at the wash bucket, Pa come up to me. He didn't say nothing about the slapping, that he was sorry he done it, but his face looked kinda draggy. "My head's aching like someone cracked me with a mesquite log," was all he said.

I didn't look up at him. I just kept rubbing yellow lye soap around and around my face in big circles.

"You could take some calomel for that head." There was a lot of things Pa coulda done to make things better.

"Ain't a mite in the house."

No, and not a mite of flour 'r coffee 'r bacon neither. For three weeks we'd been living offa fried squirrels and jackrabbits and even possums and coons that me and the other boys'd shot with our .22s. Ma'd been raising some chickens, but coons and hawks'd got a lot of 'em and the rest we found one morning with their legs up in the air, dead from some kind of sickness.

Pa went on: "I was gonna ask Mister Pike for a little more credit at the store, but weren't no use, him talking the way he did. I tell you, Willis, banks is the scourge of the Earth. Land companies, too. I dunno what that war over the niggers did but make us all slaves."

"McCutcheon and them," I said, "they ain't gonna be chewing too much gristle this year."

Pa snorted. "Lucky with that rain, all that was. But what'cha think they gonna have left over when Pike's done with 'em? Hundred-fifty dollars, I'd say. Maybe hundred-seventy five. Won't be enough to spit at."

I rinsed my face and picked up a towel and looked at my old man outa the corner of my eye.

"Hey, Pa," I said, "what'd you think of that automobile?"

"Show-offy thing. Makes me sick."

15

"Ain't just show," I said back, "if it takes that old boy over ten times the ground, half the time. Makes him a lot more money that-a-way."

"Lemme tell you what the Bible says about money, Willis." Pa snorted again. "It's the root of all evil, what it is. That's what the Bible says about money."

I didn't see that a'tall. Seemed to me the reason Pa was so down on money, he didn't have none. "No need pickin' cotton, then," I said, "if money's so plumb evil."

"Where'd you get that sass from, Willis?" Pa shot me a look. "You got more sass in you than all your brothers put together, an' half your sisters, too. You take my word for it — folks'd be a lot better off if they quit messing with money and went back to trading, like when I was a boy. Mister Pike c'n be damned! Come Monday, me and you and Dock 'r going in to Trade Day."

I knowed that was coming. "Trade Day" was the first Monday of every month in Rising Star, like in most of the other towns in West Texas. On Trade Day, you took things into town that you didn't want no more—horses, wagons, chickens, plows, whatever—and traded 'em for things you did want. Or tried to. Pa could get more lathered up over Trade Day than a revival preacher over Glory up yonder, by and by.

"Yeah, Mister Pike c'n be damned." Pa said it again. "An' thank God for Trade Day."

What's he thanking God for?, I thought. He's already traded off our two best plows, and Ma's milk cow, and—

—and what for?

—for two old buzzard-bait horses.

"What we got to trade besides them plugs?" I pointed out the window, towards two jug-headed horses standing just outside the yard gate, their ribs sticking out like the slats in a fence. They was such sorry horses they'd hardly lifted their heads when Mister Pike's machine had come a-roaring and a-rattling down our road. A respectable horse woulda reared or bolted, or both. Pa's plugs just stood there.

"They ain't plugs! Them horses 'r good breeds." Now Pa was mad all over again. "Trouble with you, Willis, you think you know ever'thing, and you don't know nothing. Yessir, them horses 'r good breeds. Jus' look at that one's withers. All they need is a little corn..."

16

A little corn, shit. He poured corn into 'em, trying to make 'em into working horses, when the animals that really did the work—our two poor mules—got nothing but grass and weeds. And no telling how many hours Pa spent with a bacon rind rubbing the skinny asses on them horses, trying to get 'em to shine. But no matter what he did they always stayed hidebound. They was just sorry horses. Pa was the worst horse trader in the whole state of Texas.

"If you ain't gonna take in them plugs," I said, "what'cha gonna trade?"

"I'll find something." Pa's eyes shifted around. "There's always something somebody wants."

TWO

Early the next Monday, it was just peeping daylight, me and Dock loaded Ma's Singer sewing machine into the back of our wagon. Ma stood in the doorway watching us. There wasn't a tear in her eyes. But her jaw looked tighter even than when Mister Pike come.

"Pa shoulda been the woman, and I shoulda been the man," she said to me. "Then maybe we'd a-got somewheres."

That sewing machine was Ma's pride and joy. She'd bought it for two dollars from a traveling salesman, it was used, outa her own egg money. Before Ma had that Singer, she'd sewed ever'thing on her fingers. For two grownups and eleven kids! She'd sit sagged in that old rocking chair, the cloth spread out over her lap, her needle going in....and....out, in....and....out. When Ma got that machine, it was like the load of a elephant'd been lifted off her back. It had a foot pedal, and when she pumped it up and down, it'd go lickety-split, lickety-split....

I was standing right next to Ma that morning when Pa'd told her he was gonna take it in. "If you c'n think of anything else to take, lemme know," Pa'd said to Ma. "We cain't give up no more plows, otherwise we gotta give up farming."

That was the truth. God's awful truth.

"Go ahead and take it." Ma was kneading dough she'd made from flour she'd walked all the way over to the McCutcheon's to borrow. Neighbors was pretty helpful to each other them days, but Ma said she could hardly look 'em in the eyes no more, she was so ashamed about it, always borrowing, always borrowing.

And then Ma slammed that dough down on that table so hard they musta heard it all the way to Rising Star. "But if you're gonna take my machine in, Jim," she said, "you're gonna take in them two horses. And you bring back another horse, we're gonna eat it."

Pa knowed that Ma meant business. So soon as we loaded up

Janetta Pecos "Ma" Newton

that Singer, we tied both them plug horses behind our wagon.

Our mules was pokey, and you'd be pokey too if you was a mule and had to pull a wagon and two horses and live on grass and weeds instead of corn. By the time we got to Rising Star, the whole town was a-bustling. Rising Star wasn't too different from most other small Texas towns back then. The streets was dirt with deep old wagon ruts criss-crossing all over 'em. Horses and mules made little rivers of piss and little hills of dung all over them streets, and when you walked across 'em, you had to watch your step and swish away the flies. There was as many Baptists and Methodists as there was flies in Rising Star, and so there wasn't no saloons on Main Street. But there was five churches, a couple of livery stables, a small hotel, a couple of blacksmith shops, a barber shop, two banks, and two general merchandise stores that sold ever'thing from oats to coffins to Carter's Little Liver Pills.

First place we went to was Hermann's General Store, and Mister Hermann, a big fat German, oohed and "yah-yahed" over Ma's sewing machine and give us ten pounds of flour and two pounds of coffee and four pounds of bacon for it. And then Pa went and traded his two plugs for six sacks of corn and, well, one new gimpy horse. My old man couldn't help hisself. He was horse-crazy. He hated cows, God knows why. Grandma give us a milk cow one time and right away Pa traded her off for a horse. He just couldn't live without a horse. Only this new wheybelly was even scrawnier'n the last two. Dock shook his head when he seen that horse and whispered to me so Pa couldn't hear, "That plug's already dead. He jest won't lie down."

Right before we headed back for home, me and Dock left Pa to trade some wild-bee honey for two jackknives, and Pa left the wagon to jaw with some old boys standing on a corner. Well, don't you know it, that old horse, he was tied to a wheel on that wagon, he come right on back to life. He raised his head and stretched his neck over the sideboard and ate up half a sack of the corn that Pa'd just bought.

When we finally got home, and Ma seen that sorry horse, she didn't say nothing right off. Even after Dock blabbered about the corn. She fed us a good supper and give us fresh-baked biscuits from the flour. Afterwards, like she always did, she told the kids a story from the Bible and then one of her Wild West outlaw tales. Ma read ever' outlaw story that come along outa them dime magazines that

Jim "Pa" Newton

was passed from farm to farm. And being that she had a camera memory, like me, she knowed 'em all by heart, word for word—like about the James boys, or the Kid, or Dirty-Face Charley, or Butcher-Knife Bill. The story that night was about Lee Sage, sometimes knowed as Wampus Cat.

But while Ma was telling about Wampus Cat, I seen something strange. Her eyes, which was most times big and round, narrowed down to slits and her voice dropped so low I could hardly make out what she was saying. Then, after all the other kids'd gone off to bed, and it was only me left, she picked up one of them outlaw magazines from offa the floor and set it on top of her mother's Bible and said something that knocked me square in the chest. "You know, Willis, if I was a man, I guess I'da been a outlaw myself."

***

It was the next day, when we was out picking cotton again and my whole back was aching like somebody'd hammered on it with a plank, I straightened up a little to get the kinks outa my spine, and who should I see riding into our field but Eddie Munson. He was on a bareback mule, a big old gray thing, and he was a-coming on at a jog. Eddie was eighteen, two years older'n me, only he didn't look much like a man yet. He was a real string bean. His legs was so long and skinny they was swinging to and fro like somebody at the end of a hangman's rope. And that mule's ears was a-flopping back and forth with each jog, keeping time with Eddie's legs.

I could hardly believe what I was seeing. It wasn't six weeks before that Eddie'd run off from his Pa's farm, nobody'd knowed where to.

"Whoa, Eddie!" I yelled, and I pulled my hat offa my head and waved it in the air. Was he headed home?

The Munson family lived about five miles to the south of us. They was working somebody else's land, like us. Except they had better mules and they had a milk cow and their kids went to school. Old Man Munson was a pretty good farmer and this year his cotton'd started a-breaking open like popcorn in late July. Them bolls was big and full, and before Eddie run off, I never seen nobody so happy as Old Man Munson, 'cause to a cotton farmer that's been working day-break to nighttime—plowing, planting, chopping 'n cultivating, putting up with too much rain or not enough, fighting ever' kind of bug and worm you can think of, or setting quiet in his house time and time again while hail storms knocked ever'thing down outside—there ain't nothing prettier in the whole world than cotton bolls a-popping open, telling him, finally, in spite of ever'thing, he's got a crop.

That just goes to show how diff'rent kids think from their folks. All them white bolls made Eddie sick at his stomach. When he seen that big, pretty crop, he knowed there wasn't gonna be no more fishing, no more swimming, no more hunting. Just hard backbreaking work in that patch. Ever'body in a family back then was expected to pull their share. Ever'body eats, ever'body works. Wasn't no arguing about it. And that's how come Eddie run off like he done. But now here he was, clomping right up to me.

"How'r ya doing, Willis?" He squinted down at my shot-up foot. "What'd you do t'that foot?"

"Don't matter," I said back. "Your old man's about to skin you for boot leather, Eddie. Where the hell you been?"

"You tell me what's wrong with that foot, I'll tell you where I been."

I give him a smile and I told him how the Sweetwater sheriff plugged me after some trouble between my brother Jess and Pa's brother, Uncle Henry. Jess'd been saying things about one of Uncle Henry's girls, and Uncle Henry said they was damn lies, and he throwed a stick of cordwood at Jess. That made me throw a big rock at Uncle Henry, and that rock knocked him offa his wagon and when he fell he banged his head on the ground and he got mad and set the sheriff on me.

"I seen the dirt fly right next to my foot," I said. "Big lead bullet."

Eddie shook his head. He knowed I never did walk if I could run, and he knowed I never let my uncle give hell to my brothers. My brother Jess was two years older'n me, but he was a easy, lazy tumbleweed that hardly ever stood up for hisself. And my Uncle Henry was meaner'n dirt.

"Okay," I said, "that's my story. What's yours?"

He didn't say nothing right off. Just lifted up one skinny leg and crooked it over the mule's withers like you do when you want to give yourself a rest. That mule looked like it was glad to be resting itself and not a-jogging in that hot sun, it slumped its back and closed its eyes like it was gonna take a nap. I kept a-looking at Eddie's face, trying to figure out what he was up to. He had a thin face, with lots of freckles, and a sandy mustache that he was real proud of. His face didn't tell me a thing.

"C'mon, Eddie. Where you been?"

I could tell there wasn't nothing Eddie wanted more'n to tell me. He seemed kinda tickled with hisself. Only before he said anything, he throwed his eyes this-a-way and that-a-way, like he was scared somebody'd hear him.

"I been in Abilene," he said low. "Only now I'm running from the laws. Near killed a man."

Near killed a man? Skinny old Eddie?

"Don't blow me no windies, Eddie."

"Ain't no windy, Willis." He tugged on his mustache and hiked up his eyebrows. "Soon's I got to Abilene, see, I got me a job at the yards. Shoveling dung. And ever'thing was going fine 'til it come Trade Day. That's when I run across some brass knucks. Oh, boy, was they pretty! Shiny as ever'thing. I bought 'em. Then it come Saturday night, see. I got to drinking with this old boy from the yards, he went to calling me some things, I ain't gonna say what, and before I knowed it, them brass knucks'd hopped right on outa my pocket."

Eddie punched the air to show me how he socked that old boy.

"Knocked him cold. *Cold!* Eee-ah! I never knowed how hard them brass knucks is. Didn't wait for the law to show up. Jus' jumped on Julep here and blowed."

I shoulda knowed it. Eddie was green when it come to drinking whiskey. That poison can make a man plain stupid.

"What'cha gonna do now?" I asked.

"Ain't going home. 'S'all I know."

"Wouldn't if I was you."

He shrugged his shoulders. "I liked running off from my old man, and I'll be happy t'stay run-off."

Well, that I understood.

I'd run off before myself, lots of times. Sooner or later, I always come back home. But I loved that feeling, that run-off feeling. I'd sneak out in the middle of the night, hop a freight, go wherever it was going—east, west, north, south, I didn't care. Lots of times, one of them dirty-rat brakemen'd spot me and try to knock me off with a rock, or hit me with one of them hard oak brake clubs, but soon as I was old enough to have sense, I started packing me a little pistol.

They didn't knock me off after that.

One of the best times I ever run off, it was the first day of June, and I'd hopped a freight to out near Thurber, forty miles to the north-east, where the soil is clay and cakey and red. It was black as pitch when I hopped offa that train, but pretty soon a thin line of red light begun stretching out to the east and the reddest ball of a sun I ever seen come peeping up over the horizon. Far as I could see, ever'thing went from dead black to red—the red sun, that ball of fire, rising up over a field of red dirt, a-glinting in the first light of day, and, right in front of me, a big mound of dirt that'd blowed up agin a fence-line. All you could see of that fence was one shiny wire sticking up.

I looked at that little shiny fence wire sticking up outa that red mound, and I looked at all that red dirt stretching out to forever, and I looked at that old red fire-ball of a sun, and there was just some-thing about it. I said to myself, "Now, that's a picture I'll never for-get." And I never have. Ever' time it come the first day of June, for near seventy-five years, I've thought on that sun.

All of a sudden, it was like Eddie's mule had kicked me in the head. I looked over at Pa. He was busy with his one row, humped over, his back to us. I leaned over to Eddie and dropped my voice: "I'm coming with you."

Eddie looked over at Pa. "Don't know."

"C'mon. Let's go," I said. "Pa couldn't chase down a slug if it was stuck on his big toe."

Eddie dropped his leg off the mule's withers. He looked exactly like a bareback Injin now, long skinny legs dangling down. "Hop on, then!"

THREE

That was my first real getaway. On Eddie Munson's slow old mule.

We headed west, towards where the sun sets. Only it wasn't long before I begun to wonder just what I was getting away from.

On all sides, ever'where I looked, there was white, white, white.

There was pickers in ever' patch, sometimes as many as ten or fifteen. They was mostly farm families, kids and grandfolks, too, with sometimes neighbors helping out. Only the biggest farmers could afford to hire hands. Some of the pickers was stooped over as they moved on down the rows. That's how us Newtons did it. Others of 'em was shuffling along on their knees. That's how our neighbors, the McCutcheons, did it. Stoopers went faster, but their backs was more likely to ache. 'Course, if you picked on your knees, you had to pad 'em good with cotton over leather to keep your kneecaps from getting ground down to chalk.

No matter which way the pickers was working, their heads was down, you can't pick cotton without looking at it. But if they was close to the road, Eddie and me'd give out with a "hi-i-i-yaaaaa," and they'd straighten up and look to see who was yelling, and when they seen us, they'd give a wave. You could tell they was glad somebody had give 'em a break from what they was doing, and we'd wave back, and I'd give that mule a kick, to show off a little.

At first, before we'd covered much ground, I kept twisting around to make sure we wasn't getting trailed.

"Eddie," I said. "My old man reads sign."

Eddie's head spun around on his skinny neck. "I thought you wasn't worried about your Pa."

I shrugged. "He can track a rabbit."

"Your Pa?"

"He used to be a cowboy. He's just pokey. But if he catches us, he's gonna be hot."

"Oh, hell, Willis! You telling me that now?"

"We can lose him. See that road, up yonder?" I pointed to a dirt road a hundred feet ahead of us. "Let's hit on down that one. We'll light a shuck over to Onion Creek, wade upstream, and get rid of our tracks. Then we can circle on back and head on out."

"Where'll we go then?" Eddie asked.

"Let's go to Fort Worth."

Eddie's head spun around again. *"Fort Worth?"*

"Why not? Jess says it's Sin City up there. He's been."

"I've sinned already, Willis. I just want a job."

"You're yeller."

"Look, if we go to Fort Worth, we couldn't sin the way we'd wanta sin. It costs money, that kinda sinning. And the only jobs they got up there 'r slinging dung at the yards. You wanta sling dung?"

"You done it in Abilene."

"Yeah, and look where it got me. I say we head on over to Stephenville."

"Stephenville?"

"Pickers 'r getting six bits a hundred there. I heard it from four of 'em."

I groaned. "Goddammit Eddie, I ain't going nowhere they're picking cotton."

"Well, you see anything 'sides cotton, you lemme know." He waved his hand around in a circle. "And you know any other kind o' work this time o' year, other'n slinging dung, lemme know that too."

To tell you the truth, I didn't know. Them days, cotton was about the only crop in Texas a farmer could get cash money for, and cash money was what most ever'body wanted, and needed. I started to say maybe we could get a job at a gin stand, like Hank Tobin, but I stopped myself. Gin jobs didn't pay a helluva lot more'n picking cotton, and, to my mind, the pay wasn't worth the risk. Ever' cotton town in Texas had at least two or three one-armed men in 'em from gin accidents. Poor old Griff Henson! He lost both of his arms. He was reaching in to clean out some lint one day, and he couldn't see too well what he was doing, and the saws come over and sliced off both his arms. Right above the elbows. Griff figured out how to keep on working, though. He'd plow by throwing the reins of the mule around his neck, and then, with the stumps of his arms, he'd pull them reins to the right or to the left. When I was ten, Pa used to hire me out to help Griff, at twenty-five cents a day. Mostly I had to feed him at lunch-time and give him some water when he was thirsty. I liked Griff, I did. He was a good-natured old boy, in spite of what'd happened to him. What I hated most about that job was having to open Griff's pants and pull out his pecker when he wanted to piss. Worse'n that, I had to wipe his ass with a corncob.

"Look at it this way, Willis," Eddie said to me. "It's a helluva lot better picking cotton for somebody for six bits a hundred than picking it for your old man for nothing."

***

By the time we got to Stephenville, sweat had drained all the water outa us and our stomachs was flapping up against our backbones. When we went to the first gin in town, we seen cotton wagons lined up for near half a mile, and we figured it'd be no problem a'tall getting a job. We was wrong. Every farmer said nothing doing, they had plenty of pickers. Bad news, too, they was paying only four bits a hundred, even less'n Rising Star.

I was so hacked at Eddie, I like to gutted him. "You ain't no better'n a mud cat, boy," I said. "Somebody throws you a line, you swallow it whole. We don't get something to eat quick, I'm gonna drop dead."

But when we hit on over to the other gin in town, the farmers waiting in the wagons give us the same story. I went into the office of the gin and begged the owner for a job, any kind. I told him we hadn't ate since yesterday morning.

"Where you boys from?" the man asked, kinda suspicious-like.

"Rising Star."

"Best advice I can give you is go back where you come from."

Well, we was standing around, my mind a-churning over what to do next, both our stomachs a-growling, when we had a change in our luck. Over come a big fat farmer the size of Jonah's whale in the Bible. He asked if we wanted a job and I like to hugged him. Which woulda been a hard thing to do.

" 'Course," the fat man said, tying Eddie's mule to the back of his wagon, "I'm gonna expect you to stay with me 'til the end of the season. And your pay's forty cents a hundred."

"Forty cents?" Eddie reached over to untie his mule. "Ever'body else's paying four bits."

"Take it or leave it. Can't pay no more."

Eddie give me a look and I give the farmer a look. That fella was so big and round that just climbing up onto his wagon made him huff and pant and grunt. Somebody at his place must be cooking good meals.

I hooked my foot in the side of the wagon. "Git on in," I said to Eddie.

***

The farmer's name was Jonathan Mallory. Of course, we called him "Mister Mallory" when we was talking to his face. Like Eddie said, working for somebody for something, no matter how little, is a lot better'n working for your old man for nothing. To give the boar his due, Old Man Mallory had good cotton, full and silky to the hand, and I figured if I worked hard I could have me a nice chunk of money by the end of the season.

In fact, I couldn't wait to get into the field at the first crack of day, when I'd hit them tall pretty green plants and the dew'd get all over my face and hands and clothes until I was as wet as if I'd a-jumped into a mule trough. I woulda worked seven days a week if they'd let me. But the Mallorys was church people and they wouldn't allow us to work on the Lord's Day.

"Us" means four men pickers and three girls. The men lived in the hay loft and was fed three a day by Missus Mallory. Beans, potatoes, eggs, hard bread, a little meat or chicken once a day—not the best-tasting stuff but plenty of it. No wonder Missus Mallory looked like her husband's twin. Under her chin there was at least half a dozen layers of hog fat.

The girl pickers come from neighbor farms and went home at night. I figured Old Man Mallory hired 'em because he could get 'em even cheaper'n the men. Two of the girls was thick-waisted and ugly as sin, with a lot of hair on their legs. But the other one was a looker, pretty and full and fresh as the Mallory's cotton, big old breasts poking out in front like musk melons. Her name was Carrie Sikes. The way she walked and talked and looked at you was enough to make the Devil hisself turn somersaults. I couldn't keep my eyes offa her.

After a while me and Carrie was working further and further away from all the others, 'til we was so far off we could flop down in that high cotton and start hugging and kissing. Even with all the

29

sweat on her she tasted and smelled sweet as honeysuckle and she got me more worked up than I ever been in my life. And that's when I first come down with the ailment. It's what the cowboys call getting "skirt-tied."

**

All in all, I stayed around Stephenville more'n a year. That girl kept me guessing, but she knowed just what to do and just what to say to make me stick around and hope for more. So that's what I done, stuck around, picking cotton and plowing cotton and planting cotton and thinning cotton and chopping cotton, and picking cotton again. Eddie stuck around too. For him, it was just for the hell of it. Between the cotton seasons, we got us bad jobs in Stephenville, mending picket fences, or washing dishes at the café. But always when Old Man Mallory called for us, we'd be back on his farm.

Then something happened that changed ever'thing.

One Saturday morning the Mallorys went to town and bought theirselves a automobile: a Franklin Light Roadster. I couldn't take my eyes offa it. It didn't look quite as much like a buggy as Mister Pike's Oldsmobile. The engine was in the front, not in the back, and there was a big round steering wheel, not just a rod. The company that made them Roadsters said they was good at climbing hills and didn't "puff or snort."

The fat man, of course, didn't know much about operating a automobile. At first, to show it off and how proud he was of it, he tried to drive it ever'where around the place, out to the fields where we was working, and round the pastures where the cows and horses was. One time, when he was coming out to the field, he couldn't stop and he went right into the cotton and mowed down two rows of plants before the runaway machine bumped and jerked to a stop.

Later, to top things off, Old Man Mallory was tearing around the house, practicing turns, when his wife's favorite laying hen come trotting right on across the yard, "cluck, cluck, cluck." Well, that Franklin Light Roadster plowed right over that hen and stopped her clucking cold. Old Man Mallory started calling that dead chicken ever' bad cuss-word he knowed, and Missus Mallory come rushing outside and started a-crying, more about her husband's being a religious man and using them words than about the flat hen.

But it wasn't just the automobile that had me worked up. It was also the Mallorys' old horse buggy. They'd put the buggy away in a far corner of the barn and hung up the harness on nails like they never thought they was gonna use that stuff ever again. I'd never got very excited over the Mallorys' buggy before. But thinking about that buggy as *my* buggy, well, that made all the diff'rence. Maybe, I thought to myself, they'd sell me the old buggy cheap, now that they didn't need it no more.

"You want it, huh?" Old Man Mallory said when I asked him. "Damn fine, that buggy. Chase and Smith, Baltimore. And I always kept it top-notch. But a buggy's no good without a horse."

"Won't need no horse. I'll use Julep. Eddie don't mind."

"Well, hundred dollars, then. Not a penny less. Twenty down, work off the rest."

Greedy son-of-a-bitch! He knowed how much I wanted that buggy. And he made me sign a paper saying I was legally binded to pay that hundred dollars. But I signed it. Then I spent some of my picking money for paint and varnish and oil, and when I got through with that buggy it was pretty and shiny as the carriage Mister Pike used to drive. Least, I thought so when I showed it finally to Carrie and asked her if she'd like to take a drive with me come Sunday.

"Well, maybe."

It was enough to take the starch outa any man. All this time she's been hugging and kissing me ever' chance we got, and now she says, "Well, maybe."

I looked at Carrie like I didn't know her.

"Where'll we go?" she asked.

"Oh, around. Maybe take it down by Smokey Creek, have us a little picnic supper. Build a fire."

"Well, lemme think." She kept running her tongue over the edge of her lips. I could hardly stand it, the suspense and all and me watching that mouth of hers twist and turn, them lips so wet and cherry ripe.

"No, I don't think I c'n do that," she said finally.

"Why not?"

"Well, for one thing, Daddy wouldn't want me doing that. Too much temptation, us being down there by ourselves."

"Temptation?" I couldn't believe what she was telling me.

"You know what I mean," she said. "If you wanta take me some place come Sunday, why don't you take me into Stephenville? They got revival meetings ever' Sunday for the next month. Preaching and

Bible at ten o'clock."

Goddamn Baptists!

Sunday morning I took Carrie into Stephenville. I couldn't stand not being with her that day. The revival meeting was in a tent they'd set up on a vacant lot in the middle of town, with benches and chairs for the people to set down on. The preacher was a skinny, horse-faced man and he pounded his fists and sang hymns and ever' so often he'd holler: "Come on home to Jesus, sinners! Come on home to Jesus!" And that'd set the people to a-hollering back: "Jesus, I'm a-coming home! I'm a-coming home!" and some of 'em was going into fainting spells and falling down on the ground.

I spent most of the meeting scraping dirt out from under my fingernails.

Afterwards, we went to the depot to watch a train come in. Trains was the only things that made much noise in Stephenville, besides preachers and sinners. And back then, trains was the only exciting things that ever happened in them small towns. So when the Frisco passenger train come into Stephenville, tooting and huffing and puffing out steam, half the town was there to watch it.

Later on, it was near two o'clock, me and Carrie went on back to Main Street to a café to eat their fifteen-cent Sunday dinner special. Carrie seemed to be having a good time and I was starting to feel some better about things.

What I never coulda guessed while we was setting at that café, eating roast chicken and collards and grits and biscuits and white gravy and sour cherry pie, was that my life was just a hair away from turning 'round a whole new bend.

***

It was after we'd ate the last bit of our pie and Carrie had took off to the toilet. I told her I'd be with the buggy, and that's where I was, rubbing the mule on his rump to give him some company when I heard a voice behind me.

"Nice rig you got here."

I turned around and a tall man was standing there, and I could tell right off he wasn't nobody from Stephenville, he was too slicked-up. He was wearing a dudey suit covered from top to bottom with yellow and black checks. A brown derby was setting on his head, and he had a long mustache that was all oiled and pointed. And he was chewing one of them fat, eight-cent cigars.

"What you do for a living, kid?" the man said to me.

"What else? Cotton."

The man's eyes moved up and down my rig like he was eye-balling a gal.

"Doing okay for a cotton picker. How much you make?"

I didn't much like the man's questions. Why'd he want to know so much about some skinny-kid cotton picker? Only I knowed it wasn't gonna be no trouble for him to find out how much they was paying pickers around Stephenville, so I give him a answer. Except I told him a little lie.

"Six bits a hundred. Why you asking?"

"Jus' come in from outa town. Frisco from Dallas, you mighta seen it. And I'm looking to find me a partner. Pays real good, my business. Only it's a traveling affair, and I don't have no hooves and I don't have no wheels. What I need is somebody with a rig. You wanta talk?"

"What's your pay?"

"Lemme put it to you this way. You'll make more in one day in my business than you make all week long cracking your spine in them cotton fields." He flicked some dry ashes offa his cigar and looked me straight in the eye. He had pale, marble-blue eyes, they was so pale it was like I could see right through 'em.

"What kinda job is it?"

"It ain't a job, kid. What I got here is a business. And that's a big diff'rence there. A big diff'rence." Now the man was all smiles. I never seen anybody look so happy about his work. "I got what you'd call a 'entertainment' business. What I do is, I take games of chance out into the country, out to pickers and other farm hands like your-self that don't have no opportunity for entertainment like they do in the city. Now let's supposing you and me become partners. Daytime, while ever'body but us is out in that hot sun, working like the devil, you and me don't have a thing in the world to do. We take it real easy, look over the newspaper, maybe take a few drinks o' corn. Then, come evening, when the pickers are done in the fields, and they're through with their suppers, that's when we drive out to one of their camps and set up. Poker, faro, monte, keno, chuck-a-luck. And then, if what they want is something a little diff'rent, we roll a little craps."

"So you're talking about betting?"

The fella took off his derby hat and with a handkerchief wiped the sweat off the brim.

" 'Course that's what I'm talking about. If there isn't nothing at stake, don't got you much excitement, do you now? Might as well be playing tiddly-winks. Sometimes the stakes run up into the hundreds. That's how come it's a good thing to set up the games on payday, or soon's thereafter as you can."

The thought of gambling as a business was something I'd never thought of for myself—and yet the idea got a-hold of me right off.

"I been playing pitch and poker since I was old enough to pick up a deck of cards," I said.

"Look, kid. I'm gonna run the games, not you. But you drive me in this rig of yours, I'll divvy up the winnings. Twenty-five percent."

I didn't answer him right off. If the stakes run into the hundreds, twenty five percent'd be damn good.

"S'pose there ain't no winnings?" I asked. "S'pose we lose?"

The man winked. "Don't you be worrying over something silly like that. I'm an honest man, I can honestly guarantee you there'll be winnings. Say, here we are talking about being partners, and we haven't even traded names."

I held out my hand and told another little lie. "Wade Russell."

"Good to know you, Wade. Sid Jenkins, best gambler west o' New Orleans."

We shook.

All the time I was thinking, Old Man Mallory's worse'n a hog. A hog's a hog because God wanted it to be so fat, so human beings could have something for lard. But Old Man Mallory was cheating us, working us cheaper'n anybody else. He'd charged me too much for the buggy, too. As for Carrie—hell, I was bound to up my odds with Carrie if there was some silver dollars rattling in my pockets. And I wouldn't be getting 'em following a mule's ass or picking cotton!

What I didn't know right then, though I suspicioned it, was that Mister Sid Jenkins had a few different names of his own. He was also Mister Harry Harrison, Mister Tom Jones, Mister Richard McDougall, Mister Roscoe Turner, and Mister Dudley Rather, depending on where he was and who he was talking to. It took me a while to find all that out. All I knowed was, on that street in Stephenville that afternoon, I'd made a business deal with Mister Sid Jenkins, a honest gambler, and I was on my way to earning something a little better'n chicken feed.

"Good to meet you, Mister Jenkins. You got you a partner and a mule named Julep."

FOUR

I can still see it, like it was in a picture show.

That first night in the cotton-pickers' camp with Mister Jenkins. Cotton. Cotton. Cotton. Cotton. Piled high, like banks of snow, in the slatted wagons. Musta been a half dozen or more of them wagons parked at the edge of the field. Big sheets of canvas was stretched between 'em, like tents, to cover the long cotton sacks that the pickers slept on. But they wasn't sleeping now. They was all in a knot at the edge of a campfire, kneeling on a stretched-out sack. And they was rolling dice on it. All the men. Maybe 20 or so of 'em. Where was the women? All over behind one of the wagons, like they didn't wanta see what the men was doing. Besides, their work wasn't over yet. They was washing dishes from supper, nursing babies, patching pants and raggedy cotton sacks, and doing all the other things that women had to do back then.

A young picker, no more'n sixteen or seventeen, shook up the dice. Shook 'em so hard they rattled. Like by rattling 'em he could tell 'em what to do.

"Eighter from Decatur,
County Seat o' Wise...
Seven come eleven....
Buy Baby some new shoes!..."

The dice flew sideways across the sack. Mister Sid Jenkins, he was in shirt sleeves with bright red suspenders, set back on his heels and watched 'em roll over and over.

Box cars.

Mister Jenkins raked in the pile of coins and bills with his long thin fingers. He pulled 'em close to him like a woman'd cuddle a baby.

"Sorry, boy," he said. "It ain't what you say to the dice, it's how you say it."

Up went the dice to his mouth.

"Now, listen, you boneheads!"

He barked at 'em, whistled at 'em, swirled 'em around in his hands, made love to 'em.

"Eighter from Decatur,

County Seat o' Wise...

Bring me the luck o' the wise men....

The luck o' the wise men!"

Down went the dice, over, and over, and over. A five, a deuce.

He raked in the money again. Them pickers was dirty and sweaty and dog-tired from ten hours in the field. They just looked at each other, and I could hear the grumbling. They didn't like it, this dudey stranger who come into their camp at night with his dice and cards and his luck of the wise men. Who took two games outa three.

"Lemme see them dice," somebody says. He was a mule of a man, big-chested, with hands that could break a mesquite log in two.

I'm setting in the circle with the pickers and all they know about me is that I'm the one that drove him up in a buggy at sunset. Me and Mister Jenkins showed up just as they was finishing work for the day.

A dice game? Poker? Blackjack? Hell yes!

They was happy about it at the time. They was tired to death of nothing but cotton, dawn to dusk. Anything, anything, that wasn't picking cotton sounded good. From the moment we got there you could see 'em loosening up, straightening up, the blood in 'em flowing faster, a chance t' win as well as lose. HELL, YES!!!

I was beginning to squirm. Was them dice loaded? If they was, and the pickers found out about it, we was goners. They'd tear us apart, piece by piece, like hound dogs'll grab a rabbit and shake it and tear off a leg, then another leg, and then the head.

The big man rolled the dice around in the palm of his hand and throwed 'em down.

A six, a four.

He picked 'em up and throwed 'em down again.

Two fours.

"Satisfied?"

"I dunno. They seem all right."

"Then how about a game of poker? Use your cards. Anybody here got a deck o' cards?"

Who in a bunch of sun-black cotton pickers'd have a deck of cards? They used his, but only after he made 'em look the cards over up close, front and back, this way and that, to make sure they wasn't marked.

It was after midnight, the big old yellow moon had circled halfway around the sky, before we drove off. They was mad, cussing a blue streak. But they said to come back the next night, that maybe their luck'd change.

"See," Mister Jenkins said, "they got their money's worth, else why'd they tell us to come back? We get back to the hotel, we'll count it up, you'll get your share. Bet we got sixty dollars. Maybe more."

I couldn't see that stack of bills no more, they was setting in Mister Jenkin's oak-wood cash box. Only I knowed they was there. It was hard to believe it, a stack of bills that high outa only one night's work. Them pickers'd lost buckets of sweat to get that money, and all Mister Jenkins done was to flick his wrist.

I wanted to know: "Was them dice loaded?"

His shoulders tensed up. Now there was a scowl on his face. For a minute or two, even the air in the buggy seemed froze. The only sound was the clop-clop, clop-clop of Julep's hooves on the gravel. Louder'n I ever heard 'em before.

"So what?" He spit the words out, when they finally come. "They don't work for nothing, we don't either. And they're gonna be awful let down if we don't come back."

He was right there. They wanted us back. I could see it in their faces when we drove off. It was something they could look forward to the whole next day, sunup to sundown.

"Listen to me, kid. Half them pickers, they load their sacks with rocks. Cheating the farmers. I've seen 'em doing it, over and over. So what's this, huh? Just one cheat cheating another cheat."

That was true. Some of 'em did.

"Shut up," Mister Jenkins said, "and take the money."

I took it.

***

I took it, camp after camp, while we worked our way across Erath County, and then across Hood County, and Palo Pinto County, and Callahan County.

I took it until the cotton-picking season was over and the picking camps was gone. Then I took it while we worked the railroad section gangs, I took it at the cowboy outfits up in the Panhandle, and I took it at the roughneck camps around the wildcat wells.

As it come out, I never did square my debt with Old Man Mallory. Way I seen it, I'd already paid off that buggy in sweat. And, somehow, Carrie Sikes lost her tug on me in the middle of all that, when I was away from all that kissing 'n hugging 'n flopping in the grass. It works that way a lotta times, you know. Skirt-ties—the ones that ain't too sturdy to start off with—snap plumb in two when you stretch 'em a little.

'Course, family ties 'r different.

Before I knowed it, it was nineteen and oh-eight, three years since I run off with Eddie Munson. And I was feeling a pull to see my family. Not only just Ma, but Jess and Dock and Joe and all the others. Even a little bit, Pa. I'd heard they was back in Eastland County, near Rising Star. And so I talked to Mister Sid Jenkins, alias Mister Harry Harrison, alias Mister Tom Jones, alias Mister Roscoe Turner, about going to Rising Star. It was early September then, high time for cotton picking.

He said maybe. "They got enough pickers 'round there to make it worth our while, Willis?"

"More'n enough, Sid."

By that time, the gambler knowed that my real name was Willis Newton, not Wade Russell. But he didn't care. He said names was like clothes; you wore whichever one was right for what you're doing that day. By then, too, I'd worked my way up to fifty-fifty partners with that old boy, and I'd got to calling him "Sid." It hadn't took me no time a'tall to learn his tricks, like how to use a little look-ing glass, hid in a coat sleeve, so you could see what ever'body's cards was.

Anyhow, most of the farmers around Rising Star was like Pa, tenant farmers or sharecroppers. They didn't hire pickers, their fam-ilies did the work. Or neighbors helped each other. They didn't have money for gambling even if they wanted to. Their whole life was one big gamble: the sun and the rain and hail and bad seed and good seed and pink bollworms and Mex'kin boll weevils and army worms and root rot and bull nettle and four-feet-high Johnson grass. And what-ever the prices was at the gin.

But there was a few big farmers around there, too, the kind that had buggies and carriages and was starting to get automobiles, and they hired hands that lived in camps at cotton-picking time, like at

Stephenville. And when I told Sid about 'em, he said, "They got a hotel at Rising Star?" and when I said there was one, the Lone Star, he said, "Okay, then, we'll headquarter there a few days while we do the camps."

***

We drove into Rising Star at three o'clock on a Wednesday—me and Sid and a bay named Wally. I'd just got shed of Julep the mule and paid down on Wally, even though I hated horses; a horse just looked better pulling a buggy, and was faster. But Wally was winded, we'd been on the road since early that morning. Still, when we come up on the edge of Rising Star, I pulled his head up and I give him a coupla whacks with the whip and what a picture we made cutting down Main Street!

I seen a number of people I knowed, though they wouldn't a-knowed me back, all dressed up in a slick checkered suit like I had on, and with a brown mustache on my face I'd learned to oil and point. I didn't wave at them folks, or nothing like that, just set straight up and looked dead ahead, like I was in a hurry to get somewheres and had my mind on other things than waving at people.

Which is how it was.

First thing I done, I dropped Sid off at the Lone Star to get us our rooms, and then me and Wally hit on over to Mister Sullivan's Livery Stable & Funeral Service, down at the end of Main Street. Mister Sullivan was a chubby old boy with a tongue that moved twice as fast as the rest of him, and being that he did business with both the living and the dead, he knowed most of the town news and all of its gossip.

Well, Mister Sullivan didn't know me at first, but when I said who I was, and he seen it was me, behind that mustache, he "by golly'ed" me all over the map. He called me by my old nickname, "Little Snakes," which is what folks around Rising Star and Cisco'd called me from way on back. (They give me that name for snatching eggs outa hen-houses; they called my brother Jess "Big Snakes," same reason.)

"Byyyyy golly, by golly, by golly!" Mister Sullivan said. "You rascal! What a fine rig you got here, Little Snakes. You in the money?"

He didn't wait for me to answer. "Say, Little Snakes, you in the

40

money, you're sure gonna be a sight to your folks. And this horse here, oh boy! Weren't a hour ago, I'd say, maybe hour 'n a quarter, Dock come in here looking to borrow one of mine. But Old Lady Pallen passed on Monday, some kind of cancer ate her up, and the service is today, and I told Dock, 'Dock, you gotta come back later, but dunno if I c'n spare you a horse, son, even then.' "

That wasn't good news about the family. I'd had my mind set on driving out to the house the next day, since me and Sid wasn't gonna work the camps till the next night. But the thought of Pa mooning over Wally, and maybe grabbing for some of my money, made my stomach turn.

***

At the hotel, I found Sid in the dining room ordering supper. There was two women setting at the table with him, and they didn't look like the kind of women that lived around Rising Star. They was all painted up in the face, and they smelled like strong perfume.

"Willis, meet Flora and Iris. They're stopping at the hotel tonight, way to San Angelo."

"Hoddy," I said, and they nodded like they could take me or leave me.

But all the while we was eating, Iris kept looking at me and then first thing I knowed her hand come sliding on down my leg. Well, I wasn't no cowboy, but all I could think of doing when I felt them fingers a-sliding down my thigh was to hop on up, right there in that hotel dining room, and let loose with a *Yippy-ti-yi-yo, git along little dogies*!

"What'sa matter, Willis, you ticklish?"

No question about it, they was whores. But Iris was just as pretty and fresh-looking as that Carrie Sikes, and her hand on my leg had got me all worked up, no question about that. Before long she leaned over and whispered in my ear, "You could come over to my room tonight."

She put her lips right up against my ear and I was a goner.

"What'll it cost me?"

"Ten dollars. And I guarantee you it'll be worth it, and a lot more."

I reached over under the table and put my hand on her leg. Then I near swallowed my tongue.

41

There was my brother Dock, standing in the doorway, filling up the whole frame, watching ever' move I made. Dock had a crazy way of knowing things; I felt like a burglar caught in the act. But then, seeing my brother standing there in his beat-up farm clothes, looking 'bout as hangdog as them clothes, maybe thinking to hisself that nothing'd ever happened to him in his life, other'n getting bit on the head by a mad coyote, and maybe nothing more was ever gonna happen to him, other'n hard luck...and there I was, all slicked up, my hand on a lady's leg...well, I felt bad for Dock.

I quick left Iris and walked over to my brother.

"For God's sake, Willis. For God's sake!" Dock was besides hisself. He slapped me on the back so hard it shook my whole body. "What's-it with these dude clothes? An' a mustache? Oh, boy-a. That mustache!"

"I'm in a business now," I said. "Got a partner, too, one over there at the table."

"Them two heifers your partners too?" Dock let out a kind of slow, smirky horse laugh. "What you in, some kinda queer business?"

"It's a good 'un. I'll tell you that. Wouldn't be staying here if we wasn't making us some money."

"Naw, you ain't staying at the Lone Star." He didn't believe a word of it.

"Damn right I am. And soon's I'm done eating here, we'll go up and I'll show you my room right quick."

"Thanks 'n all, Willis, only I ain't got the time to go up to no hotel room. Pa's ragging on me to bring in a remnant, says I can keep what I get at the gin for it, but we ain't got nothing to pull the wagon. The old man got hisself a new horse last week, but she's lame and ain't worth the bullet to shoot her."

"How much cotton you talking 'bout?"

"Ain't but five or six hundred."

I looked over at Iris. She was shoveling the food away, not interested in us a'tall. "Take my horse. But he better be tied to that post over there by morning."

"Oh, you don't gotta worry 'bout me, 'cause I do what I say I do." He slapped me on the back again. "Say, you wanta do it with me? I'll give you halves."

"I'm gonna be busy." I threw another eye over at Iris.

Dock give another smirky horse laugh. "Well, if you get done with that 'busy' early..."

"I won't. Dock, listen, don't tell Pa it's my horse. I'll never get it back. Lemme ask you..." I held off a second, 'cause I didn't know if I wanted to ask, or not. "Pa sore about my running off?"

"Phhfew...sore ain't the word. Some of them words that come outa his mouth...I never knowed words like that. Only Pa's got other troubles now 'n all."

"Maybe I better not go by."

Dock shook his head. "You oughta see Ma, somehow, iffen you can. She gets your letters 'n all, only she's always saying you're gonna come down sick, or maybe you're kilt somewheres. Then if she don't go on! You know how she went on 'bout Brother Henry."

God, yeah.

That was the worst thing, by far, that'd ever come down on our family. Before my older brother Henry, we had three others in the family that passed on. But they was babies. Always another one come and took its place. With Henry, it was diff'rent. He was sixteen, four years ahead of me, and the sharpest of all us kids. I looked up to him, he was more like a Pa than a brother. Then he got some kind of fever that made his heart swell up like a cow udder. He was setting out on the porch one day when he just plopped over, dead. And when he passed on, with Ma it was like the whole world'd passed on with him. For months she kept her head buried in the Bible and didn't pick up a outlaw story one time. It was bad enough, having to see Henry up and die like that. It was even worse having to watch Ma grieve for him like she done.

"When Pa can't hear you, tell Ma I'm fine. Give her this." I handed Dock a ten-dollar bill.

He grabbed the money and run.

***

"Who was that crazy-looking bull?" Sid asked when I went back to the table. They was all having their dessert, apple pie and hot coffee, and Iris was eating like it was the last piece of pie in the world.

"Jus' somebody I knowed here from way on back. Nobody important."

"This pie sure is good," Iris said. "I think I'm gonna have me another piece."

I didn't see how she could eat another piece of pie, I was so raring to get up to that room and get going. Most of the whores we come across on our gambling rounds was ugly or smelly or sickly; but Iris was diff'rent, and my hopes was high. I'd done it with farm gals by then, in hay lofts or out in a cotton patch far off or one time behind a outhouse. Only I figured it was one thing to do it with a simple country girl, and a completely other thing to do it with a San Angelo whore.

Whores was what you called "professionals."

Only it wasn't nothing like I thought it'd be. No sooner'n we was up there in that room, and no sooner Iris'd unbuttoned all them buttons and pulled off all them petticoats, and no sooner I got going, it was over. Just like that! For the first time in my life I wished I didn't do ever'thing so goddamn fast! And no sooner it was over Iris took my ten-dollar bill and tucked it into a little pocket inside her brassiere and started buttoning all them buttons again.

"I gotta get me a good night's sleep," she said. "Got a long trip tomorrow."

She was in as much a hurry to get outa the room as she was to get in. I was so mad I coulda throwed her out. "That ain't fair, and you know it," I said. "Gimme another toss."

"Aw, you got your money's worth, and then some."

Sid was waiting for me in the other room. His shirt was buttoned all wrong and there was big black clouds rolling over them pale blue eyes of his. He was even madder'n I was. "Lazy trollops!" he said. "We shoulda held back the money, kicked 'em outa the rooms and dared 'em to complain to the management."

I decided right then and there my whoring days was over. Even though I'd only had one of 'em.

***

The next morning, me and Sid was having breakfast in the hotel, and the table was heaped high. There was stacks of griddle cakes, sausages, bacon, hominy grits, fried eggs, scrambled eggs, strawberry preserves, you name it, and I was going at one thing after the other, and enjoying it all in spite of what'd happened the night before, when there come a tap on my shoulder. I looked back to see who was there.

Then I took a second look. It was Dock, and he was covered all over with fuzzy white cotton lint, from the top of his head to the tips of his boots.

"What the—"

"Gotta talk private," Dock whispered fast.

When I got up from the table Sid got up too and followed us. He knowed something was wrong.

"What's the hell's going on?" I asked.

Dock was a-shaking all over, and that cotton lint was a-shaking all over with him. "It's trouble, Willis! The laws is coming! With Mel Calhoun! I reckon I didn't load it too good! And now the laws is coming!"

"The laws?" Sid begun pulling on the point of his mustache.

"Yeah! They're coming! Right now!"

I didn't ask Dock how come, or nothing else. "Go hit over to the alley behind the schoolhouse, hide in that old outhouse," I told him. "I'll figure out what's going on. Wait 'til I give you the signal. Then hit the brush."

I didn't have to tell Dock what "the signal" was. We used it all the time when we was kids, out prowling—snatching figs or pigs or whatever. You'd cup your hand around your nose 'n mouth and make a lonesome bird cry: whip-poor-weel! whip-poor-weel! whip-poor-weel!

Dock got the point, faster'n he got most things.

No sooner he was gone, in come Constable Jim O'Toole with a tall skinny guy right on his heel, and a whole bunch of stirred-up kids behind. One of them kids was my little brother Joe. He was three years older'n when I last seen him, but I knowed him by his Newton jaw. He looked jittery and jumpy, like he wanted to say something to me.

Only he didn't have no chance.

"You're under arrest, Willis Newton!" You'd a-thought that ham-hocked old constable was arresting Jesse James or Billy the Kid, he looked so tickled with hisself.

"For what?"

"For stealing my cotton, that's what for!" Mel Calhoun hollered. Mel was a tall, skinny cotton farmer with teeth that stuck out in front like a beaver, and he was so mad he was hopping from one foot to other.

"What the devil you talking about?" I said.

"You know good and well what I'm talking about!" He spun his head around that hotel eating room, and then raised his voice so ever'body else'd know what he was talking about, too. "You and Dock was bringing in a half-load, and you was passing my barn and you seen *my* cotton on the floor, and y'all just helped yourself. To make you a full bale."

"Hell, I been at this hotel all night. Ask my business partner here."

I turned around to get Sid to back me up. He wasn't there no more.

Constable O'Toole screwed up one eye. "The horse was yours, wasn't it?"

"I loaned it out."

"Aw, he's guilty as hell!" yelled Mel. He was still hopping around from one foot to the other. "Him and Dock both. Lock 'em both up! I got a witness! And next time you're stealing cotton, you might oughta load it better. Left a trail from my door plumb to the gin!"

That was more'n my little brother Joe could take. "Liar!" Joe shouted at Mel. "Willis didn't steal no cotton!"

"Nooooo—and I reckon he didn't steal no melons outa the Hayden's patch! And he didn't steal that cow from Old Man Withers! And he didn't snatch that old sow and ever' one of her six little piglets outa my uncle's..."

He never finished, cause Joe lit in. Punching and kicking.

Mel shoved him off. So hard Joe went a-sprawling.

That was it. I hauled off and let Mel Calhoun have it. Socked him square in the jaw. While he was falling, he knocked over a table and I can still see all them dishes and sausages and grits and griddle cakes and fried eggs and strawberry jam a-flying.

After he hit the ground, I booted him a time or two.

FIVE

Back in them days, in the law courts of Texas, there was a helluva diff'rence between a $49 thief and a $51 thief.

If a judge said you stole something, and that something was worth less'n $50, that was a misdemeanor and off you went to jail. Most likely for a few weeks. But if the judge said you stole something, and that something was worth more'n $50, that was a felony. And off you went to prison. Most likely for *years*.

I figured Dock had stole about $35 of Mel's cotton. That's all, just about $35 worth. That shoulda been jail time. For Dock. But after I hauled off at Mel and caused all that ruckus, and after Dock and the gambler vamoosed like they did, somebody had to pay. That somebody was me. And when Mel's jaw swole up big as a pumpkin, he said he wouldn't never be happy unless I was sent to the pen.

It took six months for the trial to even start. Most of that time I spent in the county jail, pacing around a cell that wasn't much bigger'n a two-seater outhouse. And then Mel swore in court, his clammy old hand laying flat on that Bible, that me and Dock stole $53 worth of his cotton.

Fifty-three dollars!

That sorry, lowdown bastard! I'd saved enough money from the gambling business to get me a lawyer, and we battled them charges from the county court right up to a higher court. All they had agin me was some crazy old boy that said he seen me at Mel's barn and some boot tracks at the gin that a shoemaker claimed was mine. But that witness changed his story later on, and how could that shoemaker say them tracks was mine, when it was all dry, loose sand around there?

Lies! All lies!

I was in the Eastland jail for twenty-two months and twenty-six days while the case was tried, and retried and appealed.

After all that time, I got three years in the pen.

For nothing!

***

My first year in the state penitentiary, I spent it in the town of
Rusk in east Texas. I done what I was told, and I mostly stayed outa
trouble. Then, wouldn't you know it, off I got shipped to one of
them "earn your keep" prison farms, Imperial, that was further
south, tucked out in the country under the city of Houston, just west
of the Gulf Coast. And all you could see in ever' direction you
looked wasn't nothing but cotton.

Cotton, cotton, cotton, cotton.

More'n a thousand acres of it.

All tall, bright, green cotton.

Them rows was straight as arrows, no weeds, because they had
plenty of field hands: bank robbers and petty thieves and rapists and
murderers, you name it, all working side by side. And working them
fields was even worse'n working for Pa. We'd hit the fields at day-
break, and we'd work 'til long after dusk, 'til we couldn't even see
our hands no more.

There was a hundred and fifty of us convicts, and when we
wasn't out picking, we was living in dirty clapboard barracks, and
them barracks was filled with the sourest air you ever smelled.
There was a tall bobwire fence circling them barracks, a fence high
as three men standing one on top of the other. And in two places on
that fence, there was wood-box guard posts. And in them posts was
guards packing 12-gauge shotguns, long black guns loaded with
buckshot.

'Course, if you tried to escape, and you wasn't spotted in time to
get shot, most likely you'd just traded a mess of bullet holes for a
mess of dog-tooth holes. There was a pack of redbone hounds
penned inside a little wood building next to the prison gate, and them
dogs had noses that could smell human scent ten hours old. And they
was crazy for a chase; they even run down butterflies and field larks.
And they had teeth as sharp as that bobwire.

At night, you could hear 'em a-yowling.

Sometimes, to spook us, the guards'd catch a cottontail in the
fields and they'd hold it upside down, and then they'd hit on over to
the doghouses and open the doors and let go them rabbit paws. And
the dogs'd race and scramble and fall all over each other for that cottontail, and, like as not, all that'd be left when they was done with
that thing was a few red, wet clumps of fur. The guards'd point to

them clumps, and throw their heads back and laugh like crazy men. "Won't be that much of *you* left, you sorry bastards, if you get rabbit in you."

I decided to break out.

***

But how was I gonna do it?

Most of the prison breaks I knowed about, or seen with my own eyes, was in the day, when we was all out picking in the fields, away from them bobwire fences and them hound pens and them guard posts. Could I make it by myself? Or should I find a partner? I knowed that, lots of times, convicts worked in twos when they was planning something like that. The right kinda partner could be a big help—with bribing guards, or smuggling in guns, or whatever.

The big problem was: Who can you trust among a bunch of convicts?

When I first come to Imperial, I didn't know no better and I'd talk to just about anybody. When one of 'em would ask what I was in for, I'd tell em: "For stealing $35 worth of cotton...only I didn't do it, I was innocent." Then they'd tell me they was innocent too. They hadn't killed nobody, or robbed nobody, or raped nobody, they'd all been framed. Every man in that whole prison had been nailed to the cross, just like Jesus Christ.

I soon come to hate the whole bunch of 'em. Biggest liars and snitches I ever knowed. If one of 'em told you his name was "Vernon," it mighta been "Vernon," or it mighta been "Ennis" or "Samuel" or "Jeb." You'd never know. 'Course, some of 'em had been living under made-up names so long they'd forgot what their real names was. A lot of 'em went by what was called "monikers"— names like "Hard Rock," "Banjo Ass," "Bronco Jack." And most of 'em would rat on you, sure as hell, if there was something in it for 'em. And you had to be careful who you sassed, if you was mad at somebody. You was likely to end up with a knife in your back.

Out of all them convicts, I was tight with only two of 'em.

One of 'em's name was Frank Holloway, and he didn't claim to be innocent, and I guess that's how come I took a liking to him. "I was a bank robber, and I got caught, that's all," he said. Frank come from a rich family in Mississippi, and he didn't look rough like most of the other inmates, that was nearly all poor country boys. He had a

49

thick head of black hair, black as coal, and he always combed it neat. And his teeth was straight and real white. He was older'n me, about thirty, but we was both about the same height, and he was skinny, like me. (Frank always called me "Skinny." For some reason, he didn't have no moniker. He was just "Frank.")

There was another reason I hanged with Frank. I'd never got much school 'cause my old man always had something else for us kids to do. I only gone nine weeks when I was twelve and Pa had hit off to New Mexico, hunting for God's Country. But Frank had gone all the way through high school, and his people was educated; his daddy was a gov'ment lawyer. Some of the other cons didn't like Frank 'cause they thought he acted like a know-it-all, but I never did mind all his spouting off about this or that. Like, being that his daddy was a gov'ment lawyer, I learned things about how the courts worked, and the laws.

Still, even if I liked Frank, I didn't know if he'd be any good for a break. He wasn't too tough, coming from that rich family like he did. One time while he was a-working in the fields, he just up and fainted. The sun was too much for him. The guards put him under a tree for awhile, and throwed buckets of water on him 'til he come to. 'Course then they put him right back to work again. It didn't matter to the guards if a prisoner died or not. They cared more about the mules. Inmates was for free. Mules cost money.

Anyhow, I couldn't risk it that Frank might pass out.

Des Moines Benny was the other prisoner I was tight with. I learned a lot from him, too. He'd been sent up for forgery and mail fraud. But he was a friendly guy and I played cards with him on Sundays. He had a long thin face and long thin fingers that could do things in a fine way like a woman. I liked the way he shuffled and dealt. He did it like a professional gambler, though he swore he wasn't. And I never caught him cheating. If he did cheat, he did it way better'n me or Sid Jenkins.

I liked Benny too 'cause he knowed how to softsoap the guards. Like I said before, some of them guards was more brutes than men. They'd spit in your face, or kick you in the balls, or run over you with their horses if they didn't like you. But Benny got along real good with most of 'em, I guess because he was just a natural con man. 'Course, he also knowed how to con people a helluva lot smarter than them guards.

"Outside, I'm the best in the business," he was always telling me. "You string somebody a story, see, and you give all the little details you can think of. But it's a mix, see. Ninety percent truth, ten percent lies. The truth gets 'em to take the bait. The other ten percent, that's where you fish-hook 'em."

Only I wasn't sure if Benny'd be good for a break. I needed to know him better.

It wasn't long, though, before I had me a new friend.

One morning, while we was trotting out to the fields, we passed the pull-do squad. The pull-do squad was a kind of fifth-rate work team that did jobs ever'body hated, like cleaning the crappers. That morning they was loading garbage barrels into a wagon. Our squad was all pinching our noses, the stink was so damn bad, when I seen somebody I knowed standing in the road by hisself, looking hard at us. He was the only one of that pull-do squad that was dressed in stripes. That meant he was in some kind of trouble.

I couldn't miss him.

"Dock!"

He looked direct at me.

"Willis!"

That was all we had time to say. The guards was keeping us at a trot.

I didn't get to see old Dock again until recreation time on Sunday afternoon. We was so happy to see each other, we hugged. I had a kind of special feeling for Dock, life had dealt him a bad hand. I'd never seen him with such a long face. He said he'd been working for a farmer near Cross Plains, that's where he took off to after all that cotton trouble with Mel Calhoun. And Cross Plains was where the sheriff nabbed him. The judge give him five years.

"And what'd you do to get that?" I pointed at his stripes.

"Coupla things," he said. "Last one, socked a guard. He give me a kick for working too slow, an' I give him something back."

I knowed they didn't put you in stripes unless you was "dangerous," in their minds, so God knows what else Dock did, or how many bones he'd cracked in that old guard. Dock never did have no idea how strong he was; he had a punch like a mule's kick. He told me he'd been to four other prison farms before they sent him to Imperial.

"The wardens was so glad to get shed o' me, in ever' one of them joints, they shook my hand when I left," Dock went on. "Only I tell you, Willis, this one's the rankest. What I'm thinking right now

51

is I'm gonna leave, ya'know. How 'bout you come along?"

It was like Dock'd read my mind.

"We gonna walk out the front gate?" I give him a smile.

"I'll show you. You game 'n all?"

"Hell, yeah," I said.

'Course, I figured I'd be the one showing Dock, not Dock showing me.

I was wrong.

***

A few days later, we was both in the same field picking cotton. The field was near two miles from the barracks so the guards was armed heavy with double-barreled shotguns. But the day was a hot 'un, and the guards was winking off. I could see one of 'em half asleep on his sorrel bay, fat horseflies a-buzzing around his head.

When we filled up the long cotton sacks we dragged along behind us we'd lug 'em over to the squad supervisor, who weighed 'em on a scale. Then he'd write down our names and the weight of the cotton: "Skinny" Newton, 195 pounds; "Fishhook" Jones, 136 pounds; "Bigfinger" Martin, 156 pounds.

Well, Dock'd just weighed his sack when, all of a sudden, he tucked up close to me. And in a voice so low I could hardly hear him, he said: "Stay close. When you hear me holler, come a-running." Then he passed on. All I could do was bend over again and go back to work. But I could feel my heart pick up: ker-thumpa, ker-thumpa. I knowed Dock was up to something. And from past times, I knowed about his poor judgment.

I kept watching him outa the far corner of my eye. He was picking, just like the rest of us, only he seemed to be inching his way over towards one of the guards. The guard had his shotgun resting across the pommel of the saddle and his head was slumped down, like he was taking a catnap.

If Dock was planning something, he oughta have talked it over with me first. Then we coulda done it right.

It was too late.

Dock sprung up from his row, grabbed that snoozing old guard by the arm and flipped him off his horse. Only somebody strong as Dock coulda done that. The guard come a-flying off that horse, and when he did Dock grabbed his shotgun and throwed down on him.

He stuck the gun in that old boy's left shoulder.

"Get me the belt!" Dock hollered at me.

I throwed off my sack and run over. I unhooked the guard's cartridge belt and held it in my hand.

Dock hopped on the guard's horse, I scrambled on behind.

It all come down so quick and so unexpected that the other prisoners working the rows close by didn't even know what was going on. I wasn't even sure myself what was going on. It was like I'd been sucked up by one of them crazy old Texas cyclones—and I was getting carried along with it.

Dock started screaming: "The woods! The woods!"

At first the convicts just stood like fence posts, they was so used to taking orders from the guards.

"You fools!" Dock yelled it again. "Run! Run, while you can!"

He hollered at 'em hard this time, like he was giving 'em an order, and that got about half of 'em to moving. And once they started moving, did they blow! They tore for them woods like they was running for their lives, which they was.

'Course, while all this was going on, the guard that Dock'd yanked off his horse wasn't just laying there, playing possum. He'd pulled hisself up offa the ground and started to run toward the other guards and was a-hollering: "Escape! Escape!"

I seen two guards wheel their horses and start toward us.

There'd be others, a whole army of 'em, I knowed it.

Dock aimed his shotgun up, to the sun. Blam! Blam!

The guards pulled up short.

"Woods! The woods!" Dock kept hollering at the prisoners that was still standing around, too boogered to move. "They cain't stop all of ya!"

He screamed at 'em like he was on fire.

All of a sudden, it was like he'd set the rest of 'em on fire too. They all, ever' last one of 'em, begun flowing towards the woods. They was moving in long thin streams. Whites and stripes together. And as they went, they begun to spread out so that if you was up in the sky, looking down at 'em, it woulda looked like they was one big old fan, a big old fan alive and moving in every part...

"Hot piss and vinegar!" Dock said. "Try to stop 'em now!"

Sooner 'r later, I knowed, we was all gonna pay the price for what was happening. But lemme tell you what, I don't think I ever seen such a beautiful sight in my life—all them Texans running for their freedom!

The guards begun firing at the escaping prisoners. Blam! Blam! Blam! Blam! I seen a couple of 'em go down.

Dock spun our horse around and shot off into the woods.

***

The trees was thick with clumps of underbrush. But ever' now and then we'd catch sight of somebody in white or stripes. The prisoners, once they'd hit the woods, had scattered out. Even with hounds on their trail there was only so many tracks the dogs could follow. Some'd get caught, some wouldn't.

Me and Dock was on a stout chestnut gelding. All the horses the guards rode was good and fat, better fed than the prisoners was. But even on a horse, I knowed we was leaving scent in the air—and ever' time we pushed through some brush, we was leaving scent on them branches. We was riding fast as we could, making good time in the open places, trying to skirt past the brush.

We musta rode a half-hour like that when the horse tripped over a big jagged rock and begun to limp.

Way far off, now, we could hear the hounds.

Yaaa-ooo! Yaaa-ooo! Yaaa-ooo!

Ever' bellow sent a shiver up my spine.

The horse was limping more and more. And when we come up over some big rocks, hid by some brush, he stumbled. Dock and me both had to jump off, or he woulda crumpled right down to the dirt. We yanked off the saddle and bridle and hid 'em under some bushes and give the horse a slap. He took off to the north, slow and limping, like a old man, and got swallowed up by the woods.

Yaaa-oooo! Yaaa-oooooo!

Them hounds was so close now that if we'd took off on foot, we wouldna had a chance in the world. But there was plenty of trees around us—post oaks, live oaks and pecans—some of 'em high as six men standing one on top of the other.

"Best we can do," I said, "is coon up."

A hard breeze was blowing away from the dogs, but our scent was fresh in the air, and even with that breeze, the dogs was likely to track us, even up in a tree. But what else could we do? We picked out a tall post oak and started to shinny up it. I went first; Dock was after me. Big and thick as Dock was, he couldn't shinny too fast. But ever' time I'd pull up on a limb, I'd reach down and grab his arm and give him a yank.

Yaaaa-oooo! Yaaaa-oooo!

Them dogs sounded like they was just a coupla hundred feet away. But we still couldn't see 'em.

I give Dock one last big yank. We both hugged the trunk close.

Yaaaa-oooo! Yaaaa-oooo!

Now here come the bodies that went with them barks—crashing outa the brush, a tangle of long red legs, their long ears a-flying, their long tongues a-dangling, their long noses a-dragging the ground, and then....

...they run right past our tree.

They'd overrun us.

Me and Dock was just two pairs of eyes, way up high, peeking down at 'em through a bunch of leafy branches.

"Safe," Dock whispered to me.

"I hope."

But when the dogs was about thirty yards past our tree, all of a sudden, it was like somebody'd pulled the brake on 'em. They stopped in their tracks and throwed their heads up in the air. They all sniffed. They scrambled around in a circle for a second, and then they all whipped around and run back in the other direction—towards our tree!

Damn!

We could hear horses crashing through the brush, and men's voices. Them horses hadn't been able to keep up with the dogs, but they wasn't that far behind.

Yaap, yaap, yaap.

The dogs' barks was choppier than before, and louder. They'd found what they was looking for. It was probably us.

Probably, hell. It *was* us!

Before you knowed it, they was a-raring up on our trunk, a-yowling and a-baying, like they'd treed a coon. I'll tell you what, if I'da been running with them dirty dogs instead of hugging the top of that old tree, I'da been pretty worked up myself. Yeah, them dogs had found something!

The posse that was after us knowed it too. Directly they come riding up and we could hear 'em talking down below.

"There's one of 'em up there," we heard somebody yell. "Naw, it's two of 'em!..."

Then we heard another voice that scared the shit outa me. "Come on down you sons-o'-bitches, or we'll blow you down. Count of three. One, two...."

"Sorry 'bout this, Willis," Dock said.

I didn't say nothing back. I just started on down the tree.

When my foot come down on the lowest branch, I seen four men standing at the foot of the tree. I knowed three of 'em. I said, "Jones, call off the dogs."

That set 'em all to laughing.

So I said, "Jones, I ain't coming all the way 'til you call off them dogs."

Jones hawed like a mule. Hee-haw! Haw-haw-haw! He was one of them brute fellas with big long yellow teeth that looked like a animal's.

"You're damn right you're coming down," he said. "I'll count to three, how 'bout it? One, two..."

His shotgun was aimed right at my chest.

I looked down at them hounds. They was jumping up at me with bared teeth, yelping and snarling. I knowed what I was in for. I dropped one foot toward the ground. They jerked me the rest of the way.

Now, you may not wanna hear what come next, but I still got the scars all over my legs to prove that it happened. Lemme tell you what happens when you get bit by a dog. First off, there's a loud POP! That's when the teeth is breaking through the skin. The skin is kinda tight, see, and that's what makes the pop. Then, after ever' POP! there's a yank of pain that's so sharp and so hard you feel it in the pit of your stomach. That's when the teeth is sinking on down into the muscle. Now multiply them pops and that pain by a hundred, or more, and you got a little idea of what I was going through. Them hound teeth was all over me.

Their jaws was a-snapping and their teeth was a-stabbing.

They was dogs. I was meat.

To get 'em off, I backed up agin the tree and throwed my arms out, this-a-way and that-a-way. They gnawed on my arms for a while, then they went right back to my legs. Blood was pouring outa all them teeth holes, my head was dizzy, and my gut was flipping somersaults. And oh boy! How them guards wanted me to holler, to beg for mercy! But I never peeped.

Them dogs would've chewed me to death, I'm sure of it, if

Captain Anderson hadn't rid up just then. Anderson was one of the toughest men on the prison staff. They'd outlawed whipping in the Texas prisons by then, but I'd seen Anderson use a thick leather belt called "The Bat" to slap the balls of one inmate that tried to stab another. And I seen him ride his horse right over two prisoners that had started a fight. Still, he musta had a few grains of Christian mercy left in him. When he seen them dogs a-chewing on me, he got pretty mad.

"Pull the dogs off!" he hollered at Jones. "You got him, don't you!"

SIX

It took three months for my legs to heal.

It took six months for the State of Texas to round up most of them hundred and fifty convicts that'd took to the woods.

Hunting up all them run-off inmates, it made me think of one day way back when me and Ma was riding to Rising Star. The wagon rolled over a big rut, and it joggled, and Ma's arm come flying up and hit the string of her town necklace. And a whole mess of beads, dozens and dozens of 'em, went flinging off in ever' direction.

Well, them convicts had flied off just the same way: into corners and cracks and holes all over the State of Texas. Some of 'em never got found.

The warden give me and Dock a double shot of misery to pay for his trouble.

First off, three fat guards marched us out into a dark little room and put us direct under two long boards hanging on ropes. "Raise yer left hand," one of them guards said. I raised my left hand and he pulled it up through a round hole cut in that board. He took some heavy cord and he looped it over my thumb and the board and pulled that cord real tight. "Raise yer right hand," said the guard. He done the same with that one. Then he done the same to Dock.

"Get ready, boys," the guard said, and he walked over to the thick rope that was holding the boards to the ceiling. "This here's gonna put you 'bout eight inches closer to the Lord God in his Blessed Heaven."

He yanked that rope, and up them boards went, and up went me and Dock with 'em. Only our toes was touching the ground. One of my feet was near off completely. I could catch the floor with the other one, but just barely. A pain that was dull and hard shot down through my arms, and a pain that stabbed like fire shot on up through my legs. I don't know which pain was the worst, the pain in my arms or the pain in my legs. Them dog bites on my legs was still red-fresh.

And there we hung.

Neither me or Dock said nothing for the first half hour. What was there to say? We just had our own thoughts, whatever it is people think about when they're a-hanging up by their thumbs. Like how it's strange you don't think much about how your body is put together, how the muscles and the bones and ever'thing is all hooked up, until you're rope-tied in a way that ain't natural.

It was Dock that broke the quiet at last. "Sorry 'bout all this, Willis."

I give him a look from the corner of my eye. "From here on out, Dock, you follow me."

We didn't say nothing else.

When they cut us down, my thumbs was completely numb. They stayed that way for a year.

The rest of our punishment was even worse. The warden said we had no chance in hell for parole. Then they added five years to Dock's sentence, and the same to mine. Dock's sentence was now ten years, and mine was eight.

All that for stealing $35 worth of cotton.

Eight goddamn years to be a clump in prison!

Dock took his ten years a little better'n I took my eight. But only a little better. Sooner or later, he said, no matter how many years they added to his sentence, he was gonna get out.

I wasn't so sure no more.

Eight years! I might've been able to stand it for two years. Or even three years. But eight! Here I was, twenty-three years old, in the prime of my life, raring to be out in the world doing things—and instead of that they had me behind bobwire like a wild animal in a cage.

I felt sick all over. And mad. Mad not only at Pa, but mad now at ever'body. At Dock for getting me into this mess. At the warden and guards. At the constable and district attorney and Mel Calhoun back in Eastland County. At ever'body in the whole State of Texas and in the whole world.

Except Ma.

I hated ever'body and ever'thing except Ma.

***

The worst thing about prison is it's the same thing over and over and over again. Same work: from dawn to dark. Same smells: of sweat, of piss, of stinky feet, of sour air. Same food: hog jowls and corn mush, hog jowls and beans, hog jowls and biscuits, hog jowls and hash, hog jowls and corn mush again. They brung them hog jowls in by the wagonload. You ate 'em cause you was hungry, you was always hungry, and because that's all there was.

Well, I tell you, I was gonna get outa that penitentiary, somehow. Dead or alive. By myself. No Dock.

They was just thoughts, I kept 'em to myself. But I had to feel free in some way.

When a man's caged up like we was, the tight inside of him builds up and builds up 'til he either explodes, or he blows it out a hole. I used my mind, my thinking, to blow out some of that steam. A lot of convicts did it other ways, like stabbing each other, or humping each other, or cussing each other.

Dock took to cussing.

Dock cussed the other convicts and he cussed the guards and he cussed the chapel preacher. He could cuss like a crazy man, using ever' mix of bad words you can think of, and some that didn't make no sense. He'd call one convict a "goddamn wood-pussy," and he'd turn right around and call some guard a "skim-milk flip-cock." And ever' time Dock'd cuss out somebody important, he'd get swung up by his thumbs. After a while his thumbs just went completely dead, and he never— for the rest of his life—got back the feeling.

There was only a coupla things you could do on that work farm to keep from getting bored outa your head, and that wasn't gonna get you into trouble.

Ever' so often you'd be a-picking away in the fields and outa the corner of your eye you'd see a clump of brown bouncing down them middles. And most times, that clump of brown had a little clump of white on its ass. And ain't nothing tastes better'n cottontail rabbit when all you been eating for months is hog jowls. They'd let the prison cook fry you up one if you could catch it.

If you could catch it…

But any rabbit that crossed my path was good as flipping in a pan. My fingers moved like lightning.

There was one other thing you could do to break the sameness: cotton-picking races. You'd egg on some guy in your squad to see who could pick the most pounds before quitting time. If you won, all you won was a little piece of pride. Still, that was better'n nothing.

One day, I was racing with a tall bald-headed fella named Dirty Butter, and we was going neck and neck for a while. Dirty Butter'd got that name because he hardly ever took a bath and he smelled like rancid butter. But how rank a man smells don't affect how fast his fingers move, and he was fast. Still, I was faster and Dirty Butter couldn't keep up. In the middle of the afternoon I dragged in a specially heavy sack to be weighed. The supervisor, who was a trusty, could hardly believe it when he looked at the scale.

"Got rocks in that sack, Skinny?" he asked me.

"Hell no. All pure cotton."

"Says here you already picked four hundred and ten pounds and it ain't three o'clock yet. Where'd you steal it?"

That supervisor just had to rub it in, he knowed I'd been sent to prison for stealing cotton.

"I'll tell you where I stole it," I said, and I pointed out to the field. "Right outa them burrs."

Dirty Butter was standing direct behind me with his sack. He knowed he wasn't gonna come nowhere near me, and he was looking down in the mouth. He'd picked hardly three hundred pounds that day to my four hundred and ten. Later, when he passed me in the field, he give me a look that was as sour as how he smelled. "I'm tellin' you, Skinny," he said, "if you didn't steal none of that, you better slow things on down. Other boys 'r pretty griped. You're making 'em look like loafers."

Then he smiled.

"Ain't smart to make 'em look bad."

***

He was right. It weren't smart. There was nothing the boys hated worse'n what they called a "righty boy," somebody that played up to the guards. Well, I wasn't playing up to nobody. But that didn't make no diff'rence to them soddy-mite convicts. And all that got me to thinking I'd better watch my back. Only a week before somebody throwed gasoline and a lighted match on a prisoner that'd snitched to the guards. He was burned black like barbecue.

One Sunday afternoon, when we was all walking around the yard for "recreation," I run into Frank Holloway. He was setting on a bench reading the *Houston Post*. The chaplain had give it to him. Like I said before, Frank acted like a "know-it-all," no matter what you talked about he put on like he knowed more. But it was true he'd had more school than near anybody else at Imperial, even the guards. And he was likely the only one that had much interest in what was going on outside the joint.

Anyhow, I set down next to him and I couldn't help saying how mad I was. Goddamn that Dirty Butter! Goddamn the whole bunch of 'em!

"Your first mistake," Frank said, laying that *Houston Post* down neat on his lap, "was going out with that brother of yours."

"I had to go out with him," I said. "He's my brother."

"One crazy in a family, Skinny, is one too many."

I didn't say nothing else right off. He just wouldn't get how me and Dock felt about each other. That's one thing I knowed about "know-it-alls"—lots of times, it's the simplest of things they just don't get.

Me and Dock was blood, that's all. Dock got me in hot water this time. But he got me outa hot water other times. Like one time when we was kids, me and him'd run off from home and we was right in the middle of nowhere, having a good old time knocking over jackrabbits with our .22s. And right in the middle of that nowhere, I come down with the typhoid fever. Typhoid fever is that old, slow fever that'll suck up ever' last drop of water outa you and kill you just as dead as how a bad drought'll fry up a cotton plant. Sure enough, I was so sick I died. Died just as natural as anything. And when I died, I seen the devil a-standing in front of me, clear as day, with them sharp horns on him and that crooked tail. And I went to laughing and saying, "Hey, devil, gimme a smile." Dock seen what was going on, and he set off afoot under a burning, burning August sun to find me water, and he went fifteen miles one way and fifteen miles t'other way, bringing it back, and never one time did he say how long that walk was, or how hot that sun was.

No, Frank didn't know that. And I didn't feel like telling him. I just reached down and pulled up my pants leg.

"Look at this."

I stuck my left leg straight out so he could get him a good look. I didn't wanta prove his point, that I didn't have no more sense in me than my brother. Only I liked showing off them dog-bite scars. Hell, I didn't holler, I didn't even peep, when them hounds was chewing my legs right on down to the bone. Dew poison from the cotton plants had got into some of them sores; they was red and runny and full of pus. The prison doctor who treated 'em was a horse-doctor—a vet for the prison mules—and he give me kerosene when I'd asked for some liniment.

Frank looked at my legs, but he didn't whistle or nothing. He just held up the newspaper he was reading. "Listen to this, Skinny. The Baptists and Methodists are fighting to make it a crime to drink whiskey."

He turned to another page, "And over here, it tells how women are fighting to get the vote. Lady says here if women get the vote, 'Peace will descend on this land like a morning mist.' "

He turned to another page. "But over here it tells how England and France and Germany are arguing about something that's liable to end up in another helluva big war, bigger than our own War Between the States."

He put down the paper, "Be wonderful, wouldn't it, if life were so simple? Women get the vote, peace 'descends.' But I'd say that's a piper's dream, wouldn't you?"

"Who knows?" I said. "You ain't never met my Ma."

I pulled my foot back on the ground. Frank wasn't paying me no mind. He was too caught up in his own talking.

"Well," Frank said, going on, and shaking his head, "I, for one, doubt that women are the answer to the problems plaguing this crazy world of ours. Let me say this, Skinny: The world's not all that civilized. Not like we like to think it is. Some animals live off others because they're more powerful, and it's the same with humans. If you have the power—money, guns, the laws—you live off the ones who don't."

"Tell me something I don't know, Frank." I straightened the leg of my pants.

Yeah, I knowed all that. Wasn't I setting there caged up in a pen with two red, runny, chewed-up legs 'cause somebody had more power'n me?

Only Holloway did know some things I didn't, he'd been in the penitentiary before. So I let him keep on talking.

Which he was, without me asking.

"Let's say you try that escape stunt again, Skinny. Let's say this time the dogs don't get you. You think the warden's gonna lick his pencil and cross you off his register?" He give a titter. "He'll keep after you, and he'll keep after you, and he'll keep after you. And sooner or later, one way or another, you'll be back. And you know what they can do to you for getting rabbit in you a second time?"

"I don't care."

"When you get the book tossed at you, Skinny, you might care quite a bit. That, my friend, can put you up for life."

Life? Damn! I didn't say nothing to that.

"Think about that, Skinny," Frank went on. "Think about it hard. If you haven't learned it already, you can't win by bucking the powers in this world. Not in the long run. You have to come at things from a different place." And with that, Frank tapped his head. "Only way you can do it is to outwit 'em."

He give me a toothy smile, and that was the end of it. He'd talked hisself out.

I thought to myself: if Frank Holloway is such a Smart Man, how come he's in the joint along with the rest of us dumb clucks? Only, much as I hate to say it, he did get me to do some new thinking.

***

I thought over it the rest of that day, and into the next. How there's all kinds of power, and all kinds of smarts. We seen it ever'-day out on the farm, how the bigger animals lived off the littler ones, and how mules and horses had more power in 'em than humans, but how humans ruled over 'em anyways.

Take my brother Jess. He started busting broncs when he was just fourteen, still skinny as a twig and hardly outa kneepants. And it was damn risky, that kinda work. A 1,200-pound bronc can pitch the tar outa you, and whirl the tar outa you, and then, if it wants to, drop its head and do a somersault forwards, *chile pa riba*. We knowed one fella that got rolled like that and was smashed like a watermelon.

But the crazier the horses was, the better Jess liked 'em.

No horse could do a front roll with my brother because he knowed just how to rein 'em in. Jess couldn't read a book, he hardly knowed his ABCs, but he sure as hell could read a horse. Before he ever got on one he studied ever'thing about 'em, whether they was skittery or just plain mean. How they moved their head and the muscles of their body and how much white they had showing in their eyes.

No matter how mean or tricky a bronc was, Jess could ride 'em

64

down to sweat.

So the more I run it over in my head, how somebody like me, without no power, was gonna get out of a state penitentiary that was circled by mule-faced guards and 12-gauge shotguns and a pack of dirty dogs and ten rows of bobwire and the power of the whole state of Texas, the more I begun to think of Jess and how he out-tricked some of the biggest, rankest animals that ever was born.

It took me a week of hard thinking and talking, mostly to Des Moines Benny, and then it come to me. It was a far-fetched idea. It'd be taking a helluva chance if it didn't work out. But if I wanted to get anywhere in this life, if I just wanted to get out of the joint, I had to take some chances.

I was gonna need Ma's help. I wrote her that I wanted her to visit me at Imperial, that I had to see her. I didn't tell her why because the prison people read all our letters and scratched out whatever they didn't like with a big, black pen. Ma wrote back right away; she was coming. How she got the money, I don't know. Ma was a determined person, and somehow she got it.

She was my first and only visitor.

I can still see Ma coming through that door. She had her straw town hat on, and she'd stuck some crow feathers in the band to slick it up. There was tears in her eyes.

"Willis," she said. "Son. You all right?"

There was a guard in the room. He didn't want no visitor to slip you a knife, or to even touch you on the cheek. All I could do was stand up. "I'm fine, Ma. Fine. How's ever'thing at home?"

"Fine. Fine."

She knowed I wasn't telling her the truth, 'n I knowed she wasn't telling me the truth. So I didn't ask no more questions. I come right to the point. "Ma, I want you to go see the Gov'nor for me..."

Ma's eyebrows jumped up like they had legs. "The Gov'nor?"

I told it to her fast. I wanted Ma to ask the Gov'nor to give me a pardon, 'cause I hadn't done nothing wrong in the first place to get sent up. They'd made a mistake. And Ma was a good woman, the Gov'nor could tell that right off. Besides which, I'd heard the Gov'nor was giving out pardons right and left. That anybody could get a pardon for the right amount of money, if they knowed how to do it. You didn't give it outright to the Gov'nor, that'd be bribery, but there was a way, a legal way.

I didn't tell Ma the whole story. I didn't tell her that there was a few things I'd likely have to do after she seen the Gov'nor— things that wasn't altogether straight—to make double-sure I got me that pardon. But I always think it's best to leave holes in a story, when you need to.

***

Ma told me later how things come out when she went to see the Gov'nor. She told me exact.

She said she took the Texas & Pacific to Dallas, and then the Katy to Austin. When she got to Austin and seen that state capitol building, she just stood and stared at it. It was like a palace, she said. Glittery pink granite with that big dome atop. When she finally went inside, she thought she'd never find the Gov'nor's office. But she did. And then she done just what I told her to do. She set down on a chair like she was waiting for somebody. There was a young woman setting at a desk, and the room was full of people.

For more'n an hour, Ma told me, she watched the hand on a big wall clock click around. At 2:16 p.m.—Ma could recall the time exact—the woman at the desk leaned over to pick up something she'd dropped on the floor. And Ma slid just like a garden snake into the Gov'nor's office.

The Gov'nor was a-talking on the telephone. He didn't notice Ma a'tall.

Ma told me the Gov'nor looked about like how she thought he'd look, dressed in a dark-blue suit with a dark blue vest and a white shirt with a stiff collar. He had a long sharp nose and a tall forehead. She said the rakes on his comb had made wide rows in his hair and it made his head look just like a fresh-plowed field.

Since the Gov'nor was talking hard on the telephone, Ma said she took the time to look around his office.

It was a big office, bigger'n some of the farm shacks our family'd lived in over the years. Behind the Gov'nor's desk was the head of a big Longhorn steer with horns that stuck out near three feet each. And on the walls was pictures of Texas heroes in gold-color frames. One of 'em had a card under it saying "Stephen F. Austin," and one said "Sam Houston," and another said "Davy Crockett."

Ma'd heard stories about these Texas heroes all her life, but she never did know what they looked like. She told me she walked over to the picture of Sam Houston with his long white hair and his wild

66

bushy eyebrows, and she stretched her neck forwards and looked at it hard. She started thinking about the stories she'd heard about Houston, how he was a good man but a big drunkard that was always passing out in the bushes outside that very state capitol building, when, all of a sudden, the Gov'nor's voice was right in Ma's ear.

"May I help you, Ma'am?"

The Gov'nor had put down the phone and he'd stood up and was a-walking straight to Ma.

Ma told me she gulped, then quick found her voice.

"Mister Gov'nor," Ma said to him, "my name is Janetta Pecos Newton, and I'm a widder woman with four small children and I got a big patch of cotton that needs to be picked." (Pa wasn't no more dead than the Gov'nor, but right then Pa was more use to Ma dead than alive.)

"My son, Willis Newton, is in prison," Ma kept on. "They said he stole cotton but he's completely innocent. And now I need to get Willis a pardon so he can help me with my patch."

"Willis Newton?" When the Gov'nor heard my name, Ma told me, his eyebrows pulled together and his upper lip pushed out, like he was thinking about something hard and smelling something bad, both at the same time. "Willis Newton? Isn't he the one who jumped a guard with his brother down near Imperial?"

"Wouldn't you fight back if you was innocent?" Ma answered him. "If they was trying to take away your human freedom? Them men up there..." She pointed up to the Texas heroes on the wall. "...them men fought and died for their freedom. Any red-blooded Texan would. Mister Gov'nor, Willis never stole no cotton. His brother Dock did. He confessed to it—that he done it all by hisself."

Then Ma told me she walked over to that stuffed Longhorn head on the wall and stood right next to its glass eye.

"My late husband, Jim Newton," she said to the Gov'nor, "drove well over 2,000 o' these Longhorns up to Wichita, Kansas." (Pa drove less'n 200 cattle up to Kansas. But Ma didn't think adding a coupla thousand would hurt none.)

"While they was up in Kansas, some dirty thief stole Jim's horse and money. But my husband didn't want to steal nobody else's horse, so he walked on his own two legs all them hundreds o' miles back home." (There wasn't no dirty Kansas thief. Pa got stranded up there 'cause he got dead drunk one night and gambled away all his money, and his horse.)

" 'Course, them days, they hung a man if they caught him steal-ing a horse," Ma went on. "I was hoping times was different. That a man's life is worth more'n a horse. Or $35 worth of cotton—*that he didn't steal.*"

Ma waited a few moments for all that to sink in.

"Gov'nor," she said then, "I'm gonna set right here until you either throw me out, or turn Willis loose."

The Gov'nor didn't say nothing right off. He give a long sigh.

"Tell you what I'll do, Missus Newton." he said at last. "If you can get letters from the people back in Eastland County recommend-ing clemency for Willis, letters that say a mistake's been made, I'll give your boy a pardon. Provided...provided he serves at least one more year of his sentence. That's for helping to let all those prison-ers escape. And I'll tell you right now, ma'am, if he ever gets into trouble again, lets me down, God help him!"

"Thank you, Gov'nor. God bless you."

Ma told me the Gov'nor then shook her hand and walked back behind his desk.

"Good day, Missus Newton."

But Ma made no move to leave.

"Gov'nor," she said in a slow voice, "the other boy, Dock, he ain't a bad 'un either. When he was jus' a tot, he was bit on the head by a mad coyote."

"Good day, Missus Newton."

Ma told me she thanked the Gov'nor anyhow.

***

It took more'n Ma's determination to get me out. I still needed letters from all them skunks back in Eastland County, the ones that'd sent me up to the penitentiary in the first place. And I knowed damn well what they was gonna say. But I had a plan. I wrote to 'em any-way. And they all wrote back, just like I knowed they would. On a Sunday afternoon, during recreation time, I showed them letters to Des Moines Benny. I'd been tight with him long enough to trust he wouldn't snitch.

"Read these," I said.

The first letter went like this: "To the prison warden: After what Willis Newton did to me, I'd rather see him hanging on the end of a rope than get out of prison. He's been a troublemaker since he was born. Signed, Mel Calhoun."

The next letter was close to the same. "Dear Willis: Your brother Dock is a proved thief, and there's no doubt in my mind that you are too. I wouldn't recommend anything except to keep you in prison as long as possible. Signed. Constable Jim O'Toole."

The letters from the district attorney and the judge was along the same lines.

"The rest is up to you," I said to Des Moines Benny.

Des Moines Benny, if you remember, had them long, thin fingers that could do things in a fine, careful way, like a woman. And with them long, thin fingers Benny'd got hisself a reputation as the best forger in Texas—as well as Oklahoma, New Mexico, Kansas, and Louisiana. So we borrowed some letter paper from the chaplain and Benny rewrote ever' one of them letters, in handwriting even Mel Calhoun and Constable O'Toole would've swore was theirs. Except the letters all said they was so sorry that a great mistake had been made, and that I was completely innocent.

Benny addressed all them letters to the Board of Pardons, and we sneaked them out of the penitentiary so they could be mailed from Eastland County. It was a big gamble, all right. But the chaplain had told me the board got so many letters it hardly ever double-checked 'em. And when the board read them letters, they wrote the Gov'nor that "no man ever had better recommendations than Mister Willis Newton."

***

Before I left Imperial the next year, with a full pardon from the Gov'nor, I went to say so long to Frank Holloway. Frank still had a coupla years left to go. "Skinny," Frank said, and he give me one of them toothy smiles, "I want to warn you about something, my friend. You know those scars on your legs? Well, there's a scar on your forehead now too. You just can't see it in the mirror."

"What're you talking about?"

"You're smart, Skinny. What do you think I'm talking about?"

I didn't wanta hear no more. I put out my hand. He took it but he didn't let it go right off. He kept shaking it. "When those gates close behind you over there, Skinny, you'll be back in what I call the Free World. And in the Free World, that scar on your forehead is gonna shimmer and flicker like it's on fire."

"Yeah, we'll see about that." I took my hand back. "You're gonna have you a forehead problem, too, when you get out. What you gonna do about it?"

"Oh, I don't know. Maybe go up to Tulsa. Or Fort Worth," Frank said. "I have a lot of friends both places."

"All got a forehead problem?" I asked.

Frank give me another smile.

"When ex-cons are with ex-cons, the mark of Cain doesn't show."

SEVEN

The State of Texas was even sorrier'n Pa.

It worked you to death in them fields, long as it could, and then when it couldn't no more, it chucked you out like you wasn't nothing but a bag of garbage. All me and Stone Egbert got when they let us loose from Imperial Prison Farm that third Monday in August in the year nineteen and fourteen was a crumpled-up $5 bill and a even more crumpled-up suit of citizen clothes.

Stone was a small-time larceny thief. He also had one of the biggest guts I ever seen. He'd been on short rations in the pen, like ever'body else, but he had a body that could turn water into fat: he stood only five foot six and weighed two hundred and sixty pounds. The citizen suit they give him was so small there was six inches of belly between the buttons and the buttonholes. He looked just like one of Ma's flour dumplings. With me— "Skinny" Newton—it was just the opposite. I stood five foot eleven inches high and weighed one hundred and thirty-eight pounds. My waist was twenty-nine inches around, and my chest was thirty-five. But the State of Texas give me a suit three sizes too big. You could hardly see me for the suit.

I think they knowed just what they was doing, giving us clothes like that, clothes that fit all wrong. They wanted to shame us. And to make things worse, when Stone set down in the back seat of that prison car, the rear seam of his pants split so loud I thought he'd broke wind. "Piss-dog!" he hollered. (Stone was like Dock when it come to cussing; he hung all kinds of words together that didn't have no sense to 'em.)

From the Farm, they drove me and Stone to a little town called Crabb, on the Sante Fe railroad line. They told us to be outa sight by sunset. I sure didn't want nobody to see me in them godawful clothes. Still, if you ain't never been in prison, you'll never know how good it feels to be out, a free man. Free to go wherever you wanta go, east or west or north or south. Free to pick whatever you wanta do, and how you wanta do it, and when you wanta do it.

I had no idea what the hell I wanted to do. But I felt so free I stood right in the middle of that side street and spun around like a drunk man. Stone just set down on the side of the road to cover up his ass.

"Look-it, Skinny," he said. "'Bout fifteen miles up the tracks, there's a town called Orchard. I been there lots. Little place, but it's got a big store that sells all kinds of men's clothes. I say we make us a little visit, snatch us some suits."

"We just got out."

"Oh, ain't nothing to worry about. I know that town. They ain't even got a nighthack. You want the whole world to know we just got sprung? These suits is screaming like they got mouths that we just got sprung." He was right about that.

When a freight come through Crabb heading northwest, we hopped into a empty boxcar. I'll tell you what, the sound of them wheels over that track come up to me like a old song: clickety-clack, clickety-clack. I near forgot where we just come from. But when we got to Orchard, it come back to me. Particularly when we had to hide out in brush outside town 'til it come a good dark.

"You sure there ain't no nighthack?"

"Swear it on my momma's Bible."

Late that night, when even the cur dogs of that town was asleep, we both went into the store. It was easy. Stone found him a sharp rock and pried open a big back window.

The men's suits was all hanging on three racks. I didn't know much about suits them days, which ones was sharp and which ones was doggy. But Stone did, that was his business. He started feeling 'em, and whispering: "This here's mohair. That 'un, pure silk. Oh, damn twenty sparrows! Here's some worsteds. Take your pick."

I tried on two, fast as I could. The second one fit okay. I couldn't tell what color it was in the dark, but it was soft as a baby's cheek.

It took Stone a lot longer to find hisself one, him being so short and so big around the gut and all. He tried on one suit after another. I started getting jittery. Maybe he was right about no nighthack; maybe he wasn't. And it took him fifteen minutes before he even found one that come close to fitting. There was still a inch of belly between the buttons and the buttonholes.

"When your five-spot runs out, Stone, and you ain't got no more to eat," I said, "that one'll fit you fine. Let's get the hell out."

Stone kept it on. Only he wasn't done yet. I seen his elbows start to fly. He was yanking all kinds of other suits off the rack, and rolling 'em into bundles. "I ain't gonna let my well run dry, Skinny," he said. "Or your's neither."

I seen his point.

Then, through one of the front windows, we seen a light flash up. My heart near stopped.

"Fish-dung!" Stone whispered. "Down!"

We both hit the floor.

In a minute or two, the light'd floated on.

"Stay low," Stone whispered. "He'll poke around a few minutes, then go back home, go back to sleep."

I wasn't trusting nothing that old fool said no more. But what could I do? We both inched ourselves under a rack of suits, and for the next half hour, we was just two pairs of eyes peeping out from some pants legs. But we didn't see the light no more, and I finally said, "Let's hit out." We climbed outa the back window with our bundles, took 'em over to the railroad tracks, and when the next freight come by, we dumped 'em in a empty boxcar.

When daylight come, I seen that suit I'd snatched outa the store was yellow. A bright awful yellow! But none of the other ones we'd stole was my size, so there was I was, stuck, looking like a egg yoke. When we got to a section stop called Wallis, we hopped off and sold the other suits to railroad workers laying new track. Stone seemed to know all the tricks. The workers paid us eight dollars a suit. That made $56 for Stone, $56 for me.

But what was I gonna do for a real living?

That I didn't know.

When we was done with selling them suits, we hiked on over to some Southern Pacific tracks and hooked a freight west. But when we cut up a high, rolling prairie and stopped for water at a farm town called Weimar, I shook Stone's hand and hopped off. One thing I did know: I didn't wanta go back to work for the Gov'nor and hanging out with a silly old 260-pound petty thief was running up too much of a risk.

"Good luck to ya, Stone," I said. "Maybe someday we'll meet again—down yonder."

"You're crazy, Skinny!" was the last thing Stone said to me. "With me, you could live like a king!"

You'd a-thought I *was* crazy by how they looked at me in Weimar when I went hunting for work. It was a busy town, swarming with farm wagons, packed with businesses: implement stores, drug stores, a creamery, a ice plant, banks, grocers, a dry goods store with a sign on it: "Everything here from a toothpick on up!" Well, I musta asked thirty diff'rent people if they needed a hand. But near all of 'em give long stares at my yellow suit and give me the same answer: "Nothing here. Try the gin."

Cotton. I hated like hell to go back to doing anything that had to do with cotton. But it was something to do, something to do 'til I come up with something better to do. Turns out, there wasn't no jobs at the gin, either. But there was lots of wagons milling around, all loaded high with white puffy cotton. I went over to one that had a fresh coat of green paint and looked well-oiled. That meant the farmer wasn't no sharecropper.

"Need a picker?" I asked the driver.

He was a short, stout man with a round face and a little goat beard, and when he talked, he sounded just like Mister Hermann, the big fat German grocer I knowed in Rising Star.

The farmer eyeballed me up and down. "Vat's your name?"

"Henry," I said. "Henry Hermann."

"Hermann? You a German?"

"Most of me's just American, sir. But if I had to pick a part that's closest to being German, it's these here." I held out my hands. "You won't find a faster picker 'n me. I pick two rows a time. And I ain't never kneeled once in my life. Don't goose-tail either. I pick them rows clean, and the cotton's clean, too."

The farmer looked hard at my fingers. I'd picked so much cotton at Imperial that August, the skin around my nails was red and raw. That's the way your fingers look when you pick clean like I did.

"You don't haff a suitcase or a bag?" the farmer asked me.

"Set it down in town, sir. Some tramp run off with it."

"Bad luck. Vel, jump on."

I did.

It was only by accident, mostly the farmer's good-looking wagon, that I'd asked him for a job. But, to this day, I still don't know what kinda luck that was. Sometimes I think it's too bad, you know, that life ain't like a storybook where you can just sneak a peek down a ways to see how things are gonna come out in the end. Other times I think it's best we don't got no choice but to go it page by page. Most folks'd likely get so boogered if they knowed what was coming up that they'd end up standing froze in one spot, and never move.

***

The farmer's name was Bernard Rauss. And his family was good, hard-working German folks. Their house was built of lumber and stone, and it had three bedrooms and a big, tight-wire sleeping porch that wrapped around two sides. And there was a three-seater outhouse out back.

And they owned the land they was living on.

The Rauss' farm was the cleanest, best-stocked farm I ever been on. They had a big red barn and a corn crib and a smokehouse and a chicken house. And six pear trees, two snow-flower peach trees, and a vegetable garden. There was a well and a cistern. And two milk cows and four fat old hogs.

And all around, in ever' direction you could see, there was acres and acres of tall, sturdy cotton—cotton as high as your chest.

In my whole life, I never seen a family that worked so hard as the Rausses: Momma, Poppa, all their kids, and all their kids' kids. The only Rauss child that was still living at home was a gal named Vela. She was seventeen or eighteen. The rest was married. But they all lived close by, and they all worked on their Poppa's farm, right down to the youngest grandbaby, Helga. She was only five.

There wasn't no question who was Poppa, it was Poppa. He walked with a limp, he'd been bit on the leg by a diamondback three or four years before. But he was still like the king of the family, and he told ever'body exactly what to do. Poppa said when it was time to work, and Poppa said when it was time to stop work. And after lunch, Poppa'd lay down on his bed and take a fifteen-minute nap. And while he was napping, ever'body else but Vela was supposed to nap too.

"God laid down after He made za vorld," Poppa told me that first day, "and pickin' cotton iss harder'n that, He knows it."

We rested fifteen minutes exact. No more. No less. Vela had to watch a clock.

I didn't mind none of that. Poppa Rauss could bark as loud as any of them mule-faced prison guards at Imperial, but he wasn't no dirty louse. He was just German. And he knowed how to enjoy life too. The Rausses had one of them big pine eating tables, and Momma's job was to make that table "sag in za middle." Every day the food was piled high, but on Sundays, it was like a feast: fat red sausages, fried chicken and pot cheeses, bowls of sauerkraut and hot potato salad, pumpernickel and hard dark rye bread, and pear or peach strudel. And on Sundays there was big glasses of dark beer that Poppa brewed hisself and kept cool in a underground root cellar.

Most farmers around there picked cotton even on Sundays, they wanted to get it ginned before the storms that come off the Gulf Coast in the fall. But not the Rausses. At 8:30 Sunday morning, and 8:30 on the nose, ever'body piled into the farm wagon, even me, and we drove to a little church about a mile away. The preacher didn't speak nothing but German and he sounded to me like he was clearing his throat the whole time. I just nodded my head when ever'body else nodded their heads, and I thought about other things. The better part of Sundays come later. We'd have our dinner and drink that beer and then Poppa'd get out his accordion. And Vela would pull back the rug in the living room and the whole family, sometimes neighbors too, would dance.

It was that first Sunday, during one of them pretty German schottishes, that I got stuck on Vela Ursula Rauss.

To this day, when I think of that girl, I still get a pain in my heart.

***

Vela didn't wink at me, like Carrie Sikes always did, or wiggle her things, like a lot of girls I knowed. Most of the time, she walked kinda stiff. But godamighty, she was pretty! She was tall, kinda like Ma, only she wasn't thick around the middle. She had pink cheeks and a long blonde braid. And when Vela danced on them Sunday afternoons, her braid'd swing this-a-way and that-a-way, and most of that stiffness in her just blowed right on outa the room.

Ever' now and then, it seemed like she was looking towards me. Even if I was skinny, I knowed I was pretty good-looking. I was taller'n my Pa, with thick brown hair and a straight nose and hard muscles. And when I seen Vela's eyes start to move in my direction, my heart'd pick up its beat. Other times, she'd walk right past and not even glance sideways, and I'd slump around like a sick cat.

I knowed I was only a hired hand on the place, and maybe, for her, that's all I was.

Something else. There was a neighbor's boy from two farms over, a husky blonde fella called Emil, that showed up ever' Sunday afternoon. It was like him and Vela was born to be partners, they could twist and turn and hop so perfect together. I had a suspicion that Emil was sweet on Vela, and maybe even had it in his mind to marry her.

I wanted to dance with that girl. Damn, I wanted to dance with her! But I didn't know how. Pa'd always said that shaking your body around was the silliest thing he ever heard of, and Ma'd said it was wicked in God's eyes. Well, I didn't have no faith in a God, so that part wasn't no problem, but I didn't have no faith in my feet either. So I just watched 'em hop around together, Emil and Vela, like sparrows in the springtime, and I wanted to knock that block-headed Dutchman over on his ear.

Whatever Vela thought of me, I knowed her old man liked me. Or liked my work, anyhow. Whenever I brung in a sack of cotton, he'd weigh it and then, looking a bunch of times at the number on the scale, he'd hike up them bushy eyebrows. I was picking six hundred pounds a day for that old man.

"Henry! Henry!" he said to me once. "You haff rocks in zat sack?"

"Nothing but cotton, Mister Rauss."

He pulled out a handful and looked at it careful. "No scraps. Ah, it makes a man's heart sing, see his cotton so vhite. I gotta think you 'r a German."

"No sir. Jus' American."

"Vel, you not za Irish one, I know zat. Lazy, lazy." He shook his head.

I didn't say nothing to that.

Poppa Rauss went on: "I got zis bad leg, ya. Und zo old, I get. Iff I haff two or three more pickers like you iss, I vould quit vork." And he bent over and laughed hisself silly, 'til the tears was running outa his eyes, like quitting work was the biggest joke he could think of.

"At six bits a hundred," I said back, "I figure I'll make enough money offa you to quit work too." I give a laugh with him. That was even more a joke than Poppa Rauss quitting work. Them days, the idea of a young man not working had to be a joke.

"Iff only it don't rain." That was Momma Rauss.

I turned around, and there stood Momma Rauss and Vela. They'd brung in their pick sacks and was waiting to get 'em weighed. All you could see of their faces was the tips of their noses, they was both wearing them big old stove-top bonnets, the kind that's so big and deep you gotta stick your head inside to see who's in there.

But even the end of Vela's nose looked good to me.

"Yah, yah, yah, iff only it don't rain." That was Momma again, and she was shaking her head. "Last year, ve go to pick, yah, it come za rain. Und da cotton gott yellow as Poppa's beard."

"Well, there's only one thing raining this year," I said, and I pulled my sweaty handkerchief out and mopped up my forehead. "And it ain't the sky."

This time, it was Momma that laughed. And I could tell by how she looked at me, and then at Vela, and back at me, that she liked me too—maybe was even putting us together in her head. That maybe, for some reason, she liked me better'n Emil, even though he was a German like they was. I couldn't tell that last part for sure, but the way her nose sticking outa the bonnet was flapping back and forth between me and Vela like it was, that's what I suspicioned.

***

It wasn't too long before I found out. At night I slept in the hayloft over the barn—a empty spot where they'd give me a pallet and a wash basin. And one evening, just before sunset, I was setting up there, counting out a week's wages, when a round yellow head come sticking up through the trapdoor. It was Vela. She'd climbed up the ladder and was holding a plate with a big square of Momma's pear strudel on it.

"Momma send zis."

"Come on up." I put out my hand.

"Oh no, I haff to go."

"Aw, c'mon. Jus' a few minutes." I grabbed Vela's hand and tugged a little on it. Up she come without saying nothing more. She was washed and scrubbed from after all day in the field, and I could smell a whiff of lye soap.

"Why don't you set down?" I said.

I pointed over at my pallet, it was really just a old quilt stuffed with corn shucks. Vela looked down at it, but she didn't move. She just stood there. I didn't set down either, just stood there too, holding that strudel plate. We both didn't seem to know what to say next, so we didn't say nothing. I could hear a mouse snubbing around in some loose hay, but that was the only sound there was.

Finally, Vela said something. "Poppa, he says you're za best worker he ever has."

"Ain't gonna be long before the cotton's all picked."

"Yah, but forty more acres Poppa iss going to buy. Und all za time, even in za vinter time, there is vork."

"Forty acres?" I said. "How's he gonna buy forty more acres?"

"Mister Hunter next farm, he vants to sell. Last year, za fever gott on his vife und his baby, und zey die. Und Mister Hunter, he vants to die too. He move avay, zo he can forget. Poppa und Momma, zey don't haff much cash money, but zey haff some."

"Your old man's a good farmer."

"Yah, yah." She put her shoulders back a little.

"Maybe he'd let me work them forty acres on shares?"

"Yah, yah." Her face got even pinker.

I knowed it was now or never. My knees felt like they was gonna rock out from under me. I put down the plate with the strudel on it, and I walked over to Vela and put my hands on her shoulders and I kissed her on the mouth. I did it so fast she didn't have no time to duck or go nowhere.

She still didn't move. It was like she was froze up, except for how she was breathing. Kinda like a horse after it's run hard. And her face had gone from that flushy pink to beet red.

I looked her straight in the eye. "I like you, Vela."

She didn't say nothing back. Only, "I haff to go."

At first, it was like she'd forgot where the ladder was, even though she'd just come up it. When she finally seen it, she walked over and turned around and started down it backways. I went over to her and grabbed her hand so she could hold onto something while her legs was feeling for the rungs. Her hand was slick wet.

"Henry," she said, "I haff to tell you. Emil vants to marry me."

"Emil?"

"Yah."

"Emil's a mule."

"He iss not a mule."

"Then what'd you come up here for?" All of a sudden, I was so mad I coulda spit.

"Strudel."

***

If Vela was gonna marry Emil, I didn't wanta keep staying on that farm. Only I didn't wanta take off, either.

I'd never felt that way about a girl before. Some pretty gals'll give you a itch, and if you can't have that gal, that itch'll make you feel like you're gonna die for about six hours. Then it goes plumb away. Like it was never there. Vela give me a diff'rent feeling. I can't say what it was. It was deep down. There was something so clean and pretty and sweet about her, like how the sky's so clean and pretty and washed after it's come a good hard rain. A gal and a sky are diff'rent things, of course, and a young man don't ache after a blue sky like he aches after a gal. But there's something about one of them washed skies that makes a man one-hundred percent happy to be alive on this Earth, and that's how I felt about Vela.

There was another reason I didn't wanta leave.

I didn't wanta miss the first hog killing.

Most of them German farmers around Weimar was so good at what they did, even with how hard it was to make a living offa cotton, that they could afford to keep hogs. Like I said before, the Rausses had four of 'em. Anyhow, they didn't kill any of them hogs 'til it was cold enough that the meat wouldn't spoil. But soon as it come the first norther, a bunch of Germans would get together and throw down on the first hog of the season. It was like a big party. Poppa Rauss had told me all about it. They'd stab the hog in the heart, or shoot it in the head, and hang it in a tree, and drain all the blood out into a pan. The women would take turns stirring the blood so it wouldn't clot up while the guts was took out and cleaned. The big guts was stuffed to make liver sausage, the other guts was stuffed with ground meat and salt and pepper to make other kinds of sausage. The blood was used to make "blood sausage." The main parts of the hog'd be cut into hams and bacon and ribs and chops, and they'd be cured over a wood fire. Even the hog's head would be cut up — snout, ears, tongue, ever'thing — and made into "head cheese." And the feet was pickled, what Poppa called "pig knuckles." The things that was too nasty for eating, like the balls and the bladder, they used 'em anyway. The balls was greasy and they was hung up in the barn and used to oil saw blades. The bladder'd get blowed up like a balloon with a turkey quill and dried and saved for Christmas eve. That's when the little kids'd jump on it and, BANG!, pop it like a firecracker.

I sure hated to leave the Rauss' farm before I seen one of them hog killings with my own eyes.

Yeah, it was both them things together—Vela and the hog-killing—that had me dragging my heels about taking off. But the next few days after I kissed that gal in the loft, it seemed like she didn't wanta have nothing more to do with me. She'd keep her face hid deep in that stove-top bonnet when we was out picking, and if I was north to her, she'd turn that bonnet west. If I was west, she'd turn south. If south, east. If east, north. But ever' so often, her neck'd twist towards me for a flash. And by the end of the day at the end of the week, her whole body turned plumb around and she come over to where I was at and aimed her nose right at me.

"You come Sunday?"

"I don't think so, Vela."

"Come."

"I don't dance."

"You *don*? Ur can not?"

"Same thing."

"I teach you. You come."

I went. She sounded like she wanted me there, and that give me some hope. But for most of the first hour I stood on the side and grinded my teeth, watching Vela and Emil hop and skip and whirl together. I hated that Emil. I hated him because of Vela. And I hated him because he was so much of their kind—big and strong and blond haired and German. Then I seen Vela say something in his ear, and he looked over at me, and his shoulders squared. Vela come over. She pointed outside.

"Za porch?"

Soon as we was out there, she put her arms on my waist and there we went—a-sliding, a-hopping, spinning around. Left…right…right …left…hop…hop…skip…slide. And before I knowed it, one of my legs got in the way of t'other one, and down we went—arms and legs a-tangled. And before I knowed it, I was kissing Vela and damn if she wasn't kissing me right back.

81

"How c'n you do it?" I said in her ear when the kiss was done. "Marry that mule?"

"I say zat I marry him? Nein. I say zat he *ask* to marry me. Emil iss a lazy one." And then she give me the prettiest look I ever seen in my life. "Henry, you are za one I get to loff."

***

I wanted to spend ever' second I could with that gal.

'Course, we was still picking cotton together, from dawn to dark, from can-see to can't. But I went to helping her with chores, too. When you're in love with a gal, and she loves you back, the hen-house you're sweeping out has got the sweetest chicken dung you ever smelled. And the hogs you're slopping has got the prettiest snouts you ever seen on a hog. Even the weeds in the garden ain't no problem. Them weeds got as much right to be there as you do, you think, and you give 'em their due for being strong and tough and stubborn, and you're happy to see 'em and you're happy to yank 'em.

Momma and Poppa seen what was going on, and I guess they was for it, because after the supper dishes was done, Poppa started telling me to stay for their "reading time." Sometimes, Vela'd get out the *Weimar Democrat-Gazette* and teach me spelling words. She always give me the long ones, but being I had that camera memory, all I needed was to see a word two or three times, and I could say ever' letter in it. Other times, I'd tell Vela and her folks some of Ma's outlaw stories. About bad-men like Butcher-Knife Bill and Dirty-Face Charley and Snakehead Thompson. Their eyes'd get rounder and rounder, and they'd make out like they didn't wanta hear no more, but I knowed they did.

The best part come when it was time for sleeping. Momma and Poppa was letting Vela walk me over to the barn, so long as she didn't go in it, and we'd took to inching behind that big red door and she'd let me kiss her so long as I never did wrinkle up her collar. And them kisses got me so dizzy and worked up that if that barn'd caught on fire and burned to a pile of ashes all around us, I wouldn't a-knowed it.

All that was the good luck.

Bad luck come the day after we picked the last boll of the Rauss' cotton and two weeks or so before it'd be time for the first hog-killing.

It was a Saturday, I'll never forget it. Most times, that was a work day like the others, but being that we was done with the picking, Poppa Rauss had said it was a day of rest. We was all gonna drive in the buggy to Weimar where the ladies'd buy theirselves some new hats and stockings, and Poppa, a half-keg of beer. Even though he made his own beer, he wanted plenty extra that night—a dozen neighbors had already been sent word to come drink it.

Even the mules knowed the hardest work of the year was over. They trotted all the way into Weimar and Poppa never had to pop the whip at 'em once. I had on a gray church suit (I'd got rid of that egg-yoke yellow one soon as I could), and there was eight silver dollars in my pocket to get something for Vela. It was a necklace she had her eye on at Schott's Watch & Jewelry Store.

When we got to Weimar, we drove down Main Street to Maxwell's General Merchandise Store. That's where we was going first. I hopped outa the buggy to tie up the mules. The others got outa the buggy, too, and for a minute or so we was all gathered there on the boardwalk....when all of a sudden, somebody slapped me on the shoulder from behind.

"Skinny Newton, for God's sake! When'd you get outa prison, boy?"

"*Prison?*"

All the Rausses repeated it, like they was frogs croaking together on a log.

I didn't want to turn around, but I knowed I had to do it. And there stood a big fella with a crooked nose and a coupla teeth missing in front. He was wearing bib overalls and a straw hat.

"I don't think I know you, mister." I started to walk off, but the big fella clamped a big hand on my shoulder.

"You sure knowed me good enough to flash your ass in my face when you was blowing past me down them rows."

Goddamn!

Yeah, I knowed the guy. It was Lonesome Gates, one of Dirty Butter's tight aces back at Imperial. He was a lazy old louse.

"So, Skinny," he went on, "you never answered me here, boy. When'd you get outa prison?"

Momma Rauss, she was standing the closest to me, grabbed me by the arm. "Vus you in *prison?*"

"It ain't how it sounds."

"Vus you in prison?" Momma Rauss asked it again.

I looked over at Vela. Her face was white.

"I ain't gonna lie to you. I ain't a liar. Yeah, I done some time. A little time. But I was innocent as a baby. You can go ask the Gov'nor. He'll tell you. He give me a pardon. That's how innocent I was."

"Vhy?" Vela asked. "Vhy din you tell us?"

"And you'd-a believed me?" My throat felt like somebody'd rammed a pound of cotton down it.

"Vel....you...you could haff...." Vela didn't say nothing more.

Now Poppa Rauss' face was getting redder and redder, and it looked like his whole German head was gonna blow up. "Adam und Eve, yah, they vas innocent too...Und Cain und Abel...Yah, everybody iss alvays innocent...!"

"Hell, they was the ones that stole from *me*!" I said. "More'n four years of my life! And it was a frame-up! I didn't steal no cotton! It was somebody else. He confessed to it."

"Cotton? Zat's vhat you vas in prison for? No, you didn't steal zat cotton, no!" Poppa was hollering now. "Vel, you're not going to steal my cotton! Und you're not going to steal my girl...."

"You gotta let me tell you what it was..."

But Poppa Rauss had a awful look on his face. Tears was running down Vela's cheeks.

I wasn't one to cry. Most times, when I had bad feelings I just went and sweated 'em out. But I could feel something pushing up, hard, from the back of my throat, from the same place that felt like it was stuffed full of cotton.

I choked it back.

I choked ever'thing back, turned on my heel and walked off. Walked off from Poppa and Momma, from all the Rauss grandbabies, Helga and Olga and Mina—and from Vela.

I never saw any of 'em again.

EIGHT

The train through Weimar only went two ways: east and west.
I picked west.

There was a Southern Pacific, freight, No. 277, that come in
sometime after midnight. It headed toward San Antone and El Paso
and, way on down the line, to California. I knowed I didn't wanta go
all the way to California, but, other'n that, I didn't know where I
wanted to go.

I felt like I'd been hit by one of them freight locomotives.

When No. 277 come in, I swung on up into a empty boxcar and
I set down in the doorway, dangled my legs over the side and let the
country slide by. It was a dark, dark cloudy night. There wasn't no
moon, no stars. Inside me, I felt black as that night. Vela'd blow over
me and I'd push her outa my head and, a minute later, she'd blow
over me again.

I likely woulda married that girl if it hadn't been for....

For what?

Goddamn that Lonesome Gates! Goddamn that hard-assed
Poppa Rauss!

***

That whole ride, my mind went here and there, here and there.

When I wasn't pushing Vela outa my head, I was thinking about
a letter I'd got from Ma just a week before I'd got sprung from the
penitentiary. It was a letter that I couldn't hardly believe: Ma wrote
that her and the old man had busted up.

Pa'd finally give Ma "the last straw I could take," she wrote.
Seems that he'd decided this time that God's Country was down near
the Mex'kin border, in Zavala County, where we'd gone one time
before, when I was a kid. The first time, Pa said he wanted to farm
new country, but all we found in Zavala County was horns and

85

thorns—prickly pear cactus and scrubby mesquites and wild, rangy cattle.

This time, Pa'd heard they was digging dozens of water wells into a underground lake, and turning all that dry country into a Farmer's Paradise. But, like always, he'd got ever'thing mixed-up. Them water wells cost lots of money to dig, money that Pa didn't have. And the main crop folks was growing down there was onions. Pa didn't know the first thing about growing onions. For a while there, Ma and Pa and the kids that was left was all living in a tent. That's when Ma said, "You jus' go on back north, Jim. You find God's Country, I'll read about it in a letter."

Goddamn my old man!

***

The train stopped in San Antone, to drop off some cars and pick up some others. I quick pulled up my legs and hid over in one corner of the boxcar, ready to jump out in case a railroad dick come poking around. None did. I knowed the next stop was Uvalde, about seventy-five miles west.

Uvalde's where I decided I was gonna get off.

Ma'd told me in her letter that she and some of the kids was living about forty miles from Uvalde, in Crystal City, next to the South Texas brush. And what do you know, that lazy brother of mine, Jess, was making cash money there by breaking brush country broncs for ranchers, and he was supporting Ma and what was left of our family.

Of all the people I knowed, Ma was the one I cared most about seeing.

To get to Crystal City, I had to catch a spur at Uvalde. Only I hadn't ate since early the day before, and by the time the train got to Uvalde my stomach was growling like a bulldog. I walked over to Main Street and had me a big breakfast: scrambled eggs with Mex'kin pepper sauce, sausage with Mex'kin pepper sauce, grits with Mex'kin pepper sauce, and three cups of hot black coffee. The whole thing cost me 15 cents, but it was worth ever' penny.

When a man's got a full stomach, at least he ain't altogether empty inside.

Uvalde was a pretty town, with tall leafy pecan and oak trees lining the streets and some of 'em even in the middle of the streets. If things'd been diff'rent in my life, I mighta even liked being there. There was buggies and Model Ts and people all over, going about their business. At one corner, I seen a bunch of little girls dressed in white, standing in a circle. In the middle was a skinny young fella in a black suit. "Gather 'round for the voices of angels," he was saying. "These 'r poor Baptist orphans!"

Christmas was a ways off, but the song was about how Jesus was born in a stable, and how God lives in ever'body.

I walked over and dug into my pocket, I still had them eight silver dollars in there. I felt bad for them orphans, even if they was Baptist. Their voices was soft and sweet, except for one tall girl in the back who was sticking her neck out and bleating like a calf. I felt sorry for her most of all.

Their basket was coming around and I'd just throwed a dollar in when, all of a sudden, out of the corner of my eye, I seen something I hadn't seen in a long, long time. A bright red head of hair, just as red as a peckerwood. So red you couldn't miss it if you was in a crowd of a thousand people.

Before I knowed it, that red head was right up on me.

"Red Farley! I'll be damned!"

"Well, by golly!" Red slapped me on the back. "What the hell you doing here, Little Snakes?"

I knowed Red from Cisco. His family lived on a tenant farm a few miles from us one year.

"What the hell *you* doing here?" I asked him.

He scrunched his eyes together like he was thinking hard, though I don't know how come, my question didn't call for no hard thinking. "Looking for work," he said at last. "Was picking 'round Matador, but it's all done. My life's in my knapsack here—extra pair of pants, harmonica, three pecans. And my fortune's here," he pointed to his pocket, and laughed. "Two dollars, two cents. What you been up to, Little Snakes?"

"What else? Picking. East o' here."

The basket come around again, and I throwed another silver dollar in it. Red screwed up his mouth sideways. "Oughtn't you be holding onto that?" he said.

I didn't answer him.

Now the Baptist girls was singing a song about how some kings was coming to see the Baby Jesus.

"Red," I asked him after a little bit. "Your folks have

Christmas?"

"Ma sometimes made yeast cake," he said. "But you know my Pa. Old drunk. Never knowed if it was Monday or Thursday or the Fourth of July. Y'all?"

"Hell, no," I said. "That was our moving time. We was always on our way over the fence, Christmas time."

Red give me a little smile. He knowed my Pa, like I knowed his Pa.

"So, Little Snakes," he asked me, "what'cha gonna do for work now?"

"I'm thinking. You?"

"Dunno. Maybe go to Del Rio. Fix fences, something."

"Hey Red," I said. "Wanta rob a train?"

***

I was only kinda kidding at first, but then it wasn't a joke no more. I got serious. I really wasn't caring about nothing. Just didn't care. Maybe it come from a madness deep down inside me, way way down deep, so deep down I didn't even know where it first come from. A madness at the whole stinking world.

But who knows? You think you know how come you do things, but them "how comes" is kinda like a onion. There's a top "how come," and you peel that off, and there's another "how come," and there's another under that one. You can go on forever that-a-way, asking "how come?", 'til there ain't nothing left a'tall, no answers, and no onion, either.

Fact is, right then, I didn't care about nothing.

Why rob a train? Why *not* rob a train?

Red wasn't so sure at first. He didn't say yes; he didn't say no. So I told it to him this way: "It ain't gonna be no habit, Red. We'll just do it for a one-time thing."

I already knowed something about how trains was robbed. I knowed all that from Ma's outlaw stories. Sometimes—to get a train to stop—the robbers'd block the track, and swing a red lantern, pretending they was warning the engineer that another train was stalled up ahead. Or they'd mess with the rails, loosen a few of 'em, which would make the train fly right offa the track. A lotta times they'd just do it the easy way, and that's the one I landed on. The outlaws'd wait for the train at one of its stops, a water tank or some outa-the-way station, and they'd swing on up the back of it.

Once you got on that train, all you had to do was rob it. And that wasn't so hard, if you caught the passengers by surprise, and talked rough to 'em. Or at least that's the feel I'd got from Ma's story about Little Al Jennings. Little Al was a pint-size desperado from Oklahoma—barely five feet—and here's what he said about train stickups: "Folks get so dazed that they act like trained dogs."

So which one was me and Red gonna rob?

I knowed just about ever' train in Texas. You could call out a number, and I'd tell you where it was from and where it was going.

No. 43?

Katy passenger from Chicago. Stopped in Dallas, Waco, Temple, San Antone.

No 12?

International & Great Northern freight from Laredo. Stopped in Cotulla, Pearsall, San Antone.

And so on.

I thought on all the ones I knowed, and picked the Southern Pacific, No. 9. It was a passenger, New Orleans to Del Rio, and had Pullman cars with rich folks. It stopped for water close to midnight in a country spot called Cline, about twenty miles west of Uvalde. Nobody'd be expecting trouble there.

There was something else I liked about No. 9. After it left Cline, it snaked west through miles and miles of that wild South Texas brush. That brush'd be good for our escape. In the old days, that's where outlaws and Mex'kin bandits was always hiding out from posses and sheriffs and Texas Rangers and each other in the cover of that thick brush.

To do the stickup part right, me and Red needed to get us some guns. And overcoats to hide 'em in.

I knowed where to get all that. Them days, ever' town had wagon yards where people from off the farms and ranches camped while they was buying groceries and supplies, getting tools 'r wagons repaired, and such. So we snuck into one of them yards and checked out a bunch of wagons. Sure enough, we found us two old scruffy black overcoats and a pistol. We snatched 'em. Later that night, we kicked into a hardware store and got us some rope and a knife and two .30-30 Winchesters.

***

89

Next day, me and Red headed west. It was a long walk, them twenty miles to that water stop, but I never minded hard walking. Hell, when you grow up a farm kid, the only way you get anywhere is by moving your feet. And just following a mule's ass up and down them middles took you over about twenty miles ever' day – even if you wasn't getting nowhere.

Outside Cline, me and Red hunkered down 'til it come dark, and while we was waiting, we told a few jokes. It felt good being around somebody that I knowed from when I was a kid. I think Red liked it too, you know, being around somebody that knowed him like I knowed him. Then, about 11 o'clock, fifteen minutes from when the train was due, we sneaked over near the freight house.

While we was waiting, we took off the overcoats and ripped out the linings for masks. I told Red to wrap his all over his head, like a kerchief. If we was gonna get fingered, that red hair of his woulda done it for sure. 'Course, when Red done that, he looked just like them old ladies from the Old Country you see shuffling down the streets in them little farm towns that's heavy with immigrants.

"You're looking like a grandma," I said to Red. "So I'm gonna be the head man on this one."

"Okay by me," Red said. Even if he had a drunk for a Pa, nothing bothered Red.

The train come in right on time. We was watching Red's pocketwatch. And when them wheels squealed to a stop, all the muscles in my arms and legs stiffed up and my stomach balled. But it wasn't that I was boogered. It was just my body getting ready for the go.

At 11:37, I remember the minute exact, the "highball" blowed.

I signaled Red to follow me, and we hopped onto the back car. And just as the wheels was starting to turn again, I come eyeball to eyeball with the brakeman. He was a shrunk-up old man, all bent over and crooked, but when he seen us he pulled hisself up straight as a nail.

"Hey!" he said. "You can't git on this train!"

Me and Red pulled our rifles out from under our coats. I jabbed that .30-30 in that brakeman's belly.

"The hell we can't," I said. "We're on."

The old man's chest caved in and his knees started shaking. I knowed me and Red wasn't gonna shoot him, still, most brakemen them days deserved a little boogering. Like I said way back, when I was a kid hopping trains, brakemen'd hit me with their clubs, if they could get close enough, or throw rocks at me. They was mean, dirty rats.

I give the brakeman another poke. "This is our train now."

Red tied his hands good with rope.

First car we come to was a special and there was only two men in it. One of 'em looked like a officer of the SP. Long gray whiskers, sticky and brown near the mouth from tobacco juice, and a paunch that hung over his belt like a cliff. His wallet was thick as the Bible. "I'll take that, mister," I said. And I throwed it in a coffee sack Red was carrying. No words come outa the big man's mouth but I could tell, him being a railroad man, that he took train robberies personal.

Well, I'll tell you what, when that big man pressed his lips together and give a couple of grunts, something swole up in my chest.

And it felt good, that swell.

The other fella had got so scared he was trying to push hisself under a bench, down on the floor, and you could just see the tips of his boots. Well, I tugged on the tips of that old boy's boots, and I pulled and I tugged, and I pulled and I tugged, it was like pulling a big old long bull snake outa its hole. Finally, out come two rail-skinny legs, and a big shiny silver belt-buckle, and a red-and-white checkered shirt, and the longest, skinniest neck I ever seen, and a long, bone-white face with two eyes popping outa it.

"Please don't kill me," the fella kept saying. "*Please don't kill me!*"

It made me wanta chuckle, him being so scared of nobody else but me and Red, two old farm boys.

"You wanta keep breathing, Slim," I said, "gimme your money 'n slide on back under that bench."

His wallet had a hundred dollars in it.

Then we hit the Pullmans. Pullmans was the sleeping cars on trains, with dark-green curtains that come down over the berths. Me and Red had never been in a Pullman before. We didn't know there was top berths and bottom berths, so we just robbed the bottoms. I raised the curtains, one by one, and told the folks inside, "Give us what'cha got." Then Red put the loot in his coffee sack. It was only if we found a woman alone we'd drop the curtain without taking no money. That was the code of the Old West: You don't rob a woman alone.

It was all coming natural to me—throwing just the right sharp in my voice, aiming the barrel just so, shifting my eyes here and there, here and there. 'Course, most of them passengers was so sleepy they was acting just like Little Al said—like dazed dogs.

They was throwing out pocketbooks, watches, necklaces, wallets, rings, ever'thing but the nightclothes on their backs. There was only one lady, a curly-headed gal, who give us hell and wouldn't give up her wedding ring. But her old man finally yanked it offa her finger and told her to hush up.

Then, quick as me and Red was done with the Pullmans, we pulled the cord that stopped the train and hit that wild country a-running.

NINE

Cactus, cactus, cactus.

It was a moonshiny night, near bright as day, and all you could see in ever' direction was prickly-pear cactus. Acres and acres of 'em, high as your head. They growed in clumps, their pads was big as skillets, one pad atop another atop another. And their thorns was all over, sharp as needles.

But we didn't have no choice. We had to charge right though 'em.

While we was winding this-a-way and that-a-way, getting all ripped up by them thorns, we couldn't help but wonder if some-body'd get up a posse to chase us down when the train got to the next town.

Maybe. Maybe not.

Posses was the one thing Little Al'd said he didn't like about the train-robbing business. When the laws and vigilantes and yapping dogs grows into a group and sets out on your trail, thirsty for blood.

The next town from where me and Red'd hopped off was called Spofford, about four miles down the track. But it was such a little dot on the map it probably didn't have no laws to put together a posse. And even if there was a posse after us, it'd be a job to find us. That country—the Mex'kins called it *la brasada*—was a mess of thorny brush and cactus and varmints.

I knowed it from when I was a kid.

If you wasn't careful, you couldn't go a foot without something stinging you, or biting you, or stabbing you. The thorns in them prickly pear plants'd sling right into your pants, break off and stick in your leg for days, and fester. And there was a nasty little bush called "catclaw" that had long thorns with hooks at the ends, and that'd dig in and not let go.

Then there was the rattlers, fat diamondbacks slithering all over the ground, or coiled up on rocks, like ropes. They growed so long in that brasada a five-footer was called a "baby." Some of 'em was eight feet long and fatter'n your fist. If you put your foot in the wrong place, and got bit, you'd have you a problem a lot worse'n a cactus stick.

"Watch your feet, Red," I said to him.

I set out to find us a trail.

I knowed just how to travel through that wild country so you wouldn't come outa it scratched, torn, or dead. When I was a kid, I loved prowling that brush. I always liked seeing new country, the wilder the better. The key is: you find you a animal trail—carved out by hooves or paws or claws—and follow it far as it goes, then you find you another. And lots of times, they lead straight to waterholes.

Me and Red found us a cow trail. It was about a foot wide and it snaked right through all them pears, clear and clean, like some South Texas Mex'kin had hacked it out with a machete. And that's what we walked along all night. We come to a couple of little draws and we lapped that water like we was thirsty dogs. There was crackles and rustles and crunches on both sides of us, and a couple of times I seen the glitter of little eyes in the brush, and way off, we'd hear the howls and yelps of coyotes. But we was both carrying long sticks and we kept 'em scraping the ground in front of us, and we didn't have no trouble—until daylight come.

***

Me and Red'd just waded through a little creek and we was picking up the trail on the other side, just turning a bend, when I heard something. It was low little grunts and sharp high pops—grunt-grunt, pop-pop, grunt-grunt, pop-pop.

Then, WHAMMO!

All of a sudden, the bottom part of my left leg felt like somebody'd took a knife and gashed me with it, fast and hard.

"Ayaaaaaa! Ayaaaaaaa!" I couldn't help but holler.

"What? What? What?" That was Red. He was a way behind me.

I fell to the ground, grabbed my leg, hollered again.

"Ayaaaaa!"

I was in the middle of a ambush. All around me was a dozen balls of black bristly hair, about two feet high, a-grunting and a-popping. Only thing, it wasn't really a ambush. It was more like a retreat. Fast as I seen 'em, they was gone. Crashed back into them prickly-pear stands. I couldn't see a one no more.

All they left behind 'em was a kinda musky smell in the air.

"What the hell?" Red'd caught up behind me and when he seen me on the ground, blood spurting outa a hole in my pants, he looked more boogered'n when we was robbing that train. "What the Jesus!"

"Javelinas," I said.

"What?"

"Goddamn javelinas! Herd of 'em."

"What's that?"

"Crazy little wild musk pigs." I'd forgot that Red didn't know nothing about the brush country. "They don't mess with you if you don't mess with them. But they got tusks sharp as razors, and can't see worth a damn. One of 'em blowed right into me."

"Aw, no. You okay, Little Snakes?"

Red still had that kerchief around his head, and he looked like a worried old grandma, crouched over my leg, watching that spurting blood. And I gotta say it, that gash did hurt like the devil! I knowed one old boy from way back that had a javelina tusk cut right through his hand – in through the palm and out the other side. But I checked out where I'd got stuck by the thing, and I pulled the skin this-a-way and that-a-way, and I wiped off as much blood as I could, and I didn't see no bone.

"Thanks for the worry," I said to Red. "But a pig's better'n a posse."

***

When the sun was good and up, we was eight miles or so from Spofford. It was devil's country, all right. And me and Red looked like devils ourselves, thorns all over, a bloody kerchief tied around my pig cut. I wasn't walking fast as I liked to, that stab'd give me a sore leg. But I figured we was far enough into the brush to be safe from a posse.

"Let's see what we got," I said.

We went over to a mesquite tree and I cleared away some grass and weeds from under it, and Red spilled out his coffee sack.

More'n sixty years later, I can still see that big pile on that bare spot in the middle of that brasada: men's wallets, women's pocket-books, paper money, gold and silver coins, watches, broaches, rings. And when we opened the wallets and pocketbooks, out spilled more bills, jewelry, papers, name cards, combs, and stuff that we didn't know what it was for.

For a little bit, me and Red just kneeled in front of it all.

"Jesus Christ," was all he could say.

I didn't say nothing right off. There was more money in that pile than Pa or any of them other farmers would've ever had if they worked them wore-out cotton fields until they died.

"Alright, Red," I said finally. "I'll sort the soft, you do the hard."

For the next half hour, we set that money to a-jingling and a-rattling and a-rustling and a-crinkling . We didn't have no paper or pencils to figure out exactly how much it was, so we just split it—good as we could—into two piles: silver dollar here, silver dollar there; ten-dollar bill here, ten-dollar bill there.

That other stuff, the rings and watches and such, they wasn't as easy to split up, but we done it fair as we could—one ring here, one there, one watch here, one there. The things that wasn't worth nothing—the papers and pictures and such—we stuffed down a armadillo hole.

After that, I done some rough figuring and come up that me and Red had more'n $2000 each, cash money. The rest we wouldn't know 'til we fenced it all. But it was at least hundreds of dollars more.

Was I sorry for it, for taking all that loot?

I didn't care. I just didn't care. That was the first time in my life I'd broke a federal law. But except for them two men in the special, all the folks we robbed on that train was riding in Pullmans. And anybody that's got enough money to sleep in a Pullman most likely has money to spare.

Hell, the only thing I was sorry for was that we didn't get more.

Later, I seen a story about the robbery in a newspaper and it told how we'd missed them upper berths and had passed up a little room with a rich Mex'kin man and his daughter who had $20,000 in money and jewelry. Goddamn! We'd seen that door, but we thought it was a toilet.

***

We had two piles of money, but no food.

We hit the trail again. There was plenty of game in that brush, if you was a crack shot. And I was. I could blow a rabbit's eye out at forty steps, and I could shoot a line of three or four quail's heads off with one bullet. But we had the wrong kinda guns. All that woulda been left'd be a fuzzy tail, or a coupla bloody feathers.

Finally, when our stomachs was so empty they couldn't even growl no more, we come across something we could eat: one of them big wild cows with horns more'n a yard long that even the best old cowboys couldn't get into a corral. They lived out in the brush like they was outlaws. She was grazing in a small, grassy opening, and when she heard us coming, she started to take off. But her curiosity got the best of her, and for a little bit, she stopped to see what was rustling in the brush out in that no-man's land.

My bullet hit her just above the shoulder blade. She keeled over.

I cut a hunk offa her rump and we roasted it over a fire of branches, Red had some matches in his overcoat. And I'll tell you what, that chuck tasted better'n anything I ever ate in my life. Even better'n Momma Rauss' fat pork sausages.

After we ate, we got to feeling drowsy, and while we was letting that food settle in our guts, I told Red stories. Stories all about the cowboys that worked that brush country, and how they was always risking their lives to round up the cows like the one we just'd killed.

"They call 'em brush-poppers. It's what they do, pop the brush. Just put their heads down and crash through it. They gotta dodge the limbs, so sometimes they'll be hanging on their horses one side, sometimes the other side."

"I think it's better to be a cotton picker," Red said.

But I was caught up thinking about them brush-poppers that ain't afraid to take risks. I told Red some more. How to keep from being torn to pieces, they wear thick canvas jackets and bullhide chaps and hog-snoot tapaderos over their stirrups. And wide-brim hats with chin straps. And how lots of times a thorn or limb'll drive into a brush-popper's eye or his throat. Or a big limb'll just plain kill him.

Red listened hard and then he pulled a harmonica out of his pocket. He played "Red River Valley" and "She'll be Coming 'Round the Mountain" three or four times. And we both got to feeling lonesome.

"You got a gal, Little Snakes?" Red asked when he put down his harp.

I felt something thick hop up from my gut. "Naw. You?"

"She quit me. Said my hair's too loud."

His hair *was* loud. "Your hair ain't loud, Red."

"It's loud. Gal's don't like red hair." His shoulders was slumped.

"Most gals ain't worth messing with."

"No, they ain't."

"Did'ja know, Red," I went on, "ain't hardly no Wild West out-laws that got hair your color? I must know about a hundred of 'em, and only two of 'em had red hair. Most of 'em was towheads. Or brown-headed. And nine outa ten of 'em had blue eyes. Queer thing, ain't it? Anyhow, you got them green eyes, and that red hair, so I don't think you're cut out to be a outlaw. And gals should like that."

"Lots of gals like outlaws," he said.

"With all that money you got now, Red, you ain't gonna have to worry about no gals."

We didn't say nothing else.

We was both lost in our own thoughts. We could hear some bob-white quail calling each other a ways off—ka-loy-kee, ka-loy-kee—and the answer—whoyl-kee, whoyl-kee. And a Harris' hawk swooped down nearby and we could hear its karrr, karrr, karrr. There was a few rustles and the flap,flap,flap of a tail in the brush.

That was all.

At dusk, we covered our loot with our overcoats and dropped to sleep—with our .30-30s by our sides. Next morning, we cut hunks of that chuck to take with us, and that's all we ate the next couple of days we spent fighting that brush to get to Crystal City. My leg was stiff and achy and throbbing from that javelina gash, but I didn't let it slow me up. And, thank God, nothing else stabbed us. Or bit us. Or snagged us.

No rattlers, no laws, no brush-poppers, no nothing.

If we'd run into any humans, we had a story. We even went over it a coupla times to give us something to do while we was walking.

"We're jus' two bis'ness men from San Angelo," I said, to try it out, "that's been robbed blind by that son-of-a-bitch Pancho Villa."

"Yeah, we're jus' two bis'ness men from San Angelo," Red said after me, "that's been robbed blind by that son-of-a-bitch Pancho Villa."

They was having a revolution over in Mexico, the poor folks against the rich ones, but Pancho Villa was robbing ever'body, rich people, poor people, he didn't care, and he was crossing over the Rio Grande into Texas and robbing ever'body over here too. Pancho Villa and his men was cut-throats and we was lucky we didn't really meet 'em in the brasada.

There was old white bones scattered all over that brasada. Some of 'em was human bones.

TEN

It was late afternoon when me and Red come up to Crystal City. We decided to split up and skirt the town.

We didn't figure the laws'd be hunting for the train robbers there, fifty miles from Spofford, across that brasada, but being that we was new to being federal lawbreakers, we didn't wanta take no chances. Red said he was gonna hop a freight and head west. Maybe we'd meet again; maybe not.

I watched that red head go trotting off into that red sun, and I almost felt sorry to see it go.

Then I hit off to Ma's.

I went up one dirt road, down another, and took a jog to the east, Ma'd give me directions in that letter. And before I knowed it, there I was. The house wasn't nothing to look at, just wood-frame, raw lumber, no paint on it, what they call board-and-batten, with slats nailed over ten- or twelve-inch planks to keep out the cold and the wind and the dirt. But it was a house.

There wasn't nobody out front, but just as I was walking up, something from the back that didn't sound human let out the damndest bawl of rage I ever heard. I lit on around and there I seen a square corral made of mesquite posts, and, inside it, good-godamighty!

You couldn't tell where the bronc ended and my brother Jess begun.

The horse was humping like a cat dropping from a tree, all four feet high offa the ground. It was a big old black thing, blacker'n the ace of spades, its whole body was muscles, you could see the power packed in 'em, like it was made of thunder and lightning. After it cat-backed a while, it went to sunfishing, twisting its body into a curve, so the toe fenders of my brother's saddle was touching the ground. Then it swapped ends, spinning while it jumped, so its head was a-going one way one time, its tail that way the next time. Then it started jerking back and forth, popping Jess like a bull whip, so hard it mighta busted a vessel in my brother's head 'cause blood come dripping outa his nose.

I couldn't help myself. "Grab for leather, boy!"

That's what done it.

Jess took his eyes off the head for just a flash, but long enough. Up he went, higher'n a kite.

Then KER-THUD!

The bronc kept right on pitching.

Jess let out a string of cusswords and picked hisself up offa the ground. Then, wouldn't you know it, he picked up his sweaty old Stetson, dusted it off on his leggings, put a new dent in the crown, and put it back on. All before he looked up to see who it was that'd hollered. That's the kind of crazy cowboy he was.

'Course, when Jess finally seen who it was, his mouth fell wide open and he come a-running. "Well I'll be damned! I'll be damned!"

"You shoulda grabbed for leather, boy!"

"Hell, the day I grab for leather is the day they cart me off in a box. Willis, I'll be damned!" He throwed his arms around me, then he hopped back off, there was so many cactus spikes a-sticking outa my overcoat. Then he looked down and seen my cut-up pants with dried blood around the hole. "What in the hell?"

"Son-of-a-bitch Pancho Villa."

"Hell! Pancho? That old son-of-a-bitch that fights for the poor people? You sure it was—"

"Where's Ma?"

***

What is it about a man and his Ma?

In all them outlaw stories I knowed, the last word half them Wild West bandits hollered out when they was dying was "Mother." And back in the penitentiary, I knowed about two dozen cons that had "Mother" tattooed on their arms or legs or chests. I guess it's because there ain't no sand or claw or lead in how a good mother loves her boy.

Ma was inside, stirring a big old iron pot of mustard greens on the stove, humming. And when she looked around, she let out a bawl near as loud as that horse and come a-running. "Sweet Jesus! I can't believe it!" She hugged me tight, and then the cactus sticks in my

101

coat made her hop back too. Then she seen my cut-up leg. "What in God's—?"

"It's the same old Willis, Ma," Jess cut in. "Always at the nose of a fight, and the tail end of trouble."

Ma give Jess a whack.

That night, there was more chatter than a bunch of hens around a new rooster. The other ones'd been off visiting neighbors, but when they come home there was so much ruckus that Grandbaby Seth jumped up and down, fell over flat on his face, and come up wailing. Ever'body'd growed up so much I hardly knowed 'em. My little brother Joe was near a man now, about fifteen, he had muscles in his arms and soft whiskers on his cheeks and chin.

At supper, Ma piled the table high. She'd wrung the necks off three more chickens and fried 'em all up in corn meal. And she'd made two bowls of mashed potatoes, and black-eyed peas, and greens with salt pork, and tomatoes, and hot biscuits and wild grape jelly, and for dessert, two dewberry pies oozing the thickest, sweetest juice you ever tasted.

Only problem was, all that food made me think of the Rausses and their pine table that "sagged in za middle," and even with so many ones in my family around me, Vela started blowing back up into my head. I shoved her out. She wouldn't go. I shoved her again. She wouldn't go. Finally, I just passed my plate and throwed every ounce of energy I had into eating.

Vela was all past now. Like Ma and Pa was past.

"Things ain't never been so good for me, Willis," Ma was saying, and her round Irish face was flushed pink. Her face looked more rested than I ever seen it. "Jess gits six, eight dollars a horse. Ranchers bring 'em here and come get 'em. And he's been teaching Joe. He's got the touch, Jess does. Folks say he's the best buster these parts."

"Yeah." Jess raised his coffee cup in a salute. "Ain't none better'n me."

I got a whiff of something. "What you got in that cup, Jess?"

Ma was the one that shook her head. "Oh, Jess don't drink no more."

"You ain't sipping when you're busting, are ya?" I asked.

Jess just smiled and took a long swallow. "I'm the best." He had a moon face like Ma's, and he most always had a twinkle in his eye.

Three bronc-busting brothers L. to R., Jess; Tull, holding the child;Joe

103

It was hard to believe it, Jess making money, money enough to feed a family. When we was kids, he was a big old larruping lazy boy. The old man'd whip him for not hoeing the cotton right, for cutting out the tiny little cotton plants and leaving the weeds, and then Jess'd go back and hoe it just the same way—cut out the cotton and leave the weeds.

Bronc-busting just come natural to him, I guess.

"Say, Willis," he said, "tomorrow, I'm gonna peel the bark offa five outlaws. How 'bout it? Help me out, boy. That brush is hell on horses. They use 'em up faster'n I can bust 'em."

"I ain't crazy," I said back.

"What d'ya mean by that?"

"Don't like horses," I said. "That's all."

"That means you *are* crazy." He laughed and twisted his fork in his potatoes. Joe looked up, smiled, and then went back to eating. And godamight, was that boy eating! There was a mountain of bones piling up on his plate, and a mountain of ever'thing else disappearing offa it.

It was Ma that looked worried. "Well, Willis, then what'cha gonna do?"

I shrugged. "I'm thinking."

"They're planting east of here. Maybe you could get a stake."

"I ain't gonna waste my life behind no stinking mule's ass, Ma."

"How 'bout driving a freight wagon?"

"And what's that? That's jus' following a bunch of horses' asses."

Ma frowned. "You don't need to get smart with me. That ain't a bad job, driving a freight wagon. It's what Pa's doing now, 'tween Fort Worth and Amarillo."

"Won't be for long," I said. "Railroads 'r takin' over that job."

"Well, you gotta do something. Ever'body who lives has gotta do something."

After supper, Jess and Joe went out back to meet with a rancher hauling in two new broncs. The little kids went out front to play marbles. Me and Ma stayed at the table, and we both had another cup of coffee. She saucered it, like she always done when we was kids, but when she went to blowing on it, she was blowing so hard that little waves was skittering over the top.

I could see something was eating at her.

"You got a good mind, Willis." She give a sigh and poured her coffee from saucer to cup. "I'll never forget it, how Miss Dora come up to me in town that day, come rushing right across the street. 'You can't let Willis quit, Missus Newton. You give that boy a education, there's no telling what he'll do. And you don't give that boy a education, there's no telling what he'll do either.' "

She took a sip of coffee, and give another sigh.

"I hated it that you quit."

I didn't say nothing to that.

For farm kids, school was just three months—January, February, March—between harvesting and planting times. I'd only went that one time, when Pa'd gone off to New Mexico, hunting for God's Country. I blowed through four grades in nine weeks, the teacher said I was the smartest one she'd ever had. Got ever' damn word right in that fourth speller but one. "Bulk." I spelled it how it sounded. "Bolk." Then the seat of my pants ravelled plumb out and I was ashamed to wear 'em. It didn't matter to me that I had no shoes, but when you ain't got no seat in your pants, that's a diff'rent story.

I quit.

'Course, it wouldna made no diff'rence. Pa woulda yanked me out, soon as he figured out God's Country wasn't in New Mexico, and he come back home.

"You know what Pa said about school, Ma. 'School don't give a boy sense.' "

"Pshaw. Pa's one to talk about sense. Crazy old fool!" She shook her head. "He'd let up some by the time Ila and Joe and them come along. You know Joe went into high school? He did, thank Jesus. Maybe if you'da stayed working for that old man that wanted to send you..." She stopped and shook her head again. "You're the one I worry over most, Willis. You ain't like the others. You're restless. Just like Pa."

I could feel the blood rushing to my head. "I ain't nothing like the old man."

"That one way, you are."

"I ain't like him no way."

***

I laid low around Ma's for a couple of weeks or so. I watched Jess teach Joe the tricks, how to ride them crazy-eyed broncs down to sweat, and I seen that my little brother, even if he didn't say much,

105

was a fast learner. As for me, I monkeyed around with this and that, fixed a broke-down fence, and give Joe some money to buy a hog. Then I butchered that hog the way I figured a hog oughta be butchered, and dulled four knives doing it. And after Ma got a neighbor farmer to smoke all the meat, there was a whole winter's store outa it. I even saved out the bladder and blowed it up with a turkey quill for the grandkids to bust when Christmas come.

Still, I didn't feel like I fit there.

There was a place for Jess in that ranch country, and there was a place for Joe. There really wasn't no place for me.

Then something come down that didn't give me no choice but to blow.

It was late afternoon, and Ma and the rest of 'em was off shopping in town. I was splitting mesquite logs into firewood. Swinging that ax up high as it would go. Crashing it down, WHAM! hard as it would go. Ever' muscle in my whole body was working and straining and pumping blood. Sometimes what a man needs most in this world is to just shut off his head and split a log.

WHAM! WHAM! WHAM!

I wasn't thinking, just standing there a-WHAMing, when, all of a sudden, here comes a Ford Model T, a-skidding to a stop, kicking up a big cloud of dust. The door flied open and a little body flied out. It was a man with a red face and he was a-hollering: "Where's Jess! Where's that drunk son-of-a-bitch! Gonna kill 'im!"

The man raced over and near knocked me down before he skidded to a stop. Then it was the whiskey on his breath that near knocked me down. I knowed who he was. His name was Dudley, and him and Jess had been messing around with the same woman, a dark-haired gal that worked at one of them Crystal City saloons.

"Where's that Jess? Gonna kill 'im!"

I put down my ax and wiped the sweat offa my forehead. "You ain't killing nobody, Dudley. You ain't nothing but a whiskey pickle."

"Well, this pickle's packing a pistol!" And damned if he didn't hunch down and start to pull a pistol outa his left boot.

I was faster. I had a .38 tucked into my waistband, I'd been keeping it there "just in case." I pulled it out and jabbed Dudley in the belly with it. "Jess ain't here, Dudley old boy. You're dealing with me here. And I ain't easy like my brother."

His face went white.

"Don't shoot! Don't shoot! Let's fight it out!"

Without missing a beat, he bent his head down and charged at me. It was the craziest thing you ever seen! Charged at me, and then stretched his neck out and bit me. Bit me! Square on the forearm. It drawed blood. Well, I don't know what come over me then. I reached down and grabbed Dudley's hand and popped one of his fat fingers in my jaw teeth and cut down on it. Then I ground it, and I ground it, and I ground it.

I bit him back!

He didn't go for that. He yanked his finger outa my mouth, looked at it hard, yelped, and then wheeled around and flied on back to that old dusty Model T. And he was a-hollering bloody murder the whole way: "My finger's bit off! My finger's bit off! And yur goin' to jail for it, goddamn you! Yur goin' to jail!"

Well, I hadn't bit off Dudley's finger. It was still hanging there by a couple of gristles. But I knowed it was a goner, and I knowed I was gonna be a goner, too, if I stayed at Ma's. I sure as hell was gonna get arrested, even if it was Dudley that'd bit me first. I quick put a hunk of ham in a bag, dug up my train loot from where I'd buried it, and hit into the brush.

I went about three or four miles 'til I come to a clearing that had some feed troughs for cattle, and that's where I decided to spend the night. I curled right up under one of them troughs. I don't know how come I did that, except at a time when I was starting to feel more and more cut off from ever'thing, them cows milling around—crunching cornmeal and slobbering and snorting out hot puffs of air—seemed like kinda friendly company.

And they was. All night they'd get up from where they was bedded down, and they'd come over to feed a little—up and down, up and down, all night—and for me that one night they was the best company in the world.

Next morning I walked back into Crystal City and hid behind some railroad ties 'til a freight come in, heading for San Antone.

When the engine tooted, I was ready to go. I jumped into a empty boxcar.

ELEVEN

My train loot got ate up fast, on food and places to sleep and gals and kin.

And the money I made after that sure seemed slim.

I blowed here, and I blowed there. Arkansas...to visit kinfolk. Oklahoma...to prowl around. Houston....to work on a oil derrick. San Angelo....to gamble. Mineral Wells...to rob a clothes stores. Abilene...to fence some stole stuff.

That oil job I had in Houston was lousy, dirty work that broke your back, and didn't pay but a couple of dollars a day. And you had to answer to a sorry old foul-mouthed boss. Gambling paid better if you wasn't altogether honest, but if you wasn't altogether honest, you couldn't rake in too many pots in one place before you had to scoot outa town. Robbing that clothes store had got me the biggest haul, $845, after I sold my take to a fence.

But it wasn't hardly worth the trouble.

In Austin County, I got arrested for selling them clothes and the charges, if I'da got convicted, woulda landed me in the joint again. I escaped by flinging myself outa the sheriff's car when we was going down a hill, and hitting off into some woods. I knowed it'd take them old laws a while to get their car stopped, and by the time they done it, and went to raining them woods with bullets, I was long gone.

I got shed of my handcuffs by banging 'em agin a iron spike at a train track.

Meantime, while I was blowing around, here and there, doing this and that, the country had got itself all messed up in that World War, over across the ocean. My brother Jess got called off to fight, and the ranchers wasn't bringing many horses to Joe. Things was tighter for Ma for a while, and I got to mailing her some of what I could spare.

For a while, the War pumped up the price of cotton—to thirty-

Jess Newton, in uniform during World War I.

five cents a pound—and I went back to picking, even though I'd swore off it. Then the war ended and Ma wrote she didn't need money no more. Jess'd come back home in one piece (mostly 'cause he'd never got sent no further'n New Jersey). And Joe was a good buster by then. Ma had a yardful of chickens and a milk cow name of "June," and ever'thing was took care of.

Ever'thing, but me.

***

To this day, I can still see myself squatted down on a shivery Sunday morning, hid up in some bushes near the little old German town of New Braunfels, waiting to hop that Katy No. 12. It was the second day of March, nineteen and nineteen. I was thirty years old and my life, what I was gonna do with it, was a question that didn't have no answer.

I was heading for God knows where.

All I knowed was this: I wanted something outa life, even if I didn't know exactly what that was.

What kept coming back to my head, over and over, was how most of them hard-working cotton farmers I knowed ended up when they got old. Their kids'd put 'em in a little back room and that's where they lived 'til they died. I damn sure didn't wanta die that way! I wanted something more. You watch a cow, or a horse, they'll always move over to graze where they see the grass is thicker and sweeter. Even Pa wanted something better'n he had, that's how come he was always hunting for them honey ponds and fritter trees.

I'd see where the train'd take me.

Katy No. 12 was way on down the tracks. Just a dot. Still, a way-off train dot is the prettiest dot you ever seen. Ever since I was a kid, there wasn't nothing I liked more'n waiting to hop a train. You'd glue your eyes on that dot, hold 'em there...watching it grow...and grow...and GROW...'til all of a sudden that big iron engine would explode right up on you—bells a-clanging, steam a-hissing, black smoke a-gushing, dragging a line of grumbling, swaying cars that musta each weighed as much as ten elephants.

There wasn't nothing like it in the whole world.

But when No. 12 come in, there was only a few boxcars on it, and ever' last one of 'em was locked.

I hit on over to the blinds. The blinds was the second best place to ride, after empty boxcars. That was a little platform at the front of the first car, just behind the coal tender. There wasn't no window on that car for the conductor to see anybody riding on it. And the engineer or fireman couldn't see nobody behind 'em either because the coal tender was in the way.

But when I got to the blinds, four tramps was already there. That meant I had to either ride the rods, or ride up on the roof of a boxcar.

I picked the rods.

Lucky for me, I'd thought ahead. The rods was long steel bars that run longways under the train cars to keep 'em from sagging in the middle, and you could ride on top of 'em if you had a good thick board to throw across. Well, I had me a good, thick board—I'd pulled it off a old red barn not a hour before. Still, even with a board, it's risky business riding the rods. First, you slide yourself under the car and then you lay the board sideways over them long rods and then you lay yourself on top of that board. Flat on your belly, you grab your hands onto whatever you can—a brake pipe, the queen post, whatever. The scary part comes when the train starts moving and you're looking down and watching them railroad ties and that rocky roadbed whoosh by right under your nose. If you was to slip off and fall, you'd be mashed to dough under them big, grinding wheels. That happened to a lot of hobos.

When I laid down on that board, I held onto the brake pipe so tight there wasn't a drop of blood left in none of my knuckles. By the time we pulled into San Antone, I was stiff and achy as a old man.

In San Antone, I slid on out and found me a empty Missouri Pacific boxcar. I was ready for a easy ride. That boxcar smelled like moldy corn and body stink. There was a old hobo passed out in the corner of it. He was a-snoring and a-mumbling, and ever' few seconds one of his legs'd pop up in the air and then clunk back down again. But a empty is a empty and to a train-hopper, riding in a empty is like riding in a Cadillac.

I rode north to Hearne.

***

Them days, Hearne was a crossroads. There was a big railroad yard, and a jumble of track. 'Course, you can't go no place 'til you

111

know where it is you wanta go.

North, south, east, west?

What was there for me in any of 'em?

I finally picked north. That'd point me towards Fort Worth.

Back in the pen, Frank Holloway was always talking about Fort Worth like it was one of them cities in the Bible where the roads is paved with gold pebbles. He'd told me that Fort Worth was growing fast into a big city, a city full of "opportunity," and that things was happening there. And there was supposed to be a lot of other ex-cons living and working there that wouldn't see the "mark of Cain" on you.

Maybe Frank'd be there too. Fact is, I'd heard from the grapevine that, sure enough, that's where he'd gone after he got sprung.

I already knowed a little about Fort Worth from when I was a kid. It was the biggest place near Rising Star and Cisco to do business, and it was a wild town. Full of saloons and gambling joints and bawdy houses and whore cribs. Way on back, Fort Worth was the last main stop on the Chisholm Trail before the cowboys hit on through Indian Territory, and it's where them old boys went for their last snatches of fun. And even after the trail drives stopped, all the boozing and gambling and whoring places stayed around, and that's how come Fort Worth was called "Sin City." If a farm lady's husband ever had business to do in Fort Worth, soon as he come back home, she'd check him top to bottom for signs of sinning as careful as a rancher'll look for fever ticks on a cow.

But there was a lot of other things in Fort Worth, too. Big stockyards. And it was where a bunch of railroads come together.

I was curious to see if Frank was right—if all the cow dung in that place was turning into gold pebbles.

I found me a freight on the Fort Worth Southern Pacific line. Only there wasn't no empties on it.

This time, I decided to deck a rattler, to ride up on top.

On the lid of a boxcar like that, you ain't so cramped like riding the rods. And you get to see more of the country—the fields and the cows and the birds and the clouds. Only trouble is, there ain't much to hold onto. And when that train is tearing down the tracks, a-swaying and a-bouncing, full-throttle all the way, curves and ever'thing, and when them big, heavy cars are a-shaking and a-leaning, and the ground down below ain't nothing but a flash, well, I can tell you, it's damn spooky. You ain't really that high offa the ground. But you feel like you're a mile up in the sky. With nothing to catch you if you fall.

***

I seen gold my first minute in Fort Worth.

It was on a tooth.

I'd just hopped offa that boxcar and untied my stomach when I seen a "Depot Dolly" swinging her big hips up and down the next track, a passenger line. She smiled over at me and that gold tooth give me a twinkle. Her lips was painted red and she had on a big hat with long, white, fluffy feathers and a lacy dress cut low to show off her big things. I smiled back at her, but my smile wasn't a "want it" smile, just like her smile wasn't a "for-sale" smile. Even if I'da wanted it, I wasn't gonna waste my money on a whore, and she could see right off I wasn't no moneybags. But depot dollies and train-hoppers got something in common, lots of times, living off the seat of their pants, and that's how come our smiles was just plain friendly.

I figured the best thing to do, the first thing to do, would be to see if Frank was in town.

I didn't have no address for him, but things like that never bothered me. What I done was walk around the freight yards 'til I seen a couple of shady-looking characters about to get into a boxcar. I asked 'em if they knowed where there was any hangouts for pimps, prostitutes, and ex-cons. They give me the names of some bootleg beer joints across Main Street.

But as I come up near Main Street, I got stalled out by a huge crowd of people. Hundreds of 'em! All a-cheering and a-hollering and throwing white confetti, so it looked like it was snowing. And then here come the soldiers! Lined up in six rows, clicking their heels and marching: clickity-clomp, clickity-clomp. They was the soldiers coming back from the World War, it was one of them "home parades."

I stopped to watch. It was right exciting, seeing all them soldiers in their uniforms, and all the flags a-waving. For half a hour, I just stood there and watched 'em go by. But then it come the tailend, and that was harder to swallow. They was the soldiers that had eye patches on or bandages around their heads, or was missing parts of their arms and parts of their legs or whole arms and whole legs. One of

113

'em, a blonde-headed kid, about eighteen, didn't have neither one of his legs and there was two men carrying the top half of him—and that's all there was.

And the more bad off them soldiers was, the louder them people cheered!

All I could think of was this: Poor bastards! Poor, poor, poor bastards! Did them butchered-up servicemen even know why we was fighting that war? Or was they just the ones doing the dirty work, blind, for the ones that had the say in this world? Then, another thought come to me: how it was my "bad luck" that'd saved me from maybe being a butchered-up soldier, too. And how it's hard to tell, sometimes, if bad luck is really bad luck, or just good luck with a mask on.

I didn't get drafted into that War, see, on account of that shot-up foot I'd got from that dirty Sweetwater sheriff when I was a kid. Besides that, I was a ex-con, and some of the registration boards was leery of 'em. That was all, maybe, that kept me from getting bayoneted by a Hun, or blowed to shreds by a Turk.

Well, I'll tell you what: watching them cut-up soldiers made me feel so good about my bad luck it give me fresh wind to hunt for Frank.

I crossed over Main Street and tracked down them beer joints I was told about. At the first one, the door opened just a crack. "What'ya want?" a man snarled. I musta looked like a real hayseed, I was in a sweaty work shirt and a pair of Jess' bib overalls. "Looking for a man, name of Frank. Slick hair. Straight teeth. Kinda smart-alecky."

The man slammed the door.

Same thing happened to me at the next joint, and the next one, and at one after that. But at joint number five, somebody give me the goods. It was a lady with red-dyed hair and she thought she knowed who I was talking about. She said to try looking for him at Missus Rinas' Rooming House, two blocks down, first on the left.

It was a sorry part of town, garbage in the yards and mangy dogs slinking all over. The house was a old two-story frame thing sagging ever'where, run by a thin, squeaky-voiced woman. She told me to go up the stairs and knock on Number 6. And when that door come inching open, and then swinging wide, you'da thought I was Frank's long-lost brother.

***

I'd never seen Frank in nothing but his prison clothes, so it took me a bit to get used to his new look. He had on black leather citizen shoes, they looked like they was fresh-shined. And black wool suit pants, they looked fresh-ironed. And a long-sleeve dress shirt, it looked fresh-starched. And at his wrists was cufflinks with diamonds the size of sweet peas. And something else I sure never seen on him in the joint: a arm holster with a .38.

The holster banged up agin my shoulder when Frank throwed his arms out and give me a hug.

"Well, well, well! If it isn't my old schoolmate, Mister Willis 'Skinny' Newton! *Skinny Newton!* Come on in here, boy! Come on in!"

I took a look around the room. It had gray walls with long streaks of green and brown wiggling down 'em. And it smelled like mold. Still, ever'thing was in its place, just like when we was in the penitentiary. His razor was laid out neat on a table, with a cup of shaving cream next to it. There was a newspaper folded neat on a old stuffed chair. A blanket was folded neat at the end of a narrow bed. And there was one other Holloway thing: a tin coffee pot boiling on a little kerosene stove.

In half a minute we was both drinking stiff black coffee, me setting on the chair, Frank setting on the bed, talking our heads off.

"I can't say I'm surprised to see you, Skinny," he said to me. "I had a funny feeling our paths might cross again. 'Course you never know. You just never know. But let me ask you this: You been on the square since you got out?"

"Enough."

"Well, I tip my hat to you." And he made out like he was tipping his hat though there was nothing on top of his head except neat-combed black hair.

"You, Frank?" I pointed at his diamond cufflinks.

"Oh, these are just for around the house. This part of town, they'll chop your hands off for less." He give a wink, but he didn't really answer me. He just leaned way forward. "So, why are you here?"

"Looking for work."

"Work, huh? Bad time to look. All those war boys coming back."

"I seen 'em."

"War boys get first crack at anything worth anything," he said.

"Don't surprise me."

"What kind of work do you think you might want, Skinny?"

"Something that pays good."

"Well, jobs at the packing house—if you can get one—are up to $3.25 a day. Only twelve hours a day. And they give you Sunday off."

I give him a look.

"Alright then." Frank took a big gulp from his coffee. "Let's get down to business. You want to rob a bank?"

You had to hand it to Frank Holloway. He come right to the point. Not one word wasted. And he done it without changing the look on his face, no more'n if he was asking me if I wanted sugar in my coffee.

"You still robbing banks, Frank?"

"I'm a bank robber. How can I be a bank robber if I don't rob banks?"

"So you ain't reformed?" I give a smile.

"Reformed?" Frank went to laughing so hard I thought he'd bust a gut. "Of course I'm reformed. You put a 're-' in front of a word, what does that mean? It means 'To do again.' 'To do anew.' And that's exactly what I'm doing. Formed myself right back into one helluva bank robber. Better than before. Learned a few things in the joint last time around. And I can teach 'em to you!"

To be honest, the idea of robbing a bank had come to my mind before. And to be completely honest, the idea of robbing some greedy old banker like Mister H.L. Pike didn't bother me a'tall. Them bankers never minded hurting us poor cotton farmers, so why should I mind hurting them? It seemed like most rich folks got rich by robbing from poor folks, or by working 'em to death. Even the Bible said it was gonna be harder for a rich man to get into Heaven than for a camel to go through the eye of a needle. And so most of me was saying: "Hell, yeah, let me in on a bank job!" There was only one thing niggling at me. Rich folks wasn't the only ones that kept their money in banks. Even Ma'd just opened a account at the Main Street State Bank in Crystal City.

"Lemme ask you this, Frank," I said. "You got any way of knowing whose money you're taking when you rob a bank?"

He busted out laughing all over again. So hard I thought he was gonna break another gut. "Jesus! Where'd you come from, Skinny?"

"What's that mean?"

He got up and picked up his little pot.

"Banks are insured," he said, coming over and pouring me some fresh coffee. "Nobody who's got money in 'em loses a penny. No sir. It's the insurance companies who have to pay off. And don't you know that it's the insurance companies, right along with the bankers, that have sopped up most of the money in this country. Just like you sop up gravy in a frying pan. They're shameless thieves. When Hogg was governor, you know he kicked forty insurance companies out of the state for skinning farmers? Forty of 'em! We'd just be little thieves stealing from big ones."

I set there, turning that cup around in my hands the same way I was turning over what he'd just said in my head.

Only banks I ever used in my life was old tin cans and Mason jars. But I did know something about them insurance companies. Insurance salesmen was swarming all over West Texas when I was a kid, taking money from all them poor farmers and promising 'em they was protected from ever'thing but Eternal Damnation itself. Then if you had a claim—yoooweee!—that's when they stung you. Missus Watson, she was one of our neighbors, she paid on a insurance policy for twelve years and then she got bad sick with that lung croup. But when she went to a hospital in Dallas, they said she wasn't covered. Only if she had heart trouble.

I took a swig of that coffee and clanged the cup down.

"I'm in."

"Well, you've come at just the right time! Last week I couldn't have done business with you, I already had a partner. But you know what he did? Got into a fight with a pimp. Stabbed right through the heart. Can you imagine that? Killed by a little, lousy pimp!... Oh, I've got one more question for you, Skinny. How well can you ride a horse?"

TWELVE

We was in the southeast part of Oklahoma, out in the country. There was a dried prune stuffed in my cheek, and a new Colt .45 with six lead bullets in it pressing hard into my hip. And I was about to get on a gray mare.

Soon as I throwed my leg over the saddle, I spit the pit outa that prune and I pulled my watch outa my pocket. It said 10:03. I wanted to know the time, exact, because that moment was, for me, what some folks call a "tether" moment. Ever'body's got them "tether" moments. That's a time that all the rest of your life is kinda tied to.

For me, 10:03 was the time I set the course to become a full-time outlaw.

I'll tell you right here, there was two things going through my head right then, when I swung my leg over that saddle. Once I put my mind to something, I did it and I didn't look back. If I was gonna be a outlaw, I was gonna be a outlaw. And I was gonna be a damn good one. Only I wasn't gonna be a criminal, too. It never did set right with me, the way Jesse James and some of the others would go into a bank and start shooting, killing people for no good reason. If somebody was shooting at me, and I had to shoot back, to defend myself, I'd do it. But the way I seen it, there was a big diff'rence between shooting somebody to defend yourself, and shooting somebody for no reason a'tall.

'Course, if you shot and killed somebody in a robbery, even if it was to just defend yourself, you was likely to get hanged. Old-time outlaws called that "dying with throat trouble." But I spit that last thought right outa my head. just like I'd spit out that prune pit.

***

We'd spent the night at the cabin of a friend of Frank's, a old cowboy that still did odd jobs on ranches. "We" was me and Frank

118

and a fella named Charlie. Charlie was our third man, Frank'd picked him, he was from Tulsa. I never got to know Charlie's last name. In them days, you never asked a ex-con his last name.

Next morning, that old cowboy'd saddled up three horses.

My horse was jumpy as soon as I put my boot into the stirrup. Horses know right off, I guess, when their riders don't like 'em. Well, I hated horses, that's all. Like I told you, my old man loved ever'thing there was about a horse: the creak of the saddle, the swell of their flanks, even the buzz of them black, ugly horse flies. He thought horse sweat smelled sweeter'n a lady's perfume. I thought it smelled like sweat. And I didn't like the way that gray's ears was twitching. I didn't know what it meant, but I didn't like it.

Even if my horse was jumpy at first, pretty soon her gait evened out and she settled down into a steady clippity-clop, clippity-clop. The sky was a clear, clear blue; ever' so often the brush'd open up into a pretty, green valley with rolling hills and maybe a little pond and a red farm barn and a field of corn. If I hadn't a-hated horses, I mighta even enjoyed the ride.

We rode until we was about a mile shy of a little town called Boswell, and then we guided our horses off into a field and let 'em graze while we flopped down under a tree and went over our plans one last time, so there'd be no hitch. Frank was acting so sure of hisself you'd a-thought we was going into town for a shot of whiskey.

"Remember what I told you, boys. A sharp tongue doesn't draw blood. It saves it. And after we do it, you just trot. Less attention we draw, the better. But when you get to the brush, that's when you hit it! Oh, and don't worry if there's a little shooting. It'll just be for show. Things are all sewed up."

What he meant by things being "sewed up" was this: Boswell had a crooked town marshal. And the marshal'd told Frank that, for a share of our loot, he was gonna "lose" our trail after the getaway. I hoped to hell that marshal was being straight with us. I'd heard enough outlaw stories to know that some laws was tricksters theirselves. Or they was just plain dirty. Like that old Texas Ranger, Captain Bill McDonald. Pa knowed him well. Said Captain Bill always prided hisself on being a square-shooter. Yeah, Pa said, if Captain Bill come up on somebody he wanted, he'd shoot 'em square between the shoulders, and then he'd say, "Hands up!"

***

At eleven o'clock, exact, we begun to ride into Boswell.

It was such a sleepy little town, nobody give us a second look. We was dressed up like cowboys, so we wouldn't stick out, and so we wouldn't get torn to shreds if we had to gallop through the brush on our escape. We had on high-heel boots with spurs and rowels the size of quarters; we had on bullhide leggings; we had on thick brush jackets, bandanas around our throats, and wide-brim Stetsons.

The main street was a wide road that was just dirt and ruts. There was only a few wagons and buggies on it, and one black Model T. The Model T was parked, of all places, in front of the bank. There was a half-dozen people or so wandering down the street on foot, up and down the board sidewalks. And there was one or two horsemen riding around. But ever'body looked like they had their minds on other things, and about the last thing in the world they woulda suspicioned was that the three men walking their horses slow down Main Street was about to hold up the First State Bank.

The bank was the last building on the street. A little one-story square building made of red brick.

When we was about twenty-five feet away, me and Frank got off our horses. We handed the reins to Charlie, he stayed on his horse.

"Now!" said Frank.

Quick as a flash, we pulled up our bandanas across our faces. Guns come out of our shirts and we walked fast into the bank.

There was one teller inside and four customers. One of 'em had dark brown skin, he looked like one of them Choctaw Injins that lived around them parts. The rest of 'em was white men. But ever'-body was so busy doing what he was doing, it took a while before somebody even seen us. Then the teller looked up. He was a round-faced old boy with a oiled little mustache and pink cheeks. When he seen our guns, all the blood drained outa his face, his mouth flied open, and his eyes bugged out.

"All right, ever'body, hands in the air!" Frank barked it.

Heads turned.

We didn't have to say nothing more.

I swung my pistol from one side of the bank to the other. Ever'body looked too boogered to do nothing but shake. Funny thing, soon as I seen 'em shaking like that, a calm come over me. Hell, me and Frank was the ones in charge! I'd never felt nothing like that before in my life, even when me and Red was robbing that train. On the train, we was going berth to berth; this bank, it was ever'body, all at one time. 'Course, I was still keeping my eyes a-moving and a-shifting – here and there, here and there. I didn't wanta leave no gap in my sight for somebody to throw down on me.

Meantime, Frank'd pulled a pillowcase outa his belt and went through a swinging door to where the teller was. He scooped money outa drawers and stuffed it into the pillowcase. Then he went over to the bank's safe, a little square one in a corner, with the door wide open. He scooped up ever'thing in it. Then he stuck his head in the bank's little vault, but there wasn't nothing to take. Only locked safe deposit boxes.

No sooner Frank hit for the front door, I ordered ever'body into that vault. One old farmer was slow to move. I give him a hard prod in the back with my gun.

"Git in there, mister," I said, "or I'll blow your brains out!"

The fella stepped right along. Him and the others marched, hands up, right in. Like they was schoolkids minding their teacher.

That vault was hardly big enough for the five of 'em, so they was squeezed tight. But they fit.

"You stay in there ten minutes!" I hollered. "Ten full minutes. Anybody comes out before that time, you're gonna get blowed to hell!"

I turned, jerked off my mask, and run outside. Frank was already on his horse.

"Just trot," he said.

But even while he was saying this, the teller come racing out and pointing at us and hollering: "Robbers! Jus' robbed the bank! Robbers! Somebody stop 'em!"

Frank fired a shot at the man's feet. The teller hopped up and sideways like he was doing a jig, and turned and run back in.

"Didn't you lock the vault door?" Frank said to me.

"Hell, no. They'd a-suffocated if I—"

"Oh shit! Hightail it!"

We done it, at a gallop. But folks on the street'd heard that teller a-hollering, and when I give a quick look behind us, I seen three or four men jumping on horses, and a couple more hitting over to that Model T.

My calm was gone.

Me and Frank and Charlie tore out at a gallop. We rode and we rode, 'til long after that main street'd turned into a country road lined with brush. Then Frank, he was in the lead, pulled his horse up short and raised his hand to signal me and Charlie to come close.

Frank was breathing hard.

"Better...split up...here!" he panted out. "Tonight...the trestle. That doesn't work...my place...Fort Worth!"

The trick of splitting up was one the Comanches used to pull on the Texas Rangers. Least, that's what Pa always told us kids. But it wasn't Comanches that was on my mind right then. That posse was hot on our trail. We was really gonna have to run for it!

I clucked my tongue and dug my spurs in. And me and that mare lit off down that dirt road at a hard gallop.

By now, we could hear the horsemen a piece behind us—cloppity-clop! cloppity-clop! And the Model T was right behind 'em, bouncing over the ruts just like Mister H.L. Pike's automobile.

When we come to a opening in the brush, Frank tore off to the left. Charlie was trailing behind me, maybe his horse had a sore foot or something. But the posse and automobile was gaining and all of a sudden—Pow-ww! Pow-ww!

I looked around, just in time to see Charlie fall off his horse.

Goddammit! They was shooting real bullets!

I was gonna be a goner too, if I didn't keep riding. And riding hard.

I never looked back.

I gotta give that old horse credit, when the chips was down, she sure could blow! Right then, she was my partner—not Frank or Charlie. And she was one helluva partner. She was throwing her legs out and back in a gallop that was sure and steady as a steam engine. Her front legs was coming up so high they was near to clipping her chin. Foam was coming outa her mouth. And all I had to do was rock forward with her body like I was part of her.

Before too long, I couldn't hear no hoof-beats behind me, or the rattle of that Model T.

When I come to a opening in the brush to the right, I cut into it. It led to a clearing and I loped across it and begun making a wide circle that would lead me to the train trestle where we was supposed to meet if we got split up. I seen a couple of farm and ranch houses on the way, but I skirted around 'em, and lucky for me, I didn't meet no other human.

The trestle was on the Frisco line. It was a big long bridge over a big deep gorge.

I come on it slow and cautious-like. Maybe the posse figured they had all they needed when they got Charlie. And Charlie coulda been only hurt, and not killed. To save his own skin he coulda tipped off the laws to our plans. They mighta told him they'd let him off light if he ratted on us.

But I didn't see nobody around.

***

Where the devil was Frank?

There was a thicket near the bridge. I got off the gray, tied her to a tree and lay down where I could see the trestle, but nobody could see me.

One, two, three hours went by.

I shoulda been wore out, but I wasn't. My stomach was churning outa hunger, but ever' other part of my body was twitching. And my mind was going helty-skelty: What'd happened to Charlie? And Frank! God knows. He'd got the money.

And what the hell happened with that marshal?

Damn dirty marshal'd double-crossed us! Either that, or he'd forgot to square things with the rest of the town.

One, two more hours went by.

The trees was dropping long shadows. Frank wasn't gonna show. I could feel it in my bones.

I untied the horse and pulled off her saddle and give her a whack across the rump. Strange to say it, I was almost sorry to see her go. She'd done a good job.

I crawled over to the trestle—I didn't wanta stand up, I didn't wanta be skylighted if somebody come up—and I looked down. The gorge was bone-dry, eighty or ninety feet deep. And on the bottom was huge boulders, the size of elephants. If I fell, I'd be a red splat.

But what was I gonna do, walk outa Oklahoma?

I decided to hop the first train that come by. Them days, trains—particularly freights— slowed before going over a trestle.

I lay down on the ground, on my stomach, and waited. Dark come pretty quick. Before long, it was so dark you couldn't see your hands in front of your face. And then, about a hour into that pitch-black, I heard the rails hum. And I seen a headlight throw down a kind of gold glow.

I clawed up to the edge of the roadbed.

The engine passed me and rumbled on. I was lucky: It was a freight with boxcars.

Little white splinters of light was cutting into the dark. Sparks throwed off by the wheels.

I waited my time.

The train was crawling now, but one wrong step and I'd be mashed under grinding wheels.

I jumped. I throwed my fingers around the grab-iron at the end of a boxcar. I tried to pull my boots onto a stirrup step.

All around me was black. All below me was black.

The car was bouncing and jerking, bouncing and jerking, side to side. My hands was gripping that grab-iron tight as they could. My boots kept slipping. Them stirrup steps was slick steel, slick as ice. Half the time, I was hanging on by just my fingers.

Clackety-clack, clackety-clack.

I could tell by the sound of the wheels we'd started crossing the trestle. I couldn't see the gorge, but I knowed it was down below—deep, wide, dark, mean—like the mouth of some huge animal, a-waiting.

Somehow I managed to stay on.

THIRTEEN

Nobody come when I knocked at Frank's door in Fort Worth. The landlady, the one with the squeaky-mouse voice, said she hadn't seen him in awhile. I tried again the next day, walking up all them stairs like I had a hog stuck between my thighs. My legs was stiff and sore and bowed from all that horse galloping. Still, no answer.

Finally, on the third day, the door creaked open a inch. I seen one eye.

"That you, Skinny?"

The eye seen it was me.

"Get in."

The door come open a few more inches. I slid in. Sure enough, it was Frank standing there. His hair was combed and his face was fresh-shaved and he was smiling like a idiot. It burned me up, Frank slicked up like he was, smiling like that, after the way things had went down in Boswell. Only I wasn't gonna say nothing right off. Beside, he coulda throwed it back at me, that I didn't lock the vault door. Well, hell, he was the teacher.

"You got it?" That's all I said.

"Yessir, I have it all. I have it all." He rubbed his hands together. "All but five hundred. Five hundred went to my friend. He gave us three horses, you know, and he only got one back. And that one was pretty well used up. So I covered his loss. But don't you worry, Skinny, we're rich as you are filthy."

It was true, I looked godawful. My face was prickly as scrub brush, my hair was in a greasy mat, and my clothes was sweaty and tore up. But I'd been living on my wits, and not much else, since I'd got back to Fort Worth. Frank was the one that'd slung all them money bags over his saddle. As for the loot, I couldn't help but wonder if Frank really did give his friend $500 for them two horses, or had he pocketed some of it hisself? But it wasn't time to ask that.

"Where's the money?" I asked.

"Look at this first," he said.

***

Frank's room was in order, ever'thing in its place, just like the last time I come there. And there was a pot of coffee a-boiling on the stove, just like the last time. The only diff'rence was, lying over on the bed, I seen a newspaper with a headline so big and so black you could read it across the room: "DARING MIDDAY BANK ROBBERY!"

Frank picked up the paper and brung it over to me.

There was other stories on the front page—about U.S. Army soldiers called out to knock down union strikers in Seattle, about women voting in city elections, about the batsman Frank Baker doin' good for the Yankees—but the holdup story took up more space than all the others put together. It said there was five bandits. It said the bandits made ever'body in the bank lie down on the floor and tied up their hands behind their backs. It said the bandits got away with $20,000, including $5,000 in gold.

Almost ever' word a damn lie.

"You'll soon learn, Skinny," Frank said, "that, sadly, you just can't trust the papers. They sell more extras if they exaggerate things, and they know that. Of course, it might be the bankers. They get more insurance money if they say they lost more than they did. Drives me crazy, all the crooks in this world who parade around in their stiff little collars and their tight little bowties. At least we're honest about what we do." He reached over and tapped his finger on the page. "If they only knew who we were, we'd be famous."

"Or dead," I said.

How stupid can you get?

"Too bad about Charlie." Frank shook his head like Charlie'd been his favorite brother. "Paper says he got six bullets. That's probably five more than it was. Whatever, Charlie's dead. We got double-crossed, I think, by that son-of-a-bitch marshal." He shook his head again. "Nothing we can do about it now. And there's that much more to divide up."

Well, I don't know what kinda blood Frank had running through his veins: German or Polack or Russian or Irish or what. He never would answer when I asked. But whatever kind it was, it was cold as a snake's. And I couldn't help but wonder: if my brains'd been blowed out, too, along there with Charlie's, would Frank be smiling even bigger—now he didn't have to divide up *none* of the money?

I kept watching him outa the corner of my eye. Finally, he quit staring at that headline and he went around the room pulling down all the window shades. Then he reached under his bed and brung out a paper sack. He come over to the table and turned the sack upside down. Greenbacks come tumbling out. Some of 'em in bundles. Others of 'em, loose.

"Here it is, my friend," he said. "Eight thousand two hundred and forty-four. Now, you wanta talk about the next job?"

Like always, Frank didn't waste a word. Only I wasn't wasting none either. "Count me out."

***

I'd been doing a lot of thinking them last few days. I didn't have much to do but think while I was hunting for Frank, and waiting for Frank. And this is what I'd been thinking: I liked one part of robbing banks. I liked how you asked for money, and how they give it to you. Only I hated being stupid, and the way we robbed that bank was stupid.

"Count me out," I said again. "Four thousand'll take me a long way."

Frank wrinkled up his forehead. "A long way where?"

"Been thinking 'bout cutting up to Tulsa. Papers say there's an oil boom up there. Things 'r wide open."

"Ha!" Frank give a kind of sneering laugh. "You ever see any of those oil promotors, Skinny? They're crookeder than we are. Take your money faster than we took that bank's. Besides, once you start in this kind of business, you don't leave it just like that." He snapped his fingers. "It isn't healthy."

"Robbing banks the way we done it ain't healthy either, Frank. Go ask Charlie."

"It was that fool, son-of-a-bitch marshal."

"Maybe the marshal thinks he was the smart one and you was the fool," I said back. "It's too risky, Frank, middle of the day, all them people around."

"Then you tell me how you'd do it."

To be honest, I wasn't really planning to cut up to Tulsa. But I knowed I had to shake Frank up, or he wasn't gonna pay me no mind. And I had a thought. Now that I seen how it worked, I knowed that riding horseback and going in midday was a good way to get blowed right into a casket, even if you was on a good cow horse. It's how come the James Brothers got all shot up in Minnesota, and the Dalton Boys in Kansas. You ever seen that photograph of Bob Dalton laying in his coffin? There's a river of blood pouring outa his ear, spilling all over the white lining of that coffin.

But back in the penitentiary, I'd talked a coupla times to a old boy called the Dago. He was a safecracker, and he'd told me about something called nitroglycerin. He called it "grease." Dago said railroad crews used it to blow up rocks when they was clearing right-of-way. It was soft, sloshy, slippery stuff, felt like hog lard, but it had more boom in it than dynamite. Dago'd steal some of that nitro, then break into a bank at night, do the sign of the cross on hisself—he was a good Catholic—and blow the safe door off. When you used grease, you could sneak into a bank at night, when most ever'body was asleep. And you could make your getaway in a car. A quick, quiet getaway. It wasn't as exciting as one of them Wild West getaways—but what did we want, blood spilling outa our ears, or money?

"You know a safecracker named the Dago?" I asked Frank.

"Oh, yeah." He stretched his arms out and popped his knuckles and said he knowed exact what I was saying. He asked me if the Dago'd ever told me about a partner of his, name of Skillet.

"Don't sound familiar."

"It was in all the papers," Frank said. "Poor Skillet. He was heading out to Corsicana, to meet the Dago for a job. Driving a big old Hudson. The grease was in a jar, he was holding it right here." Frank pointed where his legs come together, near his crotch. "It was tight, so it wouldn't rattle any. But right around that little town of Ennis, something happened. They think maybe the Hudson was swerving to miss hitting another car, maybe the door flew open, maybe the jar fell out. Of course, they don't know exactly what happened."

Frank leaned towards me and smiled.

"Only thing left of Skillet and his automobile was a hole in the dirt."

***

Stupid Frank. That city boy thought he was scaring the pants offa me. He didn't know me too good. I growed up on a farm. With people that took risks ever' day if they wanted to eat. Just hitching up mules was a risk. I knowed two different men that'd been killed by mule kicks. I knowed one man had his leg yanked outa the socket by a hay baler. Griff Henson got both his arms sliced off at the gin stand. It's just that some risks 'r worth it, some ain't.

"I don't like day jobs," I said to Frank again. "Day jobs, ever'-body's awake. Nights, they're snoring. And when you're on a horse, what'cha got between you and a bullet? Wind. That's it. A car's a can of steel. And I hear they got 'em now that's forty, fifty horsepower."

"Machines break down. Horses don't."

"Yeah? What about Charlie's horse?"

He didn't say nothing. But the way his mouth was twisting told me exactly what he was thinking. That he didn't like it, what I was saying, but maybe I was right. I knowed how to read people, just like Jess knowed how to read a horse. A person don't need to tell you what they're thinking. You can read it offa little things on their bodies—like how their head's jerking, or how they're squinting their eyes, or if their shoulders is tight, or how they're breathing. Sometimes, like with Frank, what you read is their mouths—if they're twisting, or twitching, or puckering; or how much of their teeth they're showing.

"Look Frank," I said, "if I'm gonna stay in with you, I wanta talk to the Dago."

His mouth loosened up, one side crept higher. "You sure he's out?"

"Got sprung last month. I hear he's in Jacksboro."

Frank banged his fist on his knee. "What are we waiting for?"

FOURTEEN

The Dago wouldna won no beauty contests. He was short as a stump, with a crooked buzzard-beak and pop-eyes. Me and Frank found him working in a hardware store in the little town of Jacksboro, northwest of Fort Worth.

When we first come up on him in the store, he pop-eyed us like a cat does when it's circling a rattlesnake. He didn't trust us. That's how lots of cons are when they're fresh outa the joint. But when we told him why we was there, and we worked on him a while, he come around.

"Well, hell, any monkey can sell nails and crapper seats," he said. "I'm the best box blower this part of the country. You wait 'n see."

I said to myself, "I will wait and see." I wasn't trusting nobody right off, not after that mess in Boswell. But the Dago did have a good rep, I knowed that from prison. And soon as he come in with us, he gave us a idea for our first mark: a little coal-mining town called Arma in the southeast corner of Kansas.

"I got people working them mines," he said. "And they say the bank's got a big payroll, and a safe setting out in the open, and the town don't got no nighthack."

The Dago swore his kin knowed what they was talking about. So finally me and Frank said okay.

Since we was gonna drive up to Kansas, the Dago said it'd be smart to get us a fourth man, somebody that knowed about fixing cars if we was ever to get in a jam. So he hooked us up with a friend of his, a ex-con from Dallas named "Slim." I got a kick outa the way the Dago introduced me and him: "Slim, Skinny; Skinny, Slim." Slim wasn't really slim, just like I wasn't skinny no more. Fact is, he was on the edge of being thick. He had a thick chest and a thick neck and even his eyelids was thick. But he wasn't bad-looking, except for a hole in his cheek, the size of a fifty-cent piece. Like somebody'd took a bite out.

I wondered what he did to get that gouge.

Still, to do the kind of work we was doing, you had to take risks with people, like you did with nitro.

I didn't have no proof that Slim was good at fixing cars, but I learned real quick that he was one helluva car thief. We was all gonna pitch in to buy a automobile when Slim said, "Why waste good money? I'll get you one for nothing." And he snatched us a green Studebaker Big-Six, right offa the street where it was parked. Stole it with a master key he'd made hisself.

Lemme tell you what, was that Studebaker slick!

That automobile was shiny dark green, as tall as I was, and nearly long as three men laying head to toe. And inside, where the driver set, there was so many levers and sticks you'd like to need three arms and three legs to run it. But old Slim, he knowed what he was doing. And that engine purred like a baby cat! Slim said it was sixty horsepower. I'd never rid in a Studebaker before, but I knowed all about 'em. They was tough, sturdy cars. I knowed that because, before it made cars, the Studebaker company had built the strongest, best farm wagons you could buy.

***

We was four men in a Studebaker Big-Six with a flat, pint-size whiskey bottle to hold the grease—but no grease.

The Dago took care of that.

He told Slim to drive us alongside the railroad tracks outside of Texarkana 'til we come to a small red building on the side of the road. There was signs on it saying, "Danger-Explosives."

The Dago said it was a felony to snatch nitroglycerin, so Frank and Slim stood lookout while me and the Dago went over to the door. The Dago used a sledge-hammer to break the lock, and in we went. The building was mostly empty, except for a couple of two-gallon cans in one corner. Tied around the caps was chains with funnels on the end of 'em. The Dago told me to hold the bottle and the funnel, he'd do the pouring.

"Whatever you do," he said, "don't let the bottle drop."

"Don't worry."

I was gripping that bottle so tight I thought it might break. But the Dago was calm as water on a cow trough. He propped hisself up on his knees and started pouring. The stuff dribbled in, slow and soft. It was hard to believe it, so much power in something that didn't look no different'n lard. But the Dago said so long as you handled nitro with respect, it was a bank robber's best friend.

"With this stuff, you can peel the doors offa safes like you was opening a can of beans," the Dago said. "Big, thick doors—they'll peel right off."

When the whiskey bottle was near full, the Dago set the big can down. Then he took the bottle outa my hands, put the cork in, and wrapped the whole thing—real careful, like a fresh baby—in a soft, thick towel he pulled outa his belt. Back in the car, he put the bottle tight between his legs. But even if it was wrapped in a towel, I didn't like how it was shaking. We was on a country road, and it was rough and rutty.

"What's it need to set that thing off?" I asked the Dago. "How big a jolt?"

"Git your mind on something else."

"Just answer me that one."

"Fifty pounds. Like, you gotta drop it on a concrete floor."

A fifty-pound jolt? That'd be a big bump, to jar something fifty pounds. But Skillet done it. And thinking about Skillet didn't make me feel too good about that bumpy road we was on. Pretty soon, we pulled off onto a good gravel highway, and the ride smoothed out. But Slim was a lousy driver. One time, we was going around a blind curve, he come right on top of a old farm wagon that was being pulled by two pokey mules. He swerved around it, but just missed hitting a Model T coming the other way.

"Would'ya take it easy!" I hollered.

"Son-of-a-bitch was eating up the whole road."

"Jesus Mary!" the Dago said, to back me up. "It ain't Old Crow in this bottle."

After that, Slim took it some slower. But I kept thinking what he'd do if we had to make us a fast getaway.

***

When I think back on it now, what come down on that first night job was so stupid I hate to even talk about it.

You ever seen one of them picture shows about the Keystone Kops? The Keystone Kops was always bonking their heads, or slipping on things, or crashing into walls, or running outa gas on railroad tracks right at the wrong time. Well, on that first job, that's just about how it was with Slim and Frank and the Dago.

The only diff'rence was: the Keystone Kops was idiot laws, and my partners was idiot thieves.

Fools, fools, fools.

When we got to Arma, we drove around 'til we found the bank. It was just a small one-story brick building in the middle of Main Street. Coulda been anything, a doctor's office or a meat market. But the Dago's kin'd said there was two hundred miners around there, and the payroll run into big money.

Then we drove out about ten miles outa town on a country road. We waited 'til midnight, when we figured most ever'body would be in bed. And when we come back, sure enough, the place was dark as a graveyard. We parked the car on the outskirts of town and hit off a-foot to the bank.

"Okay, boys," the Dago said when we come up near it, "me and Willis 'r gonna be inside on this one. You two are the outside men. And what'cha gotta watch for is if somebody's going house to house, waking people up. These little towns that don't got nighthacks, that's what they do if they think something's getting robbed."

Slim nodded, but I could tell Frank didn't like the Dago giving the orders, acting like the boss. So when the Dago handed me a little saw and told me to go up a pole to cut the telephone wires—that was the first thing he said you do on night jobs—Frank piped up and said no, he was gonna do it.

Frank grabbed the saw outa my hand and started to bear-hug his way up. It was about a thirty-five foot pole. But that old city boy couldn't get more'n five or six feet offa the ground. He was so clumsy and his arm muscles was so puny that ever' time he got a few feet up, he'd slide right back down.

I couldn't help but laugh.

Frank's lip curled up. "All right, goddammit, one of you go up and do it."

I was used to shinnying up trees. I cooned right up to the top of that pole, and sawed that big old cable clean through.

Then we went to the bank.

Frank crotched his shotgun in his arm and stood on one side. He was still hacked over being lookout, but he done it. Slim went on the other side. The Dago and me went to the back. I used a crowbar to ease a window up, and I climbed in first. The Dago handed over that whiskey bottle through the window—careful—and in he climbed.

We flicked on the flashlight.

Nothing!

Nothing!

The Dago's people had got things all wrong! There wasn't no safe setting out in the bank, waiting to get blowed. All we could make out, way in the back, was the concrete wall of a big vault.

The only thing that was gonna blow was me or Dago.

The Dago done it first. "Goddamn cousins of mine! Goddamn coal-monkeys!"

"We shoulda cased it!" was all I said back.

"It's over, I guess."

"I ain't leaving. You think your people got a pick?"

The Dago give me a look, but he took off back outa the window. It was twenty minutes before he come climbing back in.

Only good thing, he was waving a sooty miner's pick.

I shined a flashlight on him, and he crouched in front of the vault and begun to go at it. The only sounds in the bank was a cricket chirping and the Dago's pick a-pecking. Then he got a sneezing fit from all that concrete dust.

ACHEW! ACHEW! ACHEW!

"Don't sneeze so damn loud," I said.

"You can't fix how loud you sneeze."

"Well, cover your damn mouth." The minutes was ticking away, tick-tick-tick. And the Dago was only making a dent. When I heard a man's voice, coming from the window, my stomach flied into my throat.

"What's the problem in there?" a voice come barking in.

But it was only Frank. And in he come—stuffing hisself through the window.

"Lemme give it a try." He grabbed the pick from the Dago.

Peck, peck.

Peck.

Frank was the laziest thing I ever seen. He give up after just a few licks. "We can't get in."

Well, that done it. I cussed 'em all out and I grabbed the pick.

Whang. Whang. Whang.

Whang. Whang.

Whang!

Whenever I done something, I done it. I smashed the dent into a hole.

And in we climbed.

***

As things come out, we did have some good luck in all that craziness. We come on something we didn't expect in that vault: long, narrow shelves with little partitions between 'em, like in a post office. And piled high—with Liberty bonds and Victory bonds. They was bonds put out by the U.S. gov'ment to pay for the World War over in Europe, and they was negotiable. Good as money.

Then, in one corner, there she set—a pretty square-faced Packer safe.

If Dago's kin was right about the payroll, that Packer was stuffed with a helluva lot of money.

"Yessir." The Dago's eyes was all lit up. "And the vault'll muffle the sound."

Wasn't two seconds, Frank was stuffing the bonds into our loot bags and the Dago was kneeling in front of the Packer. The Dago was rushing a little, I could hear him breathing fast, and I didn't like that. But I brung him the whiskey bottle and crouched down next to him.

I wanted to watch ever' move he made.

First off, he took a bar of Proctor and Gamble soap outa his pocket. Then he mashed it in his hands 'til it was gooey, like beeswax. Then he scrunched it into the cracks around the rim of the safe door. He put in just enough to fill the outside of the cracks but left a little room behind the soap, like a tunnel. At the top of the door he pinched a little lip.

"Gimme the bottle," he said.

Real careful, I unwrapped it outa the towel and handed it to him. He took out the cork, held the bottle up agin that soap lip, and tipped it. The grease begun to slide down into the tunnel, slow and thick and smooth.

When he'd poured in enough, Dago put the cork back in and handed me the bottle. It was still more'n half full. Then he pulled what he called a "cap" outa his pocket and a length of fuse, what he called "string."

"String burns a foot a minute," he said. "You c'n cut it ten sec-

135

onds, fifteen seconds, twenty, whatever you want. It burns down to the cap, the cap explodes, sets off the grease. I'm gonna do a twenty here, give us plenty of time to get outa the vault, get against the back wall."

He cut a fuse about four inches, put the cap on it, fit it all careful into that soap lip so one end of the string could slide down into the grease.

"Jus' gotta light her up, eh, and that's it." The Dago looked up to see what Frank was doing. "You done, Frank?"

"Just about."

"Well, get done and get outa here."

Frank didn't need to be told twice. He stuffed the last bundles of bonds into his bag and scrambled outa the hole.

The Dago turned to me. "You wanta go now?"

"What do I do with the grease?"

"Hold it next to your chest. Just make sure you're against the back wall."

Hold the bottle agin my chest? More'n half full?

The Dago seen my look. "Don't worry. Nitro only blows frontways. It ain't like dynamite. Soon as I torch her, I'm back there with you, boy."

He smiled back and scratched a match. It sparkled in the dark, lighting up his whole ugly face.

Ever' hair on my body was starting to stand up on end.

I started to go out the hole, but I couldn't take my eyes offa that match. The flame was a-flickering, and the Dago's fingers was just moving right towards that string, just about to torch her and set her a-fizzing...when what do we hear? Slim, and he's a-hollering. So loud we can hear him all the way into the vault.

"Mob coming! Mob coming!"

"Jesus! We got a rank!" Now it was Frank a-hollering. His head was poking into the hole in the vault door. "Get on out! We got a rank!"

"You sure?" I asked.

"Shut up and get out!"

The Dago quick blowed out his match. I let out a groan. A 'rank' is a thief word, for when you been spotted. But something didn't set right about that "rank." I can't say what it was, but something didn't set right.

I set the half-full bottle of grease on the floor, clawed outa the hole in the vault, and run over to the window. All over the street was lights, dozens of 'em, bobbing up and down like a bunch of lightning bugs. But the lights was on the men's heads. And they was bobbing away from us, getting smaller and smaller.

They was starting to move in a little line outa town, toward the mine shafts.

"You idiot!" I looked over at Slim. "That's miners out there. Them lights is on their hats. They're changing shifts."

"You sure?" He was panting.

"Sure enough I'm going back in. We'll wait 'til they're gone and then we'll blow this thing."

"Oh no, you won't." That was Frank, and he was talking like he was the boss. "We're getting the hell outa here. We got enough."

His ass was already hanging halfway out the window, and Dago was right behind.

"Let's go!" the Dago hollered. "This place is a jinx."

Me and the whiskey bottle was all that was left. What else could I do?

***

A couple of days later, when I read about the robbery in a newspaper, it said that "Lady Luck had shined on the Arma State Bank." It said that the robbers'd got some loot, but they'd left more than $200,000 in the safe!

Good godamighty!

Can you believe it that Frank said, "We got enough," when there was more'n $200,000 right under his nose, right for the taking? Can you believe it, that anybody—a bank robber, a banker, a lawyer, anybody—would ever say, "We got enough"?

FIFTEEN

The more I was getting to see, up close, how thieves go about doing their business, the more I was thinking: it's a wonder that anything ever gets stole in this world.

It was good luck, and not much more'n good luck, that made our getaway from Arma easy as snap. Nobody'd ranked us, so nobody'd lit after us. But the way I was starting to see it, good luck and bad luck was two sides of the exact same coin, and if all you was doing was flipping coins, you was as likely to get tails as you was to get heads.

And in our business, tails was trouble.

Did I wanta keep working with a bunch of fool ex-cons? And if I did keep working with 'em, how was we gonna do things smarter? Frank was supposed to be the Smart Man, but he was a idiot.

When our car crossed outa Kansas into Oklahoma, on our way back to Texas, we pulled off the main road and went down a dirt lane into a clump of trees. Frank took charge again, like he was the president of a company. He got outa the car with the loot bag and we all crouched on the ground and watched him lick his finger and count out them bonds into four equal piles.

They added up to about $65,000.

"Well, well. I'd say we did alright," Frank said, all kinda puffed up. "I have a market in Fort Worth, he'll give me seventy-five cents on the dollar. That'll give us more than $10,000 each."

I looked at Frank square. "You blind? We didn't do nowhere close to 'all right.' That concrete vault? Ever'body boogered? And that payroll still back there?"

Frank throwed a eye over at the Dago. "We had the wrong information."

"Aw, hell, Frank," the Dago said back. "It wasn't your nose in my ass going out that window. It was my nose in your ass!" His face was all twisted. And the look he was making was enough to scare little kids. That wasn't hard for him to do. That buzzard beak. Them pop eyes.

I stood up. I wanted to look down on 'em. On all three of 'em.

"Look-it," I said, "if we do this again, we gotta use a little of what's north of our necks. We gotta go in earlier and case the town better. A helluva lot better."

Now the Dago stood up. He only come to my neck. He pointed his beak up at me. "What? You want 'em staked out for us?"

"I ain't saying we make a ruckus," I said back. "All I'm saying is, we case better. We find out the exact setup at the bank. It's got a vault, or just a setting safe? We find out about the town: if they got a nighthack, what time folks go to bed, what time they wake up. Even where's the barking dogs."

Frank was still crouched on the ground. He shuffled some of the bonds, like they was playing cards. "First time any team works together," he said, "there's gonna be a few bumps. But listen, we have a good bunch here, us four. And I think, from here on out, we can do the bigger towns." I knowed by his voice where he was going. " 'Course, if we're gonna work together, somebody's got to be in the lead. And I put the team together."

"Yeah, well, Dago does the blows." That was Slim.

Frank pressed his lips together. "We can't all be the leader."

Inside me, I was a-steaming. When it come to judgment, I had it over all of 'em, hands down. And my whole life I always was the head man. Even when I was a kid, even if it was just baseball or throwing jackknives in mumbletypeg, I was the head man. Only problem was: I was still green in this bank-robbing business.

Then I seen the Dago giving Frank a little peepy smile.

"You sure you wanta be the leader, Frank?"

"I'd say it's only fair."

"You *sure*?"

"Fair's fair."

"Good." The Dago pointed his beak down at Frank. "What's fair if you're the leader, Frank, is you do the casing. That's a leader's job, eh boys?" He looked up at me and down at Slim and back over at Frank. "And you got the whole summer, Frank. We're moving into the wrong season for blows. Gets too risky when it's hot out. People keep their windows open, walk around, take in the air. Best if we wait 'til it gets chilly again. 'Til folks hole up. So you got plenty a-time to nose around and find us some marks. Get us a good list by

September."

Frank sucked in his cheeks.

"Sounds good to *me*." It was Slim again. Now *he* stood up. "My turn. I got something else to say here, boys. Way I see it, it don't matter who's the leader, all of us has gotta follow a rule. Frank's the leader, he does the casing, fine by me. But he can't just do whatever the hell he wants. I say we gotta lay down a law."

"A law?" Frank didn't like that, I could tell.

"Law, rule, order. Whatever you wanta call it. We don't look out for each other, who's gonna look out for us? We all know it, it's a dangerous business we got here. So here's the rule. Traps shut. Nobody talks to nobody about nothing. Not to your friends, not to kin, not to skirts. And if somebody leaks, he's gotta pay the price."

The Dago throwed Slim a pop-eye. "Saying what?"

Slim pointed a finger next to his ear. "Saying this."

Nobody said nothing.

"Good," said Slim. "Let's shake on it."

***

After that Arma job, the four of us monkeyed around in Fort Worth, spending a little of our loot.

Slim was the silliest of us four. He went out and bought him three dozen shirts, all shiny silk, all colors of the rainbow: pink, yellow, blue, purple, orange, red. Some of 'em had stripes like a candy cane, some of 'em had polka dots. They was $25 each. And what a waste of good money! Putting a silk shirt on a plug like Slim was like putting lipstick on a mule.

But I did go out and buy me some new clothes too.

First off, I went to Stebbins & James, a fancy men's clothes store. And when the salesman seen the roll of bills I pulled outa my pocket, thick as my fist, he "yessired" me all over the map. He fitted me with three top-of-the-line suits—tight around the waist with big lapels, trousers skinny as pipestems. After that, I went to a haberdashery and picked up three fedoras with rolled brims and dents in the crowns—what I called "ace dude" hats. Then I went to a shoe store and bought me four pairs of low-slung, lace-up Oxfords made out of what they called "Scotch brogue" leather.

Lemme tell you what, the first time I went out in them new clothes, was I stepping high! My heels made a nice click-clack, click-clack on the wood sidewalks. And damn if I didn't look slick! I cocked that dude hat and I tipped it to ever'body and ever'thing that passed my way—men, women, kids, mules.

Meantime, I'd hardly made a dent in my share. I sent off a coupla envelopes to Ma and wrote her I'd got a "good job in oil country." And there was bundles left. Bundles and bundles. I kept 'em hid in a little iron box under the bed in a room I'd rented, and ever' so often, I'd pull that box out and pick up a few of the biggest bundles and hold 'em in my hand.

'Course, you know what kept going through my head?

I shoulda had three times more!

Hell. If it-a been *me* in the lead, that Arma State Bank woulda been all cleaned out.

***

I had some work to do.

On a hot Monday in June, I got on the telephone and called up Frank. "If you get going with that mark hunt right off," I said, "I'll help you out." Then I called the Dago. "Dago, being you're the best box-blower around, can you teach me about safes so I'll know what to look for?"

It worked with both of 'em – the slug and the stump.

The Dago got a big kick outa being my "teacher." First off, he give me a history lesson. He got some paper and drawed pictures of the way the old-time robbers worked. Way on back, see, you could just punch open a lot of the bank safes. You'd take a hammer and whang the combination off, then put a pin in there, hit a lick and, Blam! But later on, the banks got wise and put trigger locks on. When you busted the combination, you'd hear a whump!, the pins'd go in all around the door, and lock the thing up.

The Dago said it was about nineteen and oh-five, or nineteen and oh-six, that bank robbers first started using nitroglycerin.

He said the best safes to blow was square ones. Some of 'em, you do it with just one shot of grease. Others of 'em, you had to shoot a little at a time. He drawed me pictures. But the Dago said bigger banks was starting to get a kind of round safe that screwed into the walls, and that you couldn't blow. He called 'em "lugs," because they was just big round lugs of steel. Wasn't no rims in 'em to put in the grease.

Still, he said there was enough banks around with them old-fashioned square safes to keep us busy for a long time. 'Course, sometimes the safes was in vaults, like in Arma. But he said lots of vaults had flimsy doors you could blow off with nitro, just like you'd blow a safe. I told him to draw me pictures of which vaults was which; I didn't wanta have to peck through another one with a ax.

He done that.

Then me and Frank went at it.

I bought me a road atlas and drawed red circles around little towns all the way up into the Middle West. I let Frank do the driving, so he'd feel like the boss. But in ever' town we hit, I'd buy him a newspaper and tell him to relax. I wanted to do the detail work.

First off, I'd case the bank, or banks, if there was two. I'd go in with a ten-dollar bill and ask to break it. And I'd eyeball ever'thing in that bank: what kinda vault they had, what kinda safe they had, where the windows was. And when the clerk give me my change, I'd give 'em back a smile big as the moon.

If I seen it was a bank we could blow, we'd hang around the town a couple more days and I'd check out things after dark. Did the town's lights go off after a certain time? (In a lot of 'em, the electric generators got shut off at midnight.) Was there a night marshal? Where did he hang out? Was there businesses that needed people up and around at night? I'd write ever'thing down in a little yellow tablet.

Before long, I had us a list of a dozen good marks—and soon as September come around, our whole team went at it!

***

Yessir, we went at it!

We went at it in Coldwater, Kansas, and we went at it in Cassville, Missouri, and we went at it in Sleepy Eye, Minnesota.

And a bunch of other towns.

I ain't saying ever'thing went off without a hitch. A lot of roads was bad them days, and ever' so often, we'd get stuck in the mud. (Frank was never no help pushing us out.) And there was still enough bungles to make us seem like the Keystone Kops. Like one time, we was hitting a bank in north Michigan, and the little Dago seen the Northern Lights flash up in the sky—they was flashing up just as bright as day—and he thought it was a rank. He got Slim and

142

Frank all boogered, and the three of 'em run off with the soft loot and left me and all the hard behind. I had to run a half mile with a sack of silver that musta weighed a hundred and fifty pounds!

Still, with all my detail work, we was making us some money.

Before long, each one of us had $70,000. Seventy thousand dollars!

And before long, I was shooting half the safes myself.

I'll never forget the first one I blowed. It was in a little bank in Indiana that had a Packer setting out in the open. Dago held the flashlight and went over ever' step. 'Course, I already knowed just what to do. If I seen somebody do something just one time, I could do it exact. I mashed up the soap and plugged it around the cracks and dug out that little tunnel and pinched out that little lip. I picked up the jar of grease and tipped it.

"Three ounces oughta do it," the Dago said.

"I know."

I poured in about three ounces. Then I poured in another one. Then one more.

The Dago's eyes got round. "That's too much grease."

"Too much?" I said back. "I don't know what 'too much' means."

He crossed hisself. I handed him the bottle and picked up the string. I cut a twenty-second fuse. Put on a cap. Dropped one end in the nitro. Struck a match, touched it to the other end.

It set up a few white sparks and then, fiz-z-z-z-z-z-z-z-z-z-z!

"Get back behind it," the Dago said. "God knows..."

We quick went behind the safe and pressed our backs hard agin the wall.

The fire was racing up the fuse.

Fiz-z-z-z-z-z-z!

Now, it was three inches from the nitro.

Now, two inches.

Now, one inch.

Now, a half inch.

KA-BLOOOEY!

Dust flied! The safe bounced forwards! The door blowed halfways across the room! The big plate glass window in front of the bank cracked like a rifle shot!

And money flowed out like a river.

SIXTEEN.

Trouble come diff'rent than I thought it would.

It was the dead of winter, about eight months after we first put our team together. A mean norther'd just blowed up and was she a-whistling! Cold, cold, cold. We was driving down a rutty little country lane, about thirty miles north of Fort Worth.

Me, Dago and Frank. No Slim.

We was in a Model T touring car, no roof on it. Frank was driving. That Model T was a-bouncing and a-creaking. And that icy wind was cutting right through us, even though we was all in heavy brush jackets. Our teeth was a-clattering near as much as that car.

When we come to a clearing, Frank steered offa the lane. We bounced on over that open place, and then he ducked the car in a clump of trees.

"All right," he said. "Let's get it done."

We took tools outa the back. I took a grubbing hoe; Frank got a shovel; the Dago, a pick and a ax. We pushed our way through thick scrub 'til Frank pointed to a bare spot on the ground.

"There," he said.

We went at it.

At first, we was digging and hacking so hard that dirt was a-flying and rocks a-flinging and roots a-snapping. Even Frank, that lazy old louse, was kicking up a sweat. After a while, though, one or the other of us'd slow up. It wasn't that we was getting wore out. I think we was working like we was feeling about what we was doing, and that was flip-flopping.

Finally, the Dago straightened up. "I think we've got it."

"Not quite." Frank motioned him back to work. "He's not a stump like you. He's six feet."

The Dago give a snort, but went back to digging. This time, I just stuck my hoe in the dirt and leaned on it.

Frank give me a look. "Get back to it, Skinny. It's not a murder.

It's just a killing."

***

Now lemme tell you what brung all this on: After our last job, Slim'd gone out and spent $2,500 on clothes and hid another $3,500 in a old cedar trunk at his sister's house. Then what'd he do? Told his sister and her husband what was in the trunk, and where it come from. How come? God knows how come. Maybe he'd been drinking. All I know is it was one big, bad mistake. His kin was all sorry people — pimps and whores and drug-peddlers. Anyhow, one day that money disappeared. Slim knowed who took it: his brother-in-law. But when Slim wanted it back, that old boy said, "Hell, no. It ain't really yours, Slim." Before long, a dozen other of Slim's people knowed about the robberies.

One of 'em was sure to rat.

For those that don't know about it, the State of Texas in them days offered a $25 bounty to snitches.

It was a hard call, what we was about to do to Slim. But I was just as burned at that old boy as Frank and the Dago was. Slim was the one that'd preached the rule, and here he was, first one to break it! And if he done that, who knows what else he'd do? Meantime, if one of his sorry kin snitched, we could be waylaid by the laws. Maybe get sent back to the joint. Maybe get hung if there was a shootout and one of the police got killed. You could say, it was Slim's life or our lives, and when it's you agin them, who you gonna pick?

But which one of us was gonna have to lay down the law?

When the hole looked big enough, Frank come out with a silver dollar. "Everybody throw. Odd man out. You first, Skinny."

I throwed and lifted my hand. It was tails.

"Dago."

Dago throwed and lifted his hand. Heads. If Frank's dollar come out heads, I'd be the odd man.

Frank throwed.

I had my eyes glued on the top of his hand. I'll be honest, I didn't wanta be the one.

He pulled it up.

Tails!

The Dago didn't bat a eye. "Alright then. Only I ain't gonna

145

shoot him, if that's okay with you, boys. My hell is bashing. But I'll bash him 'til he's gone."

It was so cold his words come out in little white clouds.

***

So what do you do when you're waiting to kill a man?

You make you some coffee.

Frank went back to the clearing and picked up dead kindling and branches lying around, and made a little fire. And being that he had to have his coffee no matter wherever he was, he brung out a little tin pot. There was water already in it, so he just dumped in a handful of coffee grinds that come outa a paper bag.

A ways off, we could see the Dago hacking a thick branch offa a big tree. Then he chopped a three foot length. Then he crashed it agin the trunk of the tree to test it. WHAM! WHAM! It was rock solid.

Before long, we was all setting on a log in front of a crackling fire, drinking coffee. Just the smell of it, and the smell of that burning wood, was enough to make a man feel good. Only I was thinking over what was gonna happen. It was bad enough if we was gonna shoot Slim; smashing his head was something else. I was the one that'd told him to meet us in the woods. I'd made up a story with lots of detail: that we'd got a good tip on a whiskey shipment of 150 gallons; it was coming by boat up a river nearby, and we was gonna waylay it at a secret dock; that we was gonna need two cars to lug off all them gallons.

"He's late," Frank said. He seemed kinda rubbed that Slim was late for his own funeral.

"Maybe he caught on," Dago said.

"Maybe...no, what's that?"

At a distance, we could hear the chug-chug of a car motor. As it come down the lane, we could see headlights a-bouncing, two big white moons, over the deep ruts. For a little bit, we couldn't tell what kind of car it was. I stiffed up, and Frank and the Dago stiffed up too. What if Slim'd got wind of what was up and sent out some of his thug relations?

Or, if somebody'd ratted, maybe it was a decoy for the laws.

But when the car got closer, I seen it was our Studebaker Big-Six, and then I seen Slim's thick neck. He was by hisself.

146

When Slim turned off into the clearing he drove it up to the fire and got out.

"Damn country roads all look alike," he said. "Sorry. Ain't we gotta go?"

Frank handed Slim a tin cup of coffee. "We want to go over things one last time. Sit down."

"I thought we gotta be there before four."

"We'll make it," Frank said.

Slim took the coffee, but he didn't set down right off. He kept standing; his right hand was in his overcoat pocket. I think he'd got a whiff of something along with that coffee.

I smiled at Slim, to put him at his ease. "You know the dock?"

He shook his head. "I thought I was gonna follow you."

"Yeah, you are."

Now Slim's eyes was shifting side to side. "We still gonna take it to that warehouse?"

The Dago shook his head. "We're gonna bury it."

"Why you wanta bury it?"

The Dago give Slim a queer look. "Safer that way."

Frank couldn't stand it no more, the waiting. He went off a few yards into the brush and turned his back on us, like he was taking a leak.

Slim kept shifting his eyes, from Frank's backside to me to the Dago and back to Frank's backside.

The Dago acted like he was shivering. "Damn, it's cold out here. Fire's getting puny."

He walked off like he was gonna look for some wood.

Slim's eyes followed the Dago. Then he turned his head back quick to look at me. He looked me right in the eye. I looked straight back at him. He couldn't tell nothing from my eyes.

***

WHAM! Slim musta seen it coming at the last second. He ducked. The limb slammed him on the shoulder. Throwed him tumbling backwards.

"E-e-e-e-y-o-o-o-w!"

He hollered, like a cornered, snarling bobcat.

Then he was back up on his feet. Quicker'n I ever thought he could get up. And with his left hand he was pulling something outa

147

his pocket. There come a spitting, hissing sound, and a streak of red light.

Then Slim's gun jammed. He turned and run off towards the woods.

The bullet'd just glanced the Dago's left arm. "Goddammit to hell!" He tried to yank his own pistol out, but it took him a while to do it, being that he'd been shot. When he did, he fired into the dark after Slim, and kept it up until the hammer clicked empty.

Wasn't no sounds after that. Either the Dago'd got Slim, or Slim was just crouching down there, out in that brush, playing possum.

Now Frank was back, his gun out.

"Little late for that, Frank! How come I'm always looking at your ass!" The Dago give Frank a look, then went to checking out his shot. There was a trickle of blood coming outa a hole in his jacket.

Frank crab-walked sideways over to me. He said in a low voice, "You know Slim better than I do. Yell out there. Tell him to come back, we won't bother him. Then I'll shoot the son-of-a-bitch."

"Put it down, Frank," I said. "If he ain't dead already, nobody's gonna shoot him. We'll just cut him out."

The left side of Frank's top lip went up. "What?"

"We made our point."

"You kidding me?"

"It ain't worth it, Frank," I said. "It's just gonna bring down more trouble."

Frank looked over at the Dago, to get some back-up. But the Dago didn't give him none. He never liked taking Frank's side, if he had a say in it, no matter what the deal was.

Frank rolled his eyes. "Alright, but it's a bad mistake."

I hollered out into the brush, "Come on back, Slim! You brung this all on yourself. You know that. You was the one that preached that rule. But ain't nobody gonna hurt you."

Nothing.

I hollered again, "Get on back! Ain't nobody gonna do nothing. You got my word."

There was some rustling and a body—big and black in the dark—come out between two bushes. I was surprised he come back. I guess he trusted me. Or maybe he was gonna trick us.

The fire was throwing little patches of light on him. I seen he had his gun out. On the ready.

Me and Frank grabbed our own pistols. "I'm being straight with you, Slim," I said. "Use your head."

He didn't say nothing. His jaw was tight.

He inched hisself up closer to the fire.

Frank's pistol was aimed dead-eye. "Get out of Texas, Slim. You can have the car. Go back to Fort Worth, get your things, get out of Texas. Drive as far west as you can go. Go to California. Stay there."

Slim sucked in a breath and nodded.

I walked him over to the car. He musta still suspicioned something, he kept his hand on his gun. But when he finally climbed in, I told him in a low voice, "If I'da lost the toss, I don't think I coulda done it, Slim. I want you to know that. But they got a hole dug out yonder. And it ain't going nowhere. You best stay gone."

SEVENTEEN

We didn't have no choice.

After that thing in the woods with Slim, me and Frank and the Dago for once thought the same way about something. We'd move our headquarters. We didn't wanta risk that Slim's kin'd rat on us, even if they hadn't done it yet. And we couldn't know for sure that Slim'd really go off to California. Frank kept saying it was a big mistake to let him go anywheres but into that hole.

So we cleared outa Fort Worth and cut on up to Tulsa, Oklahoma.

How come Tulsa?

Back in the way old days, Oklahoma—like Texas—was settled by a lot of bad seeds. A lot of 'em was folks that'd stole something, or killed somebody somewheres else, and so they headed to Oklahoma to live, where they could be in peace. Well, a lot of them bad seeds spit out more bad seeds, and so on, down the line. And when the oil boom hit, that drawed in even more.

We'd have lots of good company. The state was swarming with thieves and ex-cons. Some of 'em was selling bogus oil leases or shares in bogus drilling companies. Others of 'em made money offa bootlegging. And there was plenty of other crooks in Tulsa, too. Ever' kind you could think of—forgers, gamblers, embezzlers, honkey-tonkers, even hit men.

It didn't take Frank two days to find somebody to take Slim's place.

Frank knowed the fella from prison, a guy that'd been in for "assault," but Frank said the guy never assaulted nobody that didn't deserve to be assaulted. Mostly, this fella was a bank robber. Frank said the guy's old "Wanted" posters called him one of the most "notorious bank burglars" in the U.S. and Canada. He had about ten aliases—A.M. Graham, Little Mizzou, Claude White, and a bunch of others—but his real name was Brentwood Glasscock.

"He's a top box man," Frank said. "And a great car mechanic. And he's got a good web of tipsters. Knows every crook between New York and San Francisco. Only problem with him is he's got stomach trouble, but he's got a wife who used to be a nurse and she takes care of him."

I didn't like the fella's looks. It wasn't that he was ugly. Fact is, he was handsome, near six foot, with a strong chin and neat-trimmed hair. But his cheeks was kinda sucked in, I guess because of his stomach trouble. And I could tell he was one of them skittery types. I could tell that by how he moved his head, like he was always shaking a gnat offa his face.

"My name's Brentwood," he said the first time we met. "But call me whatever you'd like, Willis. I answer to just about everything."

"I hear you get around," I said back.

"I have. I do." He smiled.

Well, I checked with the grapevine and even with them sucked-in cheeks and that twitchy head, Glasscock did have a good rep as a bank robber. And with Frank pushing so hard for him, finally I said okay.

***

Glasscock always wore a bullet-proof vest, and he was always looking over his shoulder. He was skittery, like I thought he'd be. But he knowed a helluva lot about grease, more'n even the Dago. Like he knowed how to blow the doors off the better-milled safes and the better-built vaults.

I was learning a lot.

None of us liked it that Glasscock always wanted to bring his wife on our trips. She was a tall, skinny blonde with round glasses and a pinched face, like she'd been eating green apples. And she was always preaching the Bible. She didn't believe in stealing. But Glasscock said he had to have her along to make sure he got his stomach medicine.

As it come out, though, Glasscock's bad gut had its good side.

He started having a hard time tolerating the nitro fumes, said that they was making him sick to his stomach. So he didn't have no problem with me and the Dago doing all the blows—with him just teaching us his tricks.

What helped even more, we got us a tipster down south that was

151

a detective with the Texas Bankers Association. The tipster knowed almost ever' bank in Texas that had one of them old, square safes. He was about to retire, see, and he wanted to make some extra cash so he could hunt and fish the rest of his life.

He sold us a list of about fifteen or twenty banks for $3,000.

For a little bit, I was leery about using them tips. How'd we know the tipster wasn't doing a double-cross? But we hit a couple of the banks on his list, just to test, and ever'thing went okay.

By the time summer break come around, my haul was up past $120,000.

A hundred and twenty thousand dollars!

Before, that $70,000 seemed like a million dollars. Now it begun to look like piker change.

And I finally was learning how to spend that money.

We was staying at the best hotel in Tulsa. I'd registered under the name "Will Reed" and when anybody asked me my business, I said "Texas oil man." Ever' inch of that hotel was first-class. Marble floors. Lamps with sparkly glass. Little bellboys that bowed at you like you was a king. I'd set on them shoe-shine stands in the lobby, they was like thrones, and goddamn, I'd feel like I *was* a king.

I had me a favorite shine boy, Booty Blue Tindle, and I liked to watch his fingers fly in and out of that polish and wax, and I'd think how my own fingers used to fly in and outa them cotton burrs.

"You ever pick cotton?" I asked Booty Blue one time.

He flicked his shine rag out so it give a loud pop. "Did a nigga pick cotton? I reckon I picked 'nough cotton to stuff this whole, entire hotel. Yessir. Only I likes this job lots better. Sun don't burns your head in here."

"The day I left the patch," I said to him, "I never did look back."

"Well, my, my, Mister Reed. You wuz a cotton picker before you wuz a oil man?"

"Yessir."

"Then we's alike, Mister Reed." He give his rag another pop. "We's both sorry ole cotton-pickers that's moved up in this big ole world. And you knows how come? 'Cause we knows how to work. The patch'll shore teach a man how'ta work. Some shine boys, aw, you might as well get a dog to lick your shoes. Me, I never do a half-job."

Booty Blue's shines was only a dime, but I'd always peel off a crisp dollar bill when I give him that dime. He was right. We *was* alike. Except that he was colored and he was still poor.

No, I wasn't poor no more. Fact is, I was moving up pretty fast to rich.

The best thing I liked to do with all that money was tip. To me, it was kinda like dealing cards. I'd peel the top bill off a roll with one finger, then I'd take that bill between my thumb and forefinger and stuff it in somebody's pocket. Or, if it was a tip for food, I'd fan the bills next to my plate. And I'd call 'em all "sir," if they was men or boys waiting on me, didn't matter, and if they was a lady I seen all the time—like a waitress or a desk clerk—I've give her a nickname. "Gimme a smile, Miss Susie Belle. Gimme a smile."

The bigger the tip, the bigger they smiled.

But even if I was staying in slicked-up hotels and eating good food and getting my shoes shined ever' other day, something was missing.

I ain't saying women wasn't around. They was, droves of 'em. Droves and droves. Most of 'em smiling. And in the big cities, our getaway car, that shiny-black Studebaker Big-Six, was better'n diamonds to pull 'em in. Just drive along a downtown street in Tulsa, Memphis, Kansas City, Omaha, and stop on the corner where gals is waiting to get on the street car. They'd jump right in with you, they would, nine times outa ten. And five times outa ten, they'd stay all night with you. I called them gals "Streetcar Sallies."

But most of them "Streetcar Sallies" was just silly, giggly girls. They had more hair than they had brains, even the ones with them new short "bobs."

***

It was when I was stopping at the Loyal Hotel in Omaha that I met Louise.

She was the cigar gal in the lobby. She was real pretty, dark complected. Only it wasn't just that. It was something about how she moved, like she knowed who she was. I was standing at the counter, wanting to buy a *Police Gazette*, and I just stood there, watching her. She was stacking some red tins of Prince Albert tobacco. Her hands was moving sure and steady. And when she finally seen me and come over, her hips rolled, like she was a woman, not a girl.

"Say, miss," I said to her when she give me my paper, "what's there to do in this city for fun?"

"You could go to a picture show."

"Besides that."

She didn't say nothing right off, and then she reached down and picked up a piece of Juicy Fruit.

"You could chew gum."

She was smaller'n most women, half the size of my Ma, but she looked me straight up in the eye. She had dark eyes, they was deep set in her face, but they was a-sparkling. She liked my looks, I could tell. And why not? That day I was wearing a three-button sports jacket with tan linen trousers and a nice straw Panama.

I took the gum and shucked off the wrapper.

"Do you know, miss," I said, "how much money Mister William Wrigley Jr. has made offa this gum? Total, I mean."

"That's a strange question."

"I got a reason for asking it."

'Course, my reason for asking it was I wanted to keep talking to that gal as long as I could. There wasn't no other customers at the cigar stand, so I put both my elbows on the counter. I smiled so she could see all my teeth.

"I could guess." She smiled back and cocked her head to one side. "But it'd just be a guess."

Well, the good thing was, I did know. And it was a good story, how that old boy Wrigley got rich offa chewing gum. I'd just read all about it in the *Chicago Tribune*.

"He's made millions," I said. "So many millions he don't know how many millions he got."

"Millions? Off nickel gum? Well, well."

"Mister Wrigley begun his life selling washing soap, see. And to get people to buy his soap, he'd give 'em a tin of baking powder as *pilon*, a little extra free thing. Then he found out folks liked baking better'n washing. So he started selling baking powder and giving out packs of chewing gum as *pilon*. Then he found out people liked chewing better'n anything."

The cigar lady smiled again. "Seems almost a crime for one man to have so much money."

"I guess it don't seem like a crime if you're the man that's got it."

"I guess not."

"Say, what's your name?"

Before she said a word, I knowed she was gonna give it to me.

"Louise. Louise Brown."

"Good to meet you, Miss Brown." I bowed from the waist. "Will Reed. From East Texas. I'm trading some oil leases 'round here. Now, I am gonna chew this Juicy Fruit, like you said, and make that Mister William Wrigley Jr. five cents richer. And then I think I will go see a picture show. But you know anybody that likes to go to a picture show by theirselves alone? How 'bout you come with me?"

"Thank you, but no."

"Why not?"

"I have an eight-year-old son. I'm a war widow."

Good godamighty, how could somebody that looked so young and so fresh have a eight-year-old son and be a widow? Only I didn't think she was lying. I said, "Bring the boy. I like kids. And I think I seen a Tom Mix picture down the street. A kid ain't a kid if he don't like Tom Mix."

"Oh, my son doesn't like Tom Mix." She laughed and pushed a piece of hair outa her eyes. "My son *is* Tom Mix."

***

The movie house was called the Wigwam and the three of us— me and Louise and her boy—drove there in a getaway car. We had us a great time. The story was about cowboys and Injins and when Tom Mix pulled out a six-shooter and blowed away a pack of Injins, the boy jumped up on his seat and started hollering.

People turned their heads all over that movie house.

That didn't bother me none, I liked a kid that knowed how to blow some wind outa his belly. But Louise got kinda upset. She grabbed the boy—his name was Lewis—down offa his seat and throwed her arm around him. "Hush, angel," she said. Then she leaned over to my ear. "You see what I mean."

I could smell her perfume; it made my head spin.

After the picture show, I took 'em for chocolate sundaes at a soda fountain down the street, and that's when I found out more about Louise. She told me she was working at the cigar stand because she'd give up her real job, second in charge of claims for the Burlington Railroad, to a veteran of the War.

"How'd you get a job like that?" I asked her.

"My father sent me to business college."

I near dropped my ice-cream spoon. Business college! I never

155

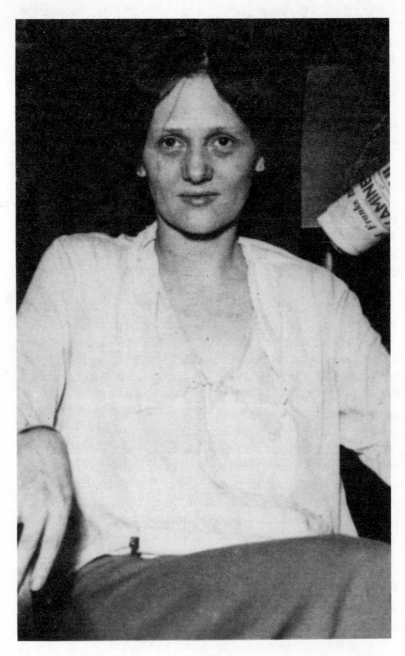

Louise Brown

knowed a woman that'd went to business college. Or any kind of college, far as that goes.

"That musta been a hard thing to do, giving up that job," I said.

"A war's a horrible thing to go through. I thought a serviceman should have it." Her eyes shifted down for a second. Then they come back up. "So, where are the oil leases you're trading, Mister Reed?"

"Oil boom's mostly in the Southwest." I coughed.

"You a millionaire?" That was the boy.

"A millionaire?"

"Yeah," he said. "Oil men are millionaires, I hear."

He clucked his tongue. He was a cute kid, dark hair like his Ma, with a round shiny face.

I coughed again. Then I laughed. The papers was starting to talk more 'n more about millionaires them days, like that Mister Wrigley. There was so much money floating around after the war, and so many big oil strikes. But back then I hardly knowed how many zeros was in a million dollars.

"I ain't one just yet, cowboy," I said back to Lewis. "But how 'bout this? First million I get, you'll be the first to know it."

"Well, if you don't got a million, how much you got then, Mister Reed?"

I dug a silver dollar outa my pocket. "I got enough to buy you a bag of them cream candies over there. Go get you some, and keep the change."

I looked at Louise and winked. And damn if she didn't wink back at me.

EIGHTEEN

Frank was still saying he was the Big Man of our team, and, for a while, even though he was a louse and a skunk, both, it quit eating at me so bad. That meant I could spend more time that summer up in Omaha, hanging around Louise.

I started really getting stuck on that gal.

She made me think about Vela, how I felt in my heart back then, except that Louise was a diff'rent kind of person. Vela was a plain, simple country girl. Louise was a city woman that'd seen things, and that knowed things.

Turns out, Louise was a German Jew who'd growed up in New London, Wisconsin. I never knowed too many Jews before. Back then, lots of people thought you shouldn't mix with Jews, just like you shouldn't mix with the coloreds. Henry Ford, the one that made that Model T, was blaming the Jews in the newspapers for just about ever'thing that was wrong in this country, like high rents and gambling and drinking and having "loose morals," and how women's skirts was getting so short and showing off the whole bottom half of their legs. To be honest, though, I liked it that Louise was a Jew. She was dark complected, like I said before, and that was new to me in a gal. And she was smart and knowed things about business. I heard that was a Jew thing too.

I coulda took Louise out ever' night of the week, if she'd let me.

Her and her boy shared a house with a married couple, and sometimes she'd leave Lewis home and I'd show her the town—take her to the best eating places, or the best speakeasies, or the best shows. I wanted to give her a taste of the good life, and I think she liked that. Other times, we'd take the boy with us, and go to supper, or a picture show.

Ever' so often, we'd just stay in and she'd cook me home-cooked food. And while the supper was getting fixed, I'd spend time with her boy. I felt bad he didn't have no Pa, though if he'd had a Pa,

158

I wouldn't have his Ma. So I only felt half-bad. Anyhow, I'd do card tricks, or tell him stories—about my people, things like that.

"Any your family cowboys?" he asked me one time.

"My Grandma Ivy."

He give a chuckle. "Ladies can't be cow-*boys*."

"In Texas, ladies are whatever they gotta be."

I didn't tell him the whole story about my Grandma Ivy. It was too rough. But I told him how my grandma's folks went to Texas from Tennessee in the 1830s when ever'body was heading West, looking for God's Country, and how Texas did look like God's Country at first. The plains was full of grass, high as your waist, with antelope and buffalo roaming, thick as ever'thing, and the streams was clear and pretty, and there wasn't no goddamn fences. And I told him how my Grandma Ivy learned how to ride a horse astride and to run cattle, just like a man. And how in them days, there was all kinds of codes of the West, but the rule most people went by was "Whatever you're big enough to take, it's yours."

"One day, in about eighteen and fifty-four," I told Lewis, "some ruffians wanted to take over her Pa's ranch. Her Pa was a religious old man and he wouldn't carry a gun. And them ruffians kidnapped him while he was belling a cow and throwed him in the Nueces River, drowned him. But my grandma sure did pack a gun. She was only seventeen, just seventeen years old, but she stood up to them ruffians with a Winchester .45-70. You wasn't supposed to kill a woman back then, 'though some of 'em done it. She was taking her chances."

"Wshew," Lewis said. "Your grandma was a tough one."

"You ever jackknifed open a prickly-pear cactus pad, cowboy? They got devil spikes all over the outside of 'em, but it's the inside of 'em, that's where they're soft and sweet. Full of mush and juice. That's what lots of Texas women 'r like. Just like that. 'Course, some of 'em's plumb the other way around. But I always walk a wide circle around that other kind."

I give a look over at Louise, she was walking outa the kitchen, and grinned. She rolled her eyes.

After supper, on them nights at Louise's, she'd send the boy up to do his schoolwork, and me and her'd play cards with that married couple: canasta, bridge, poker, whatever. 'Course, I knowed more about cards than any of 'em put together. But I always played fair. I figured if Louise caught me cheating, that'd be the end of it with her.

So all I done was throw in a little show: I done riffles and overhands, I thumbed the cards and I crimped 'em.

"You play like a gambler," Louise said to me one time.

"Yeah?" I said back. "I do a little gambling, here and there. If I get a run of dry holes. But I learned it from the best card-player in Maverick County. My Grandma Ivy. Though mostly she just used her cards to tell fortunes."

"She ever tell yours?"

"She said in June, nineteen and twenty, I was gonna get a piece of chewing gum from a lady that was gonna run circles around me."

I patted her under the table.

Lots of times, after them card games, me and Louise'd go upstairs to be by ourselves. She had a gramophone in her bedroom, and she'd pour herself some Scotch whiskey and we'd put on records. And that whiskey'd make her legs twitch.

"Dance with me, Will," she'd say.

Well, I never could quite get the hang of the dances she wanted to do. They had the damndest strange steps, with the damndest strange names, like Ballin' the Jack and the Buzzard Glide. Most times, I'd just put my arms around her waist and shuffle around a little. Then I'd kiss her on the neck to get her thinking about something else besides how my feet was moving.

Near ever' time, it worked.

I don't know what it was, but being with Louise felt right. She didn't give me a itch, she didn't make me jumpy, all I felt was good. It's what I call that "old slow feeling." I don't mean old like a old rotted peach is old, I mean old like how this old round world is old. And slow, like how a creek runs slow at the deep parts. I can't explain it more than that. Maybe some people woulda thought we was a odd pair, and God knows we looked like one, the top of that gal's head barely come up to my armpit. But something inside told me we was pretty much meant to be together—the smart little Jewish lady and the outlaw.

Only problem was, she didn't know I was a outlaw.

***

Big trouble come on a Friday night. Louise and Lewis had gone to Wisconsin to visit her folks, and I'd gone back to Tulsa for a few weeks. About 10 o'clock, the telephone went to ringing. It was Frank and he said to come over to his place, he had something important to tell me. I jumped in my car and went over there right away. A fella named Wash was there.

"Sit down, Skinny," Frank said to me.

Frank was all slicked up: pinstriped suit, silk shirt, diamond cufflinks. Wash was dressed up too, in a high-dollar suit, but his face didn't match up with the rest of him. He had the face of a monkey and a lot of wrinkles. He had a cup of coffee in his hands; it was shaking.

Frank brung me my own cup.

"The Dago's skipped town, Skinny. Wash here knows him. Says the Dago got word Slim's maybe back. It's not that he was afraid of Slim face to face. But he didn't want to be bushwhacked."

I took a slow sip of my coffee. Fact is, I'd just heard it through the underground, that Slim was back, and on the prowl.

But I didn't say nothing.

Frank kept going: "To my mind, it's no big loss. He had too many no-count relations. Bad as Slim's. Probably rat you out for *five* bucks. So I say we forget about the Dago. Wipe him right out of our minds. But summer's almost over. We need somebody to take his place." Frank throwed his eyes over to Wash. "I thought you two could meet."

I looked over at Wash too. I give him one of my dog-snarl smiles. A "dog-snarl smile" is where you stretch out your mouth, like a friendly smile, only your top lip is hiked up a little more, and a little more of your top teeth are showing. It ain't a friendly smile, but it's hard to tell the diff'rence, if you don't know how to read mouths.

"I wanta talk to Frank private here," I said to Wash.

Wash didn't say nothing, just took off.

Soon as the front door shut, I hit Frank with the questions you gotta ask about new ones: "He drink?" "Whore around?" "Keep his word?" Frank poured hisself a fresh cup of coffee and give me a dog-snarl smile of his own. His teeth was still white as snow, something that always struck me, since he never stopped soaking 'em in that black coffee. "I go way back with Wash," he said. "He's had his fingers in a lot of pies: forgery, mail fraud, dope-peddling. But the last year or two, he's been blowing boxes."

"So he's a jug-heavy?"

"Yeah."

Yeah, well, so what?

What was going through my head was something that'd been going through my head, faster and faster, for a long time. Even if we was making money, how long was I gonna be under Frank's thumb? And how long was I gonna stay alive working with a bunch of fool ex-cons? And it wasn't just my head telling me that. It was my bones, too. I think there comes a point in ever' businessman's life when his bones are "seasoned." When he can trust his bones better'n anybody or anything else. And there was something in my bones that was telling me that Wash was gonna be trouble.

I was about to tell Frank we oughta take our time, that I wanted to have a say in picking our next partner, when there come a knock on the door.

"Probably Wash," Frank said, but he was too lazy to get up. He just hollered: "Come on in."

It wasn't Wash.

***

It was three men, and they blowed into the room. One of 'em had a black hood over his head.

All of 'em had guns drawed.

Both Frank and me jumped outa our chairs and I seen a flash of arm. Frank was grabbing down for his own gun. A .32 Derringer, stuck in a holster on his leg. The man in the hood hollered: "No, you don't, Frank!" and I seen Frank lifting his hand. The man's voice sounded like Slim's. I didn't know the other two men; they was grubby and hard-eyed.

The man in the hood stuck a pistol next to Frank's ear, while his two partners grabbed Frank's gun. One of 'em took a long piece of rope from offa his belt and tied Frank's hands behind his back. Then he stuffed a bright red bandana between Frank's white teeth.

The other one come over and patted me down. I didn't have no gun on me. Then he tied my hands, too, but he didn't gag me and he said low in my ear: "This ain't about you, but keep outa the way."

I looked over at the man in the hood. "Take that fool thing offa your head, Slim. I'm your friend."

The hooded man didn't say nothing, just went out the door, I guess to make sure there wasn't gonna be no rank outside. When he come back in, he nodded his head at his partners, and the three of

162

'em marched Frank and me outa the apartment. Their car was back in the alley. A big, long Cadillac.

Frank was trying to break the ropes, but wasn't no use. He was gurgling behind that gag.

They drove us about twenty minutes up and down back roads, towards the outskirts of Tulsa. It was late, so there wasn't too many other cars around. Before long, we wasn't passing nobody. Then the driver took a dark lane up a hill. At the top, he stopped and cut off the headlamps.

It was black as pitch, no moon, no nothing.

You could just see the lights of the city way off, a-twinkling.

"You boys know where we are?" the driver said. "Pistol Hill. They say there's a good view from up here, day 'r night."

He told me to get out. Then him and the other hard-eyed man pulled Frank out and dragged him a short ways, to a tree. They leaned him up agin the trunk, and one of 'em pulled out a rope and tied Frank's feet. His partner went back to the car. He come back carrying a shovel, a pick-ax, and a little kerosene lantern. He lit the lantern. It throwed out a yellow glow.

None of 'em was paying me any mind. They was acting like I was part of their team. I was standing next to another tree. I finally set down.

I shoulda done or said something.

I didn't. But I knowed what they was up to.

In the light of that little lamp, you could see the dust and dirt and rocks a-flying. You could hear the two men grunting and huffing. Little by little, they was getting lower and lower, 'til you couldn't see their knees no more.

The whole time, Frank's eyes was popping outa his head. He was trying to say things from behind that gag, but you couldn't make out none of the words. It just come out something like: "Aaaayyyyeeeeerrrr."

Finally, one of the diggers hollered: "It's big enough. This ground's too damn hard. I ain't doing no more."

The man in the hood picked up the lantern, went over to the hole, and leaned over the edge. When the light hit it, I seen it was only about three feet long. He shrugged, come back to Frank, and crouched in front of him. Frank was making more of them sounds: "Aaaayyyyeeeeerrrr."

The man pulled his .45 outa his belt and touched the barrel to the top of Frank's right ear. He put it right up agin the top ridge of the ear. He tapped it—tap, tap, tap. Then he moved the barrel two inches down to the bottom part of Frank's ear, the fleshy part. He tapped the barrel there—tap, tap, tap. Then he moved the barrel two inches up and over to the hard bony part of the skull, right behind the back of Frank's ear. Tap, tap, tap. Then he moved it two inches over and to the right to the hard bony part of the skull right in front of Frank's ear. Tap, tap, tap.

Frank's whole body was shaking.

I kept waiting for the gunman to push the barrel into Frank's ear and blow Frank's brains out, but he didn't. Finally, he give a hand signal to his buddies and both fellas come over. One of 'em picked Frank up by the feet, the other by the shoulders. They lugged him over to the hole.

Frank's diamond cufflinks was glittering in the lamplight.

One of the men pushed Frank's legs up to his chin, and they jammed him in, ass first.

The hole was near deep enough, but not quite. The top of Frank's head, all that coal-black hair, was sticking out.

The man in the hood went over and this time he didn't waste no time tapping.

He pointed the gun down and fired two times.

PART TWO: THE FAMILY BUSINESS

NINETEEN

That was it.

I didn't want no more partners. Not if they was like Slim or the Dago or Frank. Or even Glasscock.

Frank got dug up by a rabbit hunter.

I seen it in the newspaper. A old, one-eyed colored man was up on Pistol Hill hunting rabbits when his dog got to sniffing around in some leaves and digging in some fresh dirt. The hunter got all frothed up. Thought he'd found hisself a whole case of booze buried by rum runners. He got him a shovel and he dug in. And it wasn't long before, sure enough, he'd hit something. Something hard.

It was Frank's kneecap.

I didn't like Frank. I ain't gonna make out like I did. Only I didn't wanta see him dead, either. And when I laid down to go to sleep at night, the pictures'd come up in my head and claw around in there. I'd see Frank's eyes popping outa their sockets while he watched them two men dig his grave, and I'd see the blood come a-spurting outa them two holes in his head.

I couldn't shake them pictures loose.

I'd seen people die before. But I never did see nobody die in a way that was as close to me as how Frank got it. And ever' night Frank's dead body kept a-telling me that the same thing could happen to me if I kept on working with ex-cons like I was.

Maybe it was best to move on. Somewhere further west, like New Mexico, or Arizona, or even California.

Only problem, what'd I do out there? Besides that, I didn't wanta go so far away from Louise and Lewis. And besides that, I gotta be honest here: bank robbing was hard work, but I liked it. It come natural to me, and I made damn good money at it. 'Course, money all by itself don't get your blood to pumping. You can be the richest man in the world and feel dead as a corpse if your blood ain't pumping. But bank jobs did get my blood to pumping. I had a good mind, and I knowed how to use it. I knowed how to keep it on one thing, and not let it go helty-skelty. And I had what they call "the nerve." I didn't booger easy.

But how was I gonna keep alive if all I had to work with was cowards or cut-throats?

***

The answer come one day, about a week after Frank got rubbed out, when I was setting on my bed at the Loyal, rubbing black polish on my wingtips. Booty Blue woulda give me the what-for if he seen me shining my own shoes, but my hands was needing something to do, to keep my fingers from stiffing up, and my mind was going in circles, too, when it come to me.

All of a sudden, boom!

Really, it was two booms. Two answers. And I didn't waste no time shooting a letter down to Texas with two $20 bills in it. Only one of my answers wrote me back, but that's because the other one couldn't spell too good.

The letter said they'd be up in a week on the 4 o'clock Missouri-Pacific Sunshine Special.

When the day come, I took Louise and Lewis with me to the train station. They was back from Wisconsin by then.

"Who's coming?" Lewis kept asking me. "How come it's a secret?"

"A man that shows his cards all the time is a man that don't win too many games," I said.

I poked him in the ribs and kissed his Momma on the cheek.

They was both looking good, dressed up like it was a Sunday. Louise had on a fancy little hat, and a blue dress. Near six inches of her calves was showing, but that's how women dressed in the cities. And she was wearing a diamond broach that I'd give her. The boy was dressed in a little bow tie and knickers, like a city kid, only he had a little Stetson on his head I'd give him.

At 3:56, that little Stetson started a-hopping. "Here it comes!"

And there it was, the Sunshine Special, its big old iron engine blasting into the station, bells a-clanging, wheels a-squealing, steam a-hissing, thick black smoke a-shooting way up high into the sky.

That hissing steam and that burning coal, they give your nose a tickle. And they was smells I really liked. Even living in a city, there still wasn't nothing much more exciting than watching a train come in. And, to tell the truth, this was the first time in my life I'd ever met anybody that was paying to ride one.

The engine stopped, there was more squealing wheels and steam puffing out in big clouds, and people begun pouring outa cars. Before you knowed it, there was a big crowd a-milling out on the platform. Ever'body was shaking hands and hugging and kissing and hey-heying ever'body else.

Ever'body but who I was looking for.

Damn! Did they change their minds?

"Who's coming?" The boy was jerking on my sleeve.

"It's two of 'em...and they're gonna look lost."

Then I felt Louise tapping me on the shoulder. She was pointing at two fellas who'd just got off the end car, way on down the platform. One of 'em was tall and lanky, all legs and arms and neck; the other one was shorter and squatter, with a barrel chest. Both of 'em had on high-crown Stetsons and high-heel cowboy boots. Both of 'em was lugging low-horn saddles and lumpy gunny sacks. And their heads was a-spinning around like they didn't know where in the hell they was.

"Y'all wait here," I said.

Well, I lit on over and when the stocky one caught sight of me, he throwed his head back and out come the loudest, wildest Texas yell you ever heard.

"Eeeeeeeee-hah!!!!!"

It was worse'n a Injin war whoop. One lady that was walking past us grabbed her little boy by the hand like, sure enough, wild Comanches was gonna swoop down and lift off both their scalps. Only the fella that was hollering was wilder'n any Injin.

He was a South Texas bronc buster.

Yeah, it was my older brother Jess, and, standing next to him, my little brother Joe.

"Godamighty, Jess!" I said, slapping him on the back. "You wanta get us throwed off to the hoosegow?"

"Just getting a south wind going, Willis." That moon face give me a slow grin. "Air up here in the Middle West ain't in much of a hurry, is it?"

Fact is, by then people was hurrying past us in a big circle, like they was afraid them two cowboys was gonna pull out six-shooters any second and start banging away. There was nothing like 'em on that platform. Their skin was brown as hickory nuts from that hot Texas sun and besides their hats and boots they was wearing rough, brown brush jackets and thick, dirty bullhide leggings. Both of 'em smelled like leather and sweat.

I pointed down at their saddles and gunny sacks.

"What's that?"

"What's what?" Joe asked.

"Them saddles. Whatever's in them sacks."

"What d'ya think it is? Bridles, spurs, ever'thing we'll need for that job. We brung our own gear."

"Hell, throw that damn gear away. It ain't that kinda job."

"What kinda job is it?" Joe looked mixed up.

"We'll go over that later. Right now, you see that lady over yonder? Blue dress? Next to the little boy in the hat?"

Both their necks went spinning again.

"Oow," said Jess. "A looker."

"That's my gal. And her boy. Only they don't know some things, so for right now you two are gonna be my cousins." I pointed at Jess. "We're gonna make you 'Jess Carpenter.' " I pointed at Joe. "And you're gonna be 'Joe Carpenter.' "

That throwed 'em for a few somersaults.

I went on: "Just go with the game for now, boys. Oh, and something else. This lady calls me 'Will Reed.' That's my name, see, far as what she knows. So that's what you gotta call me. 'Will Reed.' You got it?"

For the first time since my brothers got offa that train, they give me a good look, all over, side to side, top to bottom. The last time they'd seen me, I had on a work shirt and bib overalls and a straw farm hat. This time I had on a felt dude hat and a $85 mohair suit and a two-carat diamond stickpin.

"What's it *this* time, old boy?" Jess said. "Outside of Ma's jaw, ain't a inch of you looks like a Newton."

"Something smells funny." That was Joe.

"Just do me this one, boys. I guarantee you it's something good."

***

Well, Lewis was beside hisself at meeting Texas cowboys with saddles and boots and high-crown hats, and Jess and Joe, even if I'd shook 'em up, didn't flinch a muscle when I said they was my cousins. And I could tell they was pretty impressed when they seen Louise close up. They inched their shoulders back and shuffled their legs.

But they kept their manners on, called Louise "Ma'am," and turned their heads when they spit.

After a little bit, I didn't wanta take no more chances that my brothers'd let something slip about who they was, or who I was, and so I put Louise and Lewis in a taxicab and sent 'em home. And me and the boys hit on over to the Loyal. I was driving a new Studebaker Series 20 Special-Six, and the boys' eyes popped out when they seen it. Slim'd taught me how to use all them sticks and levers. That car had all-rubber tires, and I knowed how to make 'em squeal.

"Eeeeeeeee-hah!" Jess hollered again.

When we got to the hotel, my brothers was like two hounddogs checking out a new cow barn. In the lobby, they sniffed at a statue of a little nekked angel, and they sniffed at some tall palm trees in shiny pots, and they sniffed at the little bellboys that was sinking lower and lower under their saddles and gunny sacks and a fat cardboard suitcase.

"What's going on here, Willis?" Joe's eyes kept switching between round as circles, and narrow as slits. He wasn't sure what to think.

"You'll see."

When we got upstairs, Joe bounced up and down on the mattress and Jess picked up the room-service menu and whistled. I knowed he could hardly read a word on that menu, but he whistled anyhow.

"Now, you boys just settle in," I said.

That was all the sign Jess needed. He yanked open his cardboard suitcase and pulled out a tall bottle of Mex'kin tequila. He said the occasion called for a drink. With Jess, ever' occasion called for a drink. 'Course, he didn't know what this occasion was.

I told 'em.

***

Months after that, Joe told me what went on between him and Jess later that night in their room. Joe walked back and fro, side to side, for hours.

170

"You think he was kidding?" he kept asking Jess.

"Hell, no."

"Why should I wanta rob banks? I ain't never broke the law in my life."

"Well, I'll tell you what I'm gonna do," Jess said, drinking that hooch straight outa the bottle. "Come morning, I'm hitting on back to Texas. I get all the kick I need from snapping a horse."

"He'll say we're yeller."

"Let him. We go with that crazy old son-of-a-bitch, we're gonna end up hanging from a tree. Let's just get up early and cut out. He don't need to know."

"We're gonna have'ta tell him."

"How come?" Jess snorted.

"We need money for the train ticket home."

TWENTY

"You ain't yeller, are you, boys?"

Joe was right. That's exactly what I told 'em when they come knocking at my hotel door. It was just peeping daylight, and my brothers, both of 'em, was standing there with their hats on and their hands out.

Well, there's all kinds of ways to shame a man. But, back home, ain't nothing worse'n calling him just plain "yeller."

Joe hung his head. Jess just laughed.

"Aw, don't give us that bullshit, Willis," Jess said. "If we're gonna get our necks snapped, we wanta get 'em snapped the right way—by flying off a horse. Anyhow, who the hell's yeller here? You ever busted a bronc?"

"Don't be fools, boys," I come right back. "Get in here and take off them hats. You want train fare? You gotta listen first."

***

I was ready for 'em.

Yeah, I knowed, soon as the boys thought over ever'thing I'd told 'em the day before, they was gonna grouse and kick and raise all kinds of racket. And I knowed, if I wanted to turn 'em, I was just gonna have to ride it out.

I was ready to take it—and I was ready to give it.

The boys come in and set down on the edge of my bed, but they didn't take off their hats. 'Course, that didn't mean nothing. Back home, cowboys wore their hats from the minute they got up in the morning 'til the minute they bedded down at night, while they was eating and ever'thing else. Their hats was as much a part of their bodies as their arms or their legs was.

I was only in trouble if them two big old hats went back outa that door.

172

"It ain't you, is it, little brother?" I walked over to Joe and leaned down and I looked at him square. "You the yeller one?"

Joe looked away and started fingering a button on his brush jacket. "That ain't it, Willis. It's just that I ain't never broke the law in my life and I don't know how come I should start doing it now."

"For the money. You never seen money like I make in my business."

"Me and Jess don't care 'bout money like you do."

"It's human nature to want money."

"Maybe it's just *your* nature, Willis." That was Jess this time. But he wasn't talking to no button. He was looking at me straight, only half-grinning. "You was born money-hungry, and you know it. Even when you was rolling in it with that old gambler, you still wanted more. You can't fool us. We all know you went and stole that cotton with Dock."

"The hell I did!" I give Jess a straight look back.

"Well, Pa said you got just what you deserved when you got sent up and – "

"I was framed, and that's that! Look-it, this ain't gonna be forever. But me and you got a bum start, Jess, without no good schooling. And Joe didn't get it much better. And the only way folks like us can get into a good business that's legal, like the oil business, or the horse-ranching business, is to get a lotta money to start with. That's all we're doing here."

"Whoa there, old boy!" That was Jess again. "Me and Joe do plenty fine breaking horses, and a horse don't care if you graduated high school or didn't make it past the first grade. And you! You coulda gone to school if you really wanted, and you know it. How about that time you run off and ended up with that old man next county down and he was gonna send you to school if you worked his farm? Only he wanted you to wear kneepants and you wanted to wear long pants. You just never wanted nobody to tell you what to do, Willis."

I put up my hand.

Far as I was concerned, they'd got enough outa their craws.

"You're talking old history, Jess," I said. "It's time to go forward here. And I got a proposition for you, boys. No way you can lose on this one. I want y'all to try out my business for one month. Just one month. And if you don't like it after that month, fine. You got no obligation to me. I'll give you money for a first-class Pullman home, plus a thousand dollars, *pilon*. That's a thousand dollars. *Apiece.*"

They give each other a look.

***

'Course, both of 'em kicked like fuzztail broncs when I told 'em they'd have to trade in their cowboy outfits for city clothes. But, that afternoon, they let me take 'em to some men's stores and buy 'em what they needed—three-piece suits, low-slung city shoes, roll-brim fedoras.

"If you're gonna be in business, boys, you gotta look like businessmen," I said when we was back in their hotel room. "And that's what we're gonna be. We're not gonna be thugs, or kill nobody. We're just gonna be quiet businessmen. Just like lawyers or bankers or storekeepers or any other men that's in a business. All we want is the money."

Joe was setting on his bed, his shoulders slumped, his new fedora on his lap. He was thumbing the brim of that city hat so hard you could see the marks of his fingernails. Jess was setting on his bed, too, yanking off his new Oxfords and rubbing his feet like they was sore. Which they was. He hadn't been wearing no socks.

"Don't get too used to us, Willis," Jess said. "Soon's this month is up, we're putting our Stetsons back on and we're taking our thousand and we're cutting right on back to Texas."

I walked over to Joe, picked that dude hat offa his lap, and banged it on his head. Then I looked over at Jess. We was a team now, and I was the one in charge. "Get some socks on, boy. Right now, the only place you're going is a show."

"A what?"

***

Before I started in the bank-robbing business, I didn't know much about how city people entertained theirselves. In the country, folks mostly just set out on the porch and told stories—about dead kin, about big hunts, about bad scars, about ornery neighbors, about anything and ever'thing. They'd spin 'em and stretch 'em and twist 'em—you never let what really happened mess up a good story. But in the city, folks didn't have to make their own entertainment. Long as you had cash for a ticket, there was dozens of places where somebody'd do your entertaining for you. Vaudeville shows, opera houses, speakeasies, movie palaces, even something with wild city gals called burlesque shows.

The newspapers called them things "amusements." That night, I was calling 'em "tossing my brothers some oats."

It wasn't a hour later, the three of us boys was sliding into front-row seats at the Trail West Burlesque in downtown Omaha. It was a big dark room, like a cave. Only it wasn't no cave. It had a big stage in front with long purple curtains, and right under that stage, in a pit, there was a little music band. The players was tuning up their instruments, and they was screeching and snorting. And on the stage, in front of them closed curtains, there was two comics, dressed like clowns with red rubber noses, and they was slamming each other on the head with blowed-up hog bladders.

Then, crash!

There went them brass things together.

And up went the curtains!

The gals was all sizes and had all colors of hair—yellow, red, black, brown—but all of 'em was young and more'n half of 'em was pretty. And they was all lined up in a row, their arms linked together like a fence, and they was wearing little slivers of shiny pink cloth that just barely covered their things. They all had big pink hats on top of their heads and big clumps of pink feathers tied to their ankles.

Up. Up. Up.

Their legs was all kicking up, so high you'da thought they was gonna rare up and fall backwards.

I looked sideways at the boys.

I sure hoped this'd help to turn 'em. I had to have partners that wouldn't run off and leave you in a tight spot. That wouldn't knock you off when you wasn't looking to get your share of the loot. Being blood kin, we'd have that natural loyalty to each other. A lot of outlaw teams had been brothers—the Jesse James boys, the Daltons, the Youngers. It's true that Jess was lazy, a big old tumbleweed, but when we was kids and tooted around West Texas hopping freights, he never let me down. If he had a dollar in his pocket, and I wanted it, he'd give it to me, even though I was a lot more likely to have a dollar in my pocket than the other way around. Joe was a lot younger than either of us, but from what I'd seen of him and what Ma told me, he was true blue. The fact was, we was tight as a family, even if I'd run away from home all them times. Some of that family feeling was due to Ma, but most farm families was tight back then.

If ever'body didn't work, and work together, nobody ate.

Anyhow, when them burlesque gals started kicking their legs, Jess's arms started waving and now he was letting loose with a couple of them wild, hot Texas yells. Yeeee-aaaaah! Happy as a man could ever hope to be. There was only one thing that wasn't going like it was supposed to.

It was Joe.

He was setting stiff as a fence post. He wasn't smiling. He wasn't even tapping his foot.

I leaned over to him. "You okay, Joe?"

He didn't say nothing.

"You ever seen so many angels?" I asked.

Nothing.

"That blonde's a-winking at you, Joe."

Nothing.

It was then that something come to me. Joe was nineteen, tall and skinny, but with enough hard, bulging muscles to make him look ever' bit a man. By the time I was his age, I'd seen the sweet sides of plenty of gals when I was traveling with that gambler Jenkins. But maybe Joe'd never really been offa the farm. Growing up in a big family, a boy's always getting a eyeful of his sisters. Still, that ain't the same as seeing somebody you ain't kin to. And even after the World War, women out in the country was still wearing long skirts with high collars that barely give you a peek of anything, much less anything interesting.

"You okay, Joe?" I asked it again.

Still nothing.

The chorus gals had gone to singing. It was hard to make out all the words, their voices was kinda high, but it was something about a "pitter-pat" and a "raggie-tune" and a "walk down lover's lane." And ever' so often, they'd pull off their hats and bang 'em against their knees.

It took near a hour for my plan to start working.

I seen it out the corner of my eye.

Joe didn't start waving his arms like Jess was. Or howling like Jess was. Or popping up offa his seat and wiggling his hind-end like Jess was. All he done was start blinking his eyes and swallowing and sighing. They was fast little blinks and fast little swallows and short little half-sighs. They wasn't nothing nobody'd a-noticed if they wasn't looking for it. I don't think Joe even knowed he was doing it.

But, to me, it was sign:

The oats I was tossing to the boys was starting to get et.

***

Next morning, I marked our getaway route with a thick red line on a map.

The town was in Iowa, not too far southeast of Omaha, a place called Glenwood.

At first, the boys listened without saying nothing. They was both a little drooped from the night before. It was when I opened a big black bag and showed 'em the guns we was gonna take with us on the job—old Colt .45s and sawed-off shotguns—that both of 'em come back to life.

They looked at me walleyed.

It wasn't because they was scared of guns. Like all Texas farm boys they was used to handling ever' kind of gun. And they was both crack shots, like me. But it was one thing killing rabbits 'n deer 'n quail, it was something else when you figured you might be in a gun-fight with another human being.

"I ain't shooting nobody." Joe had his hat on his lap again. Thumbing the rim, and pinching it and patting it.

"You boys still don't get what I'm telling you here, do you?" I said back. "We ain't gonna be gunfighters. We do what we do real late at night, when ever'body's asleep."

"You know it well as I do, Willis," Joe said, "that there's always somebody awake at night in them country towns. Some old nighthack, or some old lady that's got the vapors."

"We got ways of handling nighthacks. And if it's a old lady, newsboy, sheriff that don't sleep too good, whatever, we just keep on driving. It's no disgrace to keep going, boys. Better to say 'There he goes,' than 'Here he lies.' "

Jess was setting with his legs wide apart, smacking a piece of Wrigley's Juicy Fruit. "What if somebody sees us anyhow, and gets a bead on us?"

"That's why we got these guns," I said right back. "For scare."

My brothers was still jumpy, that much was clear. So I pulled out one more trick. I hated horses, but I could talk horse if that's what it took. And this is what you do when you want to saddle a jittery bronc:

You grab a-hold of its ear. You chew on it.

"Listen boys. Y'all both wanna have your own ranches, right?"

Both their heads come up at that. There wasn't nothing either of 'em wanted more'n a sprawling ranch with a remuda full of hot-bloods. Only the chance of two rawhide cowboys like them ever owning a ranch like that was close to zero, no matter how good they was at busting broncs.

"Think about it," I said. "It's gonna take a lotta money to buy you land and some pretty horses, ain't it?"

Both of 'em nodded.

"You got that kinda money?"

Both of 'em shook their heads.

"Where's that kinda money gonna come from?"

Both of 'em shrugged.

"That's what I thought. Lemme tell you where that kinda money comes from, boys. It comes outa a bank. But what you think a banker's gonna do, two scruffy old cowboys walk into his office and ask him for money like that?"

They didn't answer me.

"Hell, that old banker wouldn't even give you a smile at fifty-percent interest."

I told 'em they didn't have'ta feel bad about taking the money from banks, 'cause banks do all kinds of crooked things theirselves. Like foreclosing on old widow women. Or buying stole bonds at a discount from bank robbers. When I was working with Frank Holloway and them other old boys, we never had trouble finding a banker to buy them bonds. And them bankers *knowed* they was stole.

"We'll just be little thieves taking money from big thieves."

Jess smacked his gum again. "If we're little thieves and they're big thieves, why's the laws on their side?"

"Law's always on the side of the ones that got the most money," I said right back. "And why do the bankers have all that money? By taking what ain't theirs! Same reason all them old German ladies near Cisco had all that egg business. You ever seen any of them ladies squat down on one of them nests and lay a egg? I'd sure like to see it if they do. They don't. All they do is build the hen-houses and then steal the eggs. That's what bankers 'r like."

Then I told 'em what Frank told me: Nobody really gets hurt when a bank is robbed 'cause most banks 'r insured. Besides, I told 'em, insurance companies was just as crooked as the banks. And they wasn't just thieves; they was liars!

"They'll promise you ever'thing but the moon to get you to buy the most expensive policy they got," I said. "Then just try to collect. Ha! Maybe they pay a little here, a little there, but for ever' dollar they give back, they keep five for theirselves."

Joe give me a funny look. "If the insurance companies are such big thieves, ain't they just gonna pass it on down somehow? If a bank gets robbed and they gotta pay out? And is ever'thing insured? Bank back home got robbed last year, and I seem to recollect the paper said some folks didn't get their money back."

I laughed. "You got too much going on between your ears, little brother. You gotta look at it how I look at it: Most ever'thing's insured these days, and most of them insurance companies are crooks. And something else: Them insurance companies ain't *never* planning to go straight. We are."

"Well, if we throw in with you, when is it we're planning to go straight?"

"Soon's we get enough."

"How much is that?

To be truthful, I'd never put a figure on how much I wanted to have before I give up robbing banks. Only, when Joe asked me that, a number come up. Come up right there in the middle of my head. And set there, just clear as day. But soon as I got a good look at it, with all them zeros, I decided I wasn't gonna tell it.

It woulda boogered my brothers right back to Texas.

"Tell you what, boys," I said. "You join my business, I'll let you tell *me* when you think we got enough."

TWENTY-ONE

We was all ready to hit a bank, to test ourselves as a brother team, except for one thing. We needed one more man. I knowed that four was the best number when you wanted your jobs to be a lead-pipe cinch: two to be inside men, two to be lookouts.

Luck was with us.

Three days before we was gonna pull out for Glenwood, I got a telephone call at five in the morning. And that call give me just what I wanted, though I didn't say nothing about it right off to the boys.

Two days later, the three of us set off. When I opened the throttle of that Studebaker Special-Six, it shot forward like a race horse. I felt near as good as I'd ever felt in my life. Having my two brothers with me was kinda like having our family back together again. Only this time it was me that was boss, not Pa. And we'd all put down a good breakfast that morning: thick-cut bacon, fried eggs, scrambled eggs, toast, blackberry jam, strong coffee.

And as we was cutting down that highway, I was thinking about something that was sending shivers up my spine.

I was thinking what it'd be like to have a million dollars.

***

In all the newspapers and ever'where you went them days, folks was starting to talk "millions of dollars" and "millionaires." And it wasn't just the big-name, old-time millionaires like Mister John D. Rockefeller, Mister J.P. Morgan, Mister Andrew Carnegie, or Mister William Wrigley Jr. Ever'day, it seemed, there was a story about somebody that'd growed up poor and then Blooey!, near overnight, because of some invention or some kind of deal, he was a millionaire.

20-year-old Joe in one of the gang's getaway cars, a Studebaker Special Six. Tulsa, Oklahoma.

That could've never happened before the big war over in Europe, because back then there wasn't much money going around the country. Even Mister H.L. Pike, the richest man in Eastland County, was worth only $20,000, according to what I read one time in the *Rising Star Record.* But after the big war, there was more money around because the government had been paying for the war by printing more and more money, and selling more and more Liberty and Victory bonds. And American factories was starting to sell all kinds of things—automobiles, stoves, typewriters, soap—all over the world. And lots of people was after that money, and they didn't give a damn how they got it—if they cheated the government, or rigged the price of things, or sold stocks and bonds that wasn't worth the paper they was printed on.

However they got it, more money passing around the country meant more money in the banks, and more money in the banks was what I was thinking about as we was racing down that Iowa highway. Hell, with my brothers helping me, there wasn't no reason why I couldn't get enough of that new money to make me a millionaire too. Enough to make all of us millionaires! In America, one newspaper fella wrote, nobody could dream about being a king or queen, because we didn't have no kings or queens. But ever'body, no matter how poor they was (and plenty of people *was* still poor), could dream about being a millionaire. And when folks talked about millionaires, they always made it sound like being a millionaire was greater than being a king, or even Jesus Christ.

'Course, when I was a kid, I'd never even knowed the word "million." First time I ever heard that word I was passing a old man's cotton field out in Taylor County. He was near to crying, and he was pinching something between his fingers — one of them ugly, fuzzy, black boll weevils with hump backs and long snouts. Farmers hated boll weevils more'n the Devil hisself, because of how they eat the tender little leaf buds and bore into the blossoms and baby bolls— leaving a field of empty burrs instead of soft cotton.

"There's a million of 'em! A million of 'em!" that old farmer kept saying, pinching that ugly bug. "I'm just plain ruin't!"

It was the same word, all right. But just like there's a big dif- f'rence between what folks thinks is in Heaven and what they think is in Hell, a million dollars was a altogether diff'rent thing from a mil- lion boll weevils.

Joe Newton

* * *

When we was about thirty miles into Iowa, we crossed over a river called the West Nish and turned left, heading away from the sun.

"Whoa, boy!" Jess said. "Map here says Glenwood's more north."

Like most cowboys, Jess never missed a trick when it come to directions. Cowboys did ever'thing by the sun.

"We're making a stop," I said.

Jess snorted. "You got you another heifer, Willis?"

"A bull."

"A bull?"

"Just hang onto your hat."

Jess banged his fedora. "What hat? This thing ain't a hat. It's a lid."

We rattled over some railroad tracks, and I pulled offa the road and put on the brake. I told the boys to stay in the car and I hopped on out.

"Gol-dang, Willis! How come you can't tell us nothing?" Joe said after me. "You ain't the only one in this outfit, ya know."

I walked off from the car and looked ever' which-a-way. About a hundred yards down from the train tracks I seen a stream with thick brush and tall, pretty cattails. That had to be the spot.

I cupped my hands to my mouth. "*Whip*-poor-*weel, whip*-poor-*weel.*"

Nothing.

"*Whip*-poor-*weel! Whip*-poor-*weel!*"

This time, a line of cattails went to snapping and crashing flat on their heads, like dominos a-falling, and here he comes, a-barrelling!

"Yeah-yeah-hell's-o'-fire it's me, me, me!"

Hell's-o'-fire, *who else?*

He was covered from head to toe in sticky brown mud, and he had long, spikey whiskers, and his hair was going ever' which-a-way. But he looked good to my eyes! He couldn't help it he'd been bit by a mad coyote.

He hugged me so hard he liked to crack a rib.

No sooner they seen who it was, Jess and Joe come a-running.

"Dock!" Joe said. "We thought you was still locked up."

"Broke out."

184

"Again?"

"Hell, yeah. Warden made me a trusty."

"*You?*"

Dock give a smirky smile. "I won that warden some big money, I'll tell you what. Warden seen me knock out a guard, see, and it give him the idea to have prizefights. He put me up agin the big boys, the niggers and the bulls, and I knocked 'em all out! After that, he give me priv'leges. Let me be a dog boy 'n all. Only one day, old hound trainer went off to get some smokes, left his horse without no rider on it, and that was it for me..."

Jess leaned down and come up with a pint whiskey flask that'd been strapped to his leg. "You thirsty from all that escaping?"

"I think I am."

I didn't say nothing right off. I just watched while Dock held that flask up to his mouth and poured. Agin my better judgment, I let Jess pour too. Joe passed on it, but I took a little snort, just to show Dock how glad we was to have him with us. Then, while I had my hand on that bottle, I pulled back and SLAM!

It smashed into a thousand pieces.

"Damn you, Willis!" Jess was hopping mad. "What'd you do that for!"

" 'Cause we got a job tonight," I said right back. "And in my business, we don't drink."

"You're worse'n a Baptist preacher!"

"You wanna meet up with a real Baptist preacher, Jess?" I said to him. "You keep drinking like you do, and I guarantee you you're gonna meet up with a real Baptist preacher. He's gonna be stooped over your dead body. And you ain't gonna be on your way up."

"I like down. The Devil makes better barbeque."

"I ain't kidding here, Jess. No corn. No barley. No rye. No tequila. No nothing."

He still didn't like my rule, not a'tall. But when he seen I meant business, he said, "Oh...all right," and set down on a big rock and sulked. I knowed I was gonna have trouble with Jess that way. And with Dock too, now that he'd got the taste of corn again.

Dock wasn't grousing, just hanging his head. "Aw, burr balls! I coulda drunk that whole thing by myself, Willis, and no kidding."

"Cheer up, old boy."

Back in Omaha, I'd bought Dock a fine gray suit, extra big, and a hat to match. So I give him his new outfit, along with a razor, and told him to slick hisself up. He went back through them snapped cat-tails, and when he come out, you'd a-thought *he* was the Baptist preacher.

Only I wasn't done yet. I told 'em all to set down, that I had something to go over with 'em, and that I'd buy 'em all rib-eyes soon as I was done. I went back to the car and got a big, yellow enve-lope. I pulled a big picture out.

"We don't kill people," I said. "If you kill somebody, that's when all hell breaks loose. And the public goes agin ya. I want you to know I mean it."

All three of their jaws dropped.

It was one of them doctor's medical drawings, how a man looks on the inside, if all his wrapping and skin was took off. I'd bought it off a crook doctor in Tulsa for fifty dollars. He was the one that give me the lesson I was about to give my brothers.

"Most times, boys," I said, "you'll be carrying shotguns. And we load our shotguns with Number 7 birdshot. But if I give you a pis-tol...."

I pointed to the part of the drawing that showed the man's heart. It was drawed in bright red. "A man's heart ain't way over on the left, like you might think. It's right here. Near to the middle. Look hard. You don't ever wanta shoot a man in his heart. Ever. Got that?"

The boys knowed what I was saying.

Birdshot pellets are just bitty things, see, what you use to shoot doves or quail. They wouldn't kill no human if you was careful the way you shot your gun, they'd just sting and make 'em turn tail. But the pistols was loaded with thick lead bullets. And that was a diff'rent story.

"Okay. If you gotta shoot, here's where you aim." I pointed to one of the man's shoulders in the drawing, where the bones and the gristle come together. "Just wing 'em. Don't shoot unless you have to. But if you have to, hit 'em right, if they're right-handed, left if they're lefties. Got it?"

Jess and Dock nodded.

Joe just blinked.

"All we're doing here, Joe, is getting ready for what *ain't* gonna happen."

***

186

We drove into Glenwood after dark. Wasn't much to see, mostly just one and two-story buildings on the main street. When we drove past the First National Bank, we seen a night marshal setting in a chair on one side of the building. He was a old feller, white hair and whiskers, and his chin was rocking on his breastbone.

"See that?" I said. "Naptime."

"This town's a flea trap," Jess said. "Bet nothing ever' happens here."

We stopped on a back street and switched off the car lights. Since this was gonna be the Newton boys' first job as a team, and all my brothers was green, I told Dock to wait in the car. If something went wrong, I didn't want him caught and sent back to the joint. Being that he was a escaped con, they was likely to throw the book at him.

I told Dock, if he thought me and Jess and Joe was captured, to take off by hisself. We could take care of ourselves. Then I reached under the back seat and pulled out our shotguns and pistols. One of the shotguns I give to Dock, the other to Joe. One pistol I give to Jess, the other I pocketed myself.

"Okay," I said. "First thing we gotta do, we gotta sneak up on that old nighthack and take him round back, gag him and tie him up. Joe and me's gonna do that. Jess is lookout. Somebody else comes by, talk rough to 'em."

With that, me and Jess and Joe started down the alley. It was dirt, so we wasn't making much sound. Creeping slow and easy, like cats. But just when we come up close to the back of the bank, we was just about one building away, what pops up right in front of us but a little black shadow. Kinda like a ghost.

Only that ghost was growling.

Joe turned sideways to me. "Uh-oh."

"Damn."

"He ain't gonna let us by, Willis."

It was a fearsome-looking little bulldog.

I thought quick. I knowed if we took another step forward that growl was gonna explode into a yowl, and we was gonna get bit and ranked both. If we'd a-had a lasso, one of my cowboy brothers coulda roped and jaw-tied that ugly old dog. Only we didn't have no lasso.

Then something come to me.

"Go back slow," I said to Joe, "behind the back of that store, get me that crate."

Joe turned his head and seen what I was talking about. One of them wood-slat crates they pack bananas in.

He backed up slow. That dog had its eyes glued on my little brother. But it didn't move a muscle.

Joe come back, holding the crate.

I took it and started moving, real slow, towards the dog. Its growl got deeper, coarser. Its head shot out a coupla times. Snapped back. When I'd got about a yard off, I stopped, give that dog one mean look, ragged back on my heels and...

JUMP! CLUNK!

"Okay, Jess." I motioned him over. "Somebody's gotta set on it."

"Oh, hell," he said. But he set.

Well, I'll tell you what, that bulldog was ramming and jumping and rocking the sides of that crate like nobody's business. But the box was muffling them yelps and howls. Only as it come out, our problems wasn't over. Here comes a *big* black shadow! "What the devil's going on here?" it's saying.

All that ruckus had woke somebody up. And when that big shadow come a-loping up, damned if it wasn't that sleepy old marshal!

"What you boys doin' here this time of night?"

"There's a mad dog under that crate."

"Huh? Who are you men?" He wasn't a very smart old boy. 'Cause if he was smart, he'da had his gun out—if he had a gun. He didn't have nothing.

"Well sir, we're...."

"Okay, put 'em up!" Joe yanked his shotgun out from under his coat and jabbed it into the old man's back. "You make a move, I'll blow your head off!"

Damn! You'da thought my little brother was the meanest son-of-a-bitch in the world.

The marshal throwed up his hands and went to trembling. "Aw no...don't shoot...please don't shoot me, boys...."

Outa my pocket I pulled a thin rope. I tied up the man's hands and legs. Then I put a handkerchief gag in his mouth. His eyes was just round as the moon, but he didn't make no more trouble. Didn't even sniffle.

"Come on," I said to Joe.

We left Jess setting on the dog.

***

Outside the bank I bear-hugged up a telephone pole and cut the cable.

"Ain't that gonna tip 'em off, somebody tries to use the phone?" Joe asked.

"Naw. Country town like this, something's always going wrong with the telephone."

We used a small crowbar to open the bank's rear window. And in we went. The safe was a big old Packer, easy to blow. In my overcoat I had a bottle of grease and two bars of soap. After I thumbed the soap in the cracks, I poured in the nitro and set a cap and fuse and told Joe to start heading out the door.

I lit the string and was on his heel.

We watched the sizzling fuse from a side window.

BLOOEY!!

Off flied the safe door. We run back into the bank, and there it was! Hard and soft, silver and greenbacks. Joe's jaw near dropped to the floor, he'd never seen nothing like it. We quick put the hard in one gunny sack, the soft in another. I give Joe the sack of hard.

"Let's get the hell out."

Joe took a-hold of the sack but when he tried to lift it, it near dragged him to the floor.

"Dad-gummit, Willis! It's heavier'n rocks!"

"Hell, kid," I said. "When I was your age, I could run a mile with a sack like that."

He didn't laugh. His knees was a-wobbling.

Lucky for us, we didn't meet another soul on the way to the car. We found Dock snoring in the driver's seat of the Studebaker, his jaw hanging open, just like that night marshal when we'd first rode in. I give Dock a prod with my pistol and up he woke and off we went—to pick up Jess.

Jess was still parked on top of the dog. And when he got off, he done it with a jump and vaulted over the door into the backseat just like a rodeo cowboy when he's making a running leap onto a horse.

The crate come flying up. The bulldog stood there a second, kinda stunned, before he charged. But with us all inside the car, there was nothing he could do except jump up against the door—a-banging and a-howling.

"Yowwwwwwwww!!!! Yowwwwwwwwwwwww!!!!"

189

Well, that done it.

If that nitro blast didn't wake up the town, that dog sure as hell did. Windows popped open and heads come poking out. One man wearing a nightcap hollered: "Shut up, dog!" But by that time me and the boys was tearing down that alley—and that ugly old bulldog was eating our dust.

The Newton Boys was on their way.

TWENTY-TWO

Broken Bow, Oklahoma. Mattoon, Illinois. Walnut Ridge, Arkansas.

During that fall of nineteen and twenty and winter of nineteen and twenty-one, we worked the cotton country in the South and the corn and wheat country in the Middle West. Wherever they'd been picking and ginning cotton, or wherever they'd been pulling and shipping corn, or harvesting wheat, wherever banks was full of that crop money.

We never hit 'em in a line. It was one here, one there. One here, one there. This week one in Texas, next week one in Missouri. Anywhere that'd keep the laws from figuring out it was the same people getting 'em all.

There was no problem about who was gonna be the leader, like there'd been with Frank and Dago and Slim. I was the one that'd brought us all together and I was the one that knowed all the angles. And the boys went with it. They even took to calling me "old man." "Old man" is what cowboys call the boss-man on a ranch; it's also what thieves call the leader of a gang.

Well, we wasn't no gang. We was just brothers working together in a business. But I was the head man of that business, and I give the orders, so I never did mind being called "old man." And when I give my brothers orders, like "go here" or "stay there" or "no falling asleep in the getaway car," they turned out to be real reliable. They done it and didn't go helty-skelty.

Ever' so often, Jess'd slip off to some bootleg joint and get drunk and shoot off a bunch of "windies," them Texas bull-shit stories. But whiskey's thinner'n blood, I guess, 'cause he was pretty good about stopping his drinking when we was going out on a job. He knowed if he was skunked, it could get all of us killed, him too. And he never one time got his pints of whiskey mixed up with our pints of nitro.

As it come out, Jess 'n Joe forgot all about my deadline, where I'd promised 'em a Pullman ticket back to Texas, plus a thousand dollars *pilon*, if they didn't like my business. Sometimes, Joe'd get quiet and I could tell his morals was acting up. But I'd called the deal right: soon as the boys was making good money, it was never "enough." All three of 'em, Joe too, was enjoying ever' dollar that come into their pockets and ever' dollar that leaked *outa* their pockets.

And plenty was going both ways.

After ever' job, we'd lob together the money and take out our expenses first, and then split it up even. I didn't take no extra cut. The biggest expense we had was cars. We mostly drove Studebakers, they was the most reliable, and they cost about $1,800 to $2,400. And we traded in for a new one ever' ten thousand miles, soon as the rubber on the tires wore out. It wasn't no trouble to rob the banks; the getaway was the thing.

Other expenses: The best hotels them days was twelve to fourteen dollars a night, except for the Astoria in Chicago, and that was twenty-five dollars. So that was about four hundred dollars a month for room rent. Meals was running us about six hundred dollars to a thousand dollars ever' month, with Joe at the high end, because he was young and hungry and wanted to eat! Then there was the speakeasies, the burlesque shows—and the clothes they needed to slick it up.

'Course, Dock didn't get out much since he was a escaped con and had to lay low. But both Jess and Joe was starting to buy more and more expensive suits, up to a hundred dollars each. And they was getting their hair cut sometimes ever' week. And even their fingers manicured. Can you see that? A rough old cowboy like Jess, who never took but one bath a month back in Texas, getting a manicure?

And both of 'em started chasing after gals like bucks at rutting time.

Jess was the wildest when it come to women. And it seemed like most of his dates was with them manicure gals. Some of 'em was pretty raunchy women, some of 'em wasn't too bad. Nearly all of 'em liked to dye their hair and paint their faces and lips. None of that made no diff'rence to Jess. He liked 'em all, no matter what they looked like. Just so they was women.

Joe was more particular. He said he'd rather stay in the hotel room and read a Western novel than go out with some bangtail. "I don't get it," he said about Jess. "Back home he wouldn't ride no horse that didn't look good or have a good gait. And just look at what he's taking out tonight." But Joe did his share of chasing gals too. Mostly, he'd hit on the salesclerks at the Kresge and the Woolworth five-and-dime stores. He said they was "solid girls."

There was only one thing none of my brothers liked, at first. I wanted 'em to wear diamond stickpins and diamond rings, what thieves call 'ice.' But Jess and Joe said nothing doing. And Dock said if Jess and Joe didn't care nothing about jewelry, he didn't either. So I had to educate 'em: "You get picked up for something, anything, most times it's a shakedown. You get one of them laws off in a corner and whisper to 'em, 'Look here, I got a big diamond I don't got no use for.' And nine times outa ten, they'll give you the air."

Well, damned if my brothers didn't start liking that ice a day or so after they put it on, particularly Jess and Joe. And liking diamonds didn't have nothing to do with dirty laws. It was because they seen how all that sparkle made women look at 'em twice, and sometimes three times, and four. Then it was the gals chasing after Jess and Joe instead of the other way around.

***

When I was on the road, casing towns, I didn't much care what Jess and Joe did in their free time, and I didn't worry about 'em. They knowed how to take care of theirselves. I did worry about Dock. I didn't want him roaming, gallivanting, prowling around town. Laws all over the country had his mug on yellow paper that said in big letters, WANTED ESCAPED TEXAS CONVICT. DOCK NEWTON, STOCKY, VERY STRONG, KNOWN FOR PRIZE-FIGHTING SKILLS. REWARD FOR INFORMATION.

The best thing for Dock, when we wasn't on a job, was to stay in his room. But being that he was used to doing something all the time, being cooped up in a room made him jittery and down in the dumps. So nobody was happier'n Dock when I come back to town after hunting up a bank and said, "I found some marks." He'd perk up right away and the only question he ever asked was, "You sure the money's there?"

When I come back, I always brought maps of the getaway

routes. Nearly all counties had "section maps," crisscrossed with lines and numbers, showing the little back roads on ranches and farms. Anyhow, I'd study all of 'em and draw with a red pencil the route we needed to follow, ever' crook and turn. I'd mark how far all that was on the speedometer, right down to the hundreds of a mile. I'd draw in landmarks and label 'em, like "Red Barn," "Stock Pond," "Broke Down Wagon."

Even Dock could follow them maps without no trouble. And when I showed him the maps, he'd stay up all night studying 'em, until they was second nature with him. Dock couldn't read too good, like Jess couldn't, but he'd match the pictures to the words and he knowed just what I meant. And before long, he become a pretty good getaway driver. Dock wasn't afraid of the Devil hisself. No matter how rough the road was, he wasn't afraid to put on the gas if it looked like we was being chased. Or turn a sharp corner.

***

As time went on, as our first year as a brother team moved into the next one, we started doing jobs that was a little riskier. Like in Spencer, Indiana, I decided to blow two banks in one night—at the same time. They was both on the same street, but at diff'rent corners. One had a vault; the other, a setting safe. Joe'd never blowed a safe before, but he'd watched me do it a dozen times, so I told him to take that one.

Only thing neither me or Joe knowed while we was hard at work inside each one of our banks—coming down Main Street was a farm wagon drawed by two pokey old mules. What that farmer was doing out at one o'clock in the morning we'll never know.

But he was heading right for the front of my bank.

Jess, who was doing lookout on the street, tried to head the old man off. "Hey-a, stop! Stop, you damned fool!"

The fella kept right on coming. He mighta been drunk; he mighta been half-asleep. I don't know. But clump, clump, clump. When....

BLOOEY!!

....Out flied a huge cloud of stuff outa my bank—broke glass, pieces of wood, a twisted-up lamp—right in front of that wagon.

The mules rared up so high their front legs was just a-pawing the air. And that farmer wheeled his wagon around and started barrelling down the street, helty-skelty, whipping them mules into a froth.

Only problem was, he was headed right for Joe's bank.

BLOOEY!

Joe's first shot went off. And ever'thing come flying outa his bank—window frames, doors, broke chairs and tables, pieces of rock wall.

Well, them mules stopped dead in their tracks, skidding the wagon half way across the street. Then they started to rare again. This time the farmer just jumped the hell outa his wagon and started to running to beat the devil, back towards my bank, when....

BLOOEY!!

I'd had to put another shot in the vault, and that's when the second one went off. And Jesus Christ! Off flied the vault door, and crash went ever' window in near ever' building on that block!

When I looked out the bank's window—or what was left of it— I seen that farmer wheel around and start a-hollering and race down that street so fast his legs was just a blur.

Jess was laughing so hard you'da thought he was gonna bust a gut.

Me and the boys had a better night than that farmer. Altogether, we netted $33,000. Not bad for one hour's work. And another notch toward that million dollars.

***

There was only a coupla things wrong with my life right then. For one thing, more and more of the little banks in the little towns was starting to get them round, screw-in safes we couldn't blow, and that meant that I was having to search harder and farther away for marks— from deep south Texas to western Canada.

And that little worry tied in with another little worry. Louise.

The more I was starting to care about that woman, the more I was hating to stay away on so many of them long trips. And she was starting to have some questions about my work. A couple of times she asked to see my oil-lease papers 'cause she was interested in business things.

I never could find 'em.

TWENTY-THREE

There was a cigarette burning on a little saucer next to her stove. She was stirring something in a pot. I went up behind her and give her a nuzzle. I was just back from a job in Kansas.

"Lewis let me in. I missed you like crazy, Lou."

She didn't even turn around. Just picked up that cigarette and give it a puff.

"When you start smoking, honey?" I asked her.

"I smoke now and then."

"I never seen it before."

"You're not around a lot of the time." She still hadn't turned towards me. Her voice sounded kinda chilly.

"Something up, Lou?"

"I'd like to talk. But not here. And not—" She stopped. A little Stetson'd showed up at the door, and the boy under it was saying he was hungry.

***

Louise was quiet all through supper. Afterwards, she told Lewis to go to his room. He give me a hug, but he was looking glum. Kids 'r like dogs on that. They can tell when things 'r tense. And things was tense. Though I didn't know how come.

Then Louise picked up her handbag and went out the back door. I was on her heel. Soon as we was outside, I asked her, again, what the hell was up.

"I'm not ready yet." That's all she said.

We kept walking 'til we come to a park that had some patches of grass and a couple of benches. Wasn't nobody else close by, only a couple of kids playing tag over a ways.

For a little bit, we just set and watched two squirrels, chattering and racing up and down a tree limb.

"When I was a kid, blooey!" I put my arms up like I was putting a bead on one of 'em. "I could blow a eye out at forty steps."

Louise didn't say nothing. She popped open her handbag and pulled out a pack of Camels.

"You ever ate squirrel dumplings?" I asked her.

She didn't say nothing, just lit her cigarette.

"My Ma made 'em. I can still taste 'em. 'Course if the bullet's tore up the body, the meat's spoilt. That's how come you gotta hit 'em in the eye. We had squirrel all the time. Hell, anything with four legs and paws, we ate it. Squirrel. Possum. Coon. We was just like coyotes who'll eat anything. 'Course, lots of times we didn't have enough to eat."

For the first time since we'd set down, she turned and looked at me. "I really don't want to hear any more stories about how bad you had it when you were a boy."

Then she went to puffing.

We just set there, quiet.

***

Lemme tell you about quiets. There's all kinds.

When it comes to ever'day life, the best kinds of quiets 'r what I call the "soft quiets." That's like when you're prowling the woods come a morning, maybe there's a little breeze blowing, and the sun is splintering down through the trees. I'm not saying it's altogether quiet. There could be a mockingbird up in a tree going tcack,tcack,tcack; or a armadillo pawing up some leaves. But mostly it's quiet, and quiets like that 'r the best quiets that there is.

Then there's what I call the "sharp quiets," and those 'r like when it's late at night, and maybe you're on a job, cutting a fuse or thumbing soap into a rim, and your ears 'r cocked for the laws, or a nighthack, or any sound that tells you there's trouble. Sharp quiets put a edge on your nerves, and sometimes your heart is thumping so hard you think it's booming loud as a drum, even though it ain't making a sound. But even if them quiets is sharp, you want 'em to go on, long as you need 'em.

And there's a third kind of quiet, and that's the kind you want to stop even before they get going. Those're what I call the "heavy quiets." And those're the awful quiets. That's like when two people 'r near each other, and there's some trouble in the air, something tense, but nobody's saying nothing. Oh, you want to say something, all the pistons in your head 'r going a-dukeda, a-dukeda. But you ain't saying nothing, and the other person ain't saying nothing. It's like the air is froze up. And ain't nothing worse than them heavy quiets.

Well, this was one of them heavy quiets, what me and Louise was having. Nobody saying nothing, me just watching them squirrels, her puffing on that cigarette.

After a while, I couldn't take it no more. I got off the bench and crouched in front of her.

"You gotta let me in on it, Lou."

She throwed down her cigarette. She ground on it with the tip of her shoe. She ground it and ground it. So hard there wasn't nothing left of it. Then she pressed her fingers tight around the edge of the bench.

"I'm not a widow, Will."

"What?"

"I want you to know that I'm not a widow. I'm divorced."

"Divorced? Why you been saying you was a widow?"

Her voice was shaky. "I learned a long time ago, it's a lot more acceptable for a woman to have a dead husband than be divorced. Particularly if that dead husband is a dead war veteran."

"I don't get it, honey. Why'd you think I'd care if you was divorced?"

"It scares off some men."

Well, lemme tell you what: all I could do right then was grab both her hands and throw my head back and go to laughing. That's what was making her act so crazy? A silly little lie?

"Honey, I got plenty-a scares in my life," I said to her, "but I'll tell you this, a divorced woman ain't one of 'em."

Something come to me.

"He wanting you back?" I asked. "He live here?"

"He lives in St. Louis. We don't see each other." Now her eyes was starting to blink kinda fast. "I'm telling you this because I think people who are in love need to be completely honest with each other."

"Yeah."

"I think people who are in love need to be completely honest with each other." She said it again.

I nodded my head. What could I say to that?

Now she was starting to breathe fast. Just like she was blinking fast. "Is there anything you're not telling me about your life?"

Uh-oh.

"Like what, Lou?"

She pulled her hands outa mine. She leaned down and picked up her handbag and unsnapped it. She pulled out some kind of a white envelope. She opened it up. It crackled. She pulled out a bunch of pieces of papers. They crackled too. They looked like newspaper.

"Can you tell me what these are?"

"What are they?"

"Read them."

I didn't need to read 'em. I was looking down at the headlines and that was enough. Way, way more'n enough. "Missouri Bank Takes Hit in Nightime Crime." "Airplane Used to Hunt New Braunfels Bandits." "Denver Mint Robbed of $100,000 in Brand-New Bills and Silver."

"What are these, Lou?"

"That's what I'm asking you."

"Where'd they come from?"

"I found them in that last book you gave Lewis. They were stuck in one of the middle pages."

Goddamn! It was a book about a cowhorse. I'd had it in my hotel room before I give it to Lewis, and Joe musta found it. You couldn't trust Joe if he was anywhere close to a book!

"There you go, Lou. This stuff's Joe's. He musta stole off and read it. Just marking a page, most likely. Joe's crazy like that. He's always clipping things outa the newspaper. Baseball statistics, all kinds of things...."

"Did you have anything to do with these?"

"Why'd you think that?"

"Things are starting to fall together." The muscles in her throat was hopping up and down. "All kinds of things. Like those coins."

"That money was from a oil strike, honey." I'd give her a box of silver dollars to put under a floorboard for safekeeping right before I'd left town for the Kansas trip. They was fresh-minted.

"You know where they are now, Will?"

"Where?"

"I took them to the Omaha State Bank. It was too much money to have in the house. I deposited them, right before I found these..."

She pointed to the newspaper stories.

Well, it was ever'thing I could do right then to keep my eyes straight on Louise's. Goddamn! A bank! If them bankers was ever to put two and two together...goddamn...I couldn't keep Louise's look. My eyes shifted.

She seen 'em shifting.

"Will."

For the first time in my life, I knowed what a squirrel feels like when he looks down off a limb and sees the barrel of a .22 aiming up.

***

It wasn't 'til I thought over ever'thing later, hours later, that I even remembered some of what it was that I said next. Most times, I had one of them picture memories, like I said before. But I'd be hard pressed to tell you ever'thing I said, or how I said it, or what order I said it in.

Times like that, it ain't your mind that's telling you what to do anyhow.

It's more like your bones.

I do remember that I took her hands again. And somewhere in there, I said:

"We don't hurt nobody, Lou. You gotta know that."

"It's just a business, like any other business."

"It's just 'til I can go straight. 'Til I can be that oil man."

I do remember how, in the beginning, she yanked her hands back and her whole body started shaking. She wasn't crying right off. But her body was shaking.

I do know that I told her: "I got a brain, honey. Only I didn't get no education. I wanted to go to school. Only I couldn't. You gotta understand that. You gotta think about that real hard, Lou, and understand that."

And somewhere in there, she did go to crying. She put her hands over her eyes and she went to crying. And I put my hands on her knees and held 'em there, like a little kid that's trying to hold a balloon so it don't fly off.

I told her this: "It ain't like you think, Lou. Nobody loses nothing, see. All them banks got insurance. And insurance companies is the biggest crooks in the world."

I asked her this: "You worked with all them insurance companies at the Burlington, honey. They ever put the screws on you to

200

turn down claims that you knowed good and well was legitimate?"

And she raised her head up outa her hands and said in a whisper that was worse'n if she was hollering: "Insurance companies don't stick guns in people's faces."

I grabbed her hands tight: "No, no, no. You got that all wrong. We don't shoot people. We don't hurt nobody. That ain't the way this thing works. You gotta believe me."

I leaned my face way down, right under hers, and said: "You go home, honey, and you ask your boy how he feels about me. You ask him what kind of a man I am. You can't fool a kid."

And I remember seeing two old shoes in the corner of my eye and it was a old lady walking by and then them shoes was poking right next to me and the old lady was saying: "Your wife all right, mister? Your wife need a doctor?"

"Don'cha worry, ma'am," I said back. "Somebody jus' died."

"Oh dear, God be with 'em," the old lady said. And outa the corner of my eye, I seen them two old shoes shuffling off.

All that was true, what I'd told that old lady. Somebody had just died. Will Reed, the oil man, was dead.

All that was left was J. Willis Newton, the bank robber.

TWENTY-FOUR

HUGE GUSHER RAINS OIL OVER A THOUSAND ACRES NEAR SMACKOVER!

The headline was a-hollering off the front page of the *Omaha World Herald*, and that's what snagged my eye and pulled a nickel outa my pocket.

The story told about how, used to be, Smackover was just a dumpy little old town down south in Arkansas, near the border of Louisiana. It said that, used to be, it was such a dumpy little old town where the only thing you was likely to see moving down the only street in town'd be some lazy old razorback hog.

But things was changing.

Turns out, oil drillers'd been out in a old cotton patch when a fountain of black crude come shooting up two hundred feet in the air, and raining down over a thousand acres, just like it was a spring shower. Folks said they could smell that oil ten miles in ever' direction.

Me, I was smelling that oil from *six hundred* miles north.

"This is it!" I hollered back at that headline.

I'd been reading the papers close ever' day since Louise'd found me out. If I wanted to get her back, for the long picture, I figured my best chance was to get into oil, and legitimate. I knowed there was maybe a chance she'd take me back as a bank robber if she thought over ever'thing I'd told her, and if there was enough love there. But I knowed my chances'd be a helluva lot bigger if I could show her a oil lease.

No matter how much I tried to talk to her again, she wasn't listening. She wasn't answering my telephone calls. She wasn't coming to the door when I showed up at her house. She wasn't looking at me from the cigar stand.

It was killing me, the whole thing.

Now that I knowed Louise, now that I loved her, I couldn't think of my life without her.

The papers was full of oil news. Stories about wells being drilled in Texas, Oklahoma, Arkansas, Louisiana. But most of 'em was "wildcats," the kind they drilled in new country hoping for a lucky strike. Smackover was a diff'rent story. Geologists was saying the whole area—that hard-packed red sand—might be atop a big huge lake of oil.

Fact is, I'd always had in the back of my mind that I wanted to get in on the ground floor of a oil boom. Oil could do for me what cotton, or even robbing banks, never could. If you hit her right, blooey! One day you'd be a dirt-poor farmer slicing your bacon paper-thin; next day, you'd be rich enough to buy every goddamn hog from Texas to Canada.

And I had near enough money to get into oil.

Just near enough.

The same day I seen that story about Smackover, I told my brothers to meet me in my hotel room for supper. I had room service send 'em up what the menu said was "extra-thick-cut ribeye steaks from cornfed Kansas steers." And after they'd ate them steaks, and was feeling settled in their guts, I told 'em about what I just read. I told 'em Smackover was a great deal, we might never find another one like it, but that we had to do it fast or we'd be at the tail end of a stampede.

All three of 'em balked.

"I might could-a helped you out, old man, but not now." Joe was the first one to talk. Only he kept throwing his eyes on his lap. "There's a big ranch down in Uvalde County on the block. Ain't there yet, but I'm close. Thirty-five thousand. Soon's I get enough, I'm fixing to..." Now he was talking full-time to his crotch. "...I'm fixing to head back to Texas. I been meaning to tell you."

"I'm throwing in with Joe, old man." That was Jess, only he didn't have no problem looking me square. "I been meaning to tell you."

Dock didn't say nothing. Just shook his head. I knowed what he was saying.

Yeah.

"Well, I've been meaning to tell you *this*, boys." I shook my head slow. "The laws are still trying to find somebody to pin them jobs in Hondo and Boerne on. You put up cash money like that in South Texas—big cash money—they're gonna wanta know where it all come from. And oil money's a lot cleaner'n what you got now."

Jess snorted. He pulled his Colt out and started spinning it.

"Sorry, old man. I got me a date with that blonde switchboard gal, and the only oil I want is some hair oil to slick a piece over this spot." He rubbed a little patch of bald on the back of his head with the barrel of his gun. "I didn't have this spot when I come up from Texas, and I don't much care for it."

Nothing I said could turn Jess. And Dock followed Jess, even though he didn't care nothing about buying no ranch. He just had his back up. But Joe finally give in. He said I could have half his money and maybe the rest later, depending.

That give me what I needed.

***

Just like the paper'd said, Smackover was a dumpy little place. Bad, rutty roads going into it and bad, rutty roads going outa it. And, to get into town, you had to cross over a big wide gully, called the Smackover Creek, and the bridge was a old swaybacked thing that shook and shimmied like it was just about to bust apart.

Well, that bridge shook and shimmied a lot under me 'cause I was driving over it in a big, seven-seater, $4,400 Cadillac Imperial Limousine. I'd traded in one of our Studebakers because it was a long trip to Arkansas, and I knowed if the town was booming with oil hunters, I'd likely have to sleep in my car.

Soon as I drove in, I seen I was right.

There was thousands and thousands of people swarming all over that little town: oil promotors in high-dollar suits, roughnecks and roustabouts in greasy work clothes, "oilfield doves" in not much of nothing. When I first got outa my Cadillac, I run straight into one of them doves. She was wearing a shiny pink dress and rubbing a lamp-post up and down.

"Hey, mister, you hungry? Twenty dollars, I'll make you a lemon pie."

"You keep your lemons, sister," I said back. "I gotta go about some business here."

"Oh, go to hell!"

She spit at me and started in on the next old boy getting outa the next big car. And, lemme tell you what, there was plenty of next old boys getting outa next big cars. There was only one hotel in the whole place, and it was already full up to the gills. So the townsfolk was putting up cots under ever' roof there was—in the grocery store, the beer joint, the blacksmith shop—and renting 'em for $2.50 a night. Even the barber was in on the thing. He was renting out his barber's chair in shifts, he put out a sign that said: "six hours of shut-eye guaranteed." He was charging $3 a shift, even more'n them cots. I guess because his chair was padded and leaned back.

And all around the edges of the town, there was dozens of tents set up—some of 'em filled with whole families, babies and all.

At night, I slept in the back seat of my Cadillac with a loaded .45 on my lap.

It's one of them sad facts of life: where there's lots of money, there's most likely gonna be lots of crime. The robberies was getting so bad around there, and there was so many killings from streetfights and shooting scrapes, folks was starting to call the south end of Smackover "Death Valley." And there was so many workers getting killed in accidents on the rigs, a undertaker had come to town and set up business in one of the tents. His coffins come to him in pieces from a factory—four sides, four ends, four tops, and four bottoms, and some screws and nails and hinges—and he put 'em together in that tent.

There was a new graveyard started in a field west of town, and it already had two dozen humps of fresh dirt.

But the danger didn't bother me none.

Daytime, you couldn't go one inch down that Main Street without hearing some story about somebody that knowed somebody that'd struck it rich. And turns out, a lot of that oil was coming up right near that Smackover Creek.

Well, I didn't waste no time. I bought me about $30,000 worth of "prime" creek bottom leases. Somebody give me the name of a "smart-as-the-devil" driller and I hired him on the spot. His name was Clyde. He was a short, stocky, red-faced fella, built like a wrestler, all muscles. He'd been working on derricks so long he even smelt like oil. And he knowed how to talk that oil language. Just like thieves have their own words, words that mean this and that, so do them oil people.

Clyde taught me some of them words, so my workers'd know who was the boss. He taught me that "rope-chokers" was the boys that handled the cable tools and "mud-drinkers" was the boys that did the rotary drilling and was always getting sloshed with soupy mud. "Boll-weevils" was the green workers, the farm boys fresh offa the cotton farms that you had to watch real close. Some of 'em didn't know the diff'rence between a valve and a choke. And "boomers" was the one that knowed what they was doing, they'd caught the oil fever a-whiles back, but they might be here today, yonder tomorrow.

Inside two weeks, Clyde had hired him a good crew and had three derricks up and the drills a-churning.

Like I told the boys, if you got the money, ain't nothing you can't do.

Soon as things was going good, I shot back up to Omaha to let the boys in on ever'thing, and to show them oil lease papers to Louise. I didn't know if she'd look at 'em, or if she even look at *me*. But I lit on over to the Loyal soon as I got back, and I set 'em on her lap.

"I done it, honey. I'm a oil man."

* * *

There wasn't a wisp of a cloud the day we left Omaha to go back to Smackover. And inside me, I was feeling good as that sky was clear blue. We was all heading down to look at my new wells in that new seventy-horsepower Cadillac. Me and my three brothers and Louise.

Yeah, it'd worked.

When I'd laid that lease on Louise's lap, only thing she said was Lewis'd been missing me, and that she'd sent him up to her folks in Wisconsin for the summer to get his mind on something else. She never said one word about how long we'd been apart, or what we'd talked about on that park bench. And when I give her a hundred dollar bill to hire a fill-in lady at the cigar stand, all she done was take it.

It was damn strange. Damn, damn strange! Only I was so tickled at having her back, I didn't think too hard on it—how come she was acting like she was acting. Maybe she'd had time to think over ever'thing I'd told her, and maybe it'd come to make sense. Or maybe she was just happy I was finally a oil man.

And I was, just about.

Right before we took off, I got a telephone call from Clyde, we was almost there. They was down about a thousand and five hundred feet, and folks all around was hitting oil at two-thousand.

Yessireeeeeeeeee!

Me and Louise sunk into the seats of that long Cadillac like we was millionaires already. Dock was setting in the jump seat. Jess was in the front seat with Joe, who was doing the driving. Dock was a little boogered over traveling in the daytime, thinking some law might rank him from the "Wanted" posters that'd been sent out ever'where. But I told him to quit that worrying. Wasn't no laws gonna be looking for a escaped con from Texas in a Cadillac with three men in business suits and a short lady.

We stopped overnight at rooming houses along the way, and I spent the evenings telling 'em oil stories.

I told 'em about a farmer that'd made him a half million in one week. And when the bank cashier asked him what was gonna do with all that money, that old boy spit some tobaccy juice, real straight, through his teeth, the way them old farmers do, and said in a proud kinda way: "First thing I'm gonna do is buy me a extra pair of suspenders so that I won't have to be changing 'em every Sunday to my other pants."

That story was true. I'd talked to that old farmer myself.

***

It was on the last leg of the trip, I first seen the clouds. They was over to the west of us. Parts of 'em was white and fluffy, like cotton bolls. Only they was starting to get black on the bottom of 'em, and the tops was puffing up. You could see 'em growing right before your eyes. And they was starting to get shaped like a anvil.

I didn't like none of that. We was on a paved highway right then, and my Cadillac had automatic windshield wipers—the first year they'd had them things—but the road to my leases wasn't nothing but dirt. If it come up one of them bad summer storms, that road'd turn into a soupy mudpit.

"Give her some gas, Joe," I said.

He let loose with a "Yee-haaaaaa!" and we tore down that highway and around them curves like we'd just robbed us a bank. But when we come to the turn-off, and we cut over to that little old dirt farm road, the road was rough and rutty.

Joe had to slow it down to a crawl.

It'd already rained earlier in the week, I could tell. The road was full of little gullies, criss-crossing this-a-way and that-a-way, where other folks driving down it had slided around and spun their wheels. But the only rain I wanted to see right then was black rain—squirting up from outa the ground.

There was tall pine trees on both sides of us, except when we was passing patches of cotton and corn. Some of the cotton patches was white with flowers, others of 'em was just thick with green. And workers—whole families of 'em, little kids and grownups—was bent over in the green patches, chopping weeds with long, hard hoes, just about holding body and soul together, nothing more.

Louise couldn't get over the fields that was already blooming. "So pretty," she kept saying.

"Yeah, honey," I said. "Ever'thing looks pretty from the back seat of a Cadillac."

Except black clouds.

When you grow up a farm boy, you know ever'thing there is to know about clouds. You know just how to read 'em—if they're wispy or lumpy or flat; if they're white or blue-gray or dark gray or green; if they got tails or hats or ragged bottoms; if they're sailing or strutting or whirling.

Only you didn't need to be a farm boy to read these clouds.

Now they was pitch black, and moving towards us.

Joe seen 'em too, but on that rutty road, he couldn't pick up our speed. Besides, we was starting up a high rise. And no sooner we was over the crest, lemme tell you what, them ugly black clouds blowed right outa my head.

There they was! My three derricks.

They was in the valley down below, running in a line along the banks of that creek. Looked like windmills, made out of wood, with crossbars, except they didn't have no fans on top, and they was a lot bigger and taller. Steam engines was turning the drills, all going at a steady put-put-put.

"Look at 'em, Lou!" I said. She took my hand.

We kept on the road down the rise. I told Joe to stop at a jerry-built lumber shack close by one of the derricks.

It give me a charge being so close to them working derricks. They was beautiful—big steel bits sinking into that red, red ground, cutting through hard, hard rock. And while them bits was churning, the workmen was pouring some kind of liquid down into the casings, and ever' time the drills'd sink a little deeper, mud and dirty water'd come sloshing up. Some of the workers was so covered with mud they looked like booger-men.

I seen Clyde over at Derrick No. 2; his arms was waving this-a-way and that-a-way. He was giving orders to the workers. But when he seen us, he shot right over. He had grease all over his face, and clothes, and hands.

"Hoddy, boss!"

"Hoddy, Clyde. How's it coming?"

"Real fine. No. 2 oughta be striking any time now."

"Yessir!"

"Only I tell you, boss," and the smile on Clyde's face flashed off his face, "it ain't gonna be none too soon."

Uh-oh.

"How's that?"

"Lemme show you something." He pulled out a greasy rag outa his back pocket and wiped his hands. His hands was blacker when he was done, but he didn't act like he seen it. He reached into another pocket, pulled out a map and unfolded it.

He pointed a greasy finger. "These'r your leases, the ones colored pink. These ones, the ones in blue, they're other people's leases. Almost ever' one of the blue ones has got wells that are producing. Some of 'em are right here." He pointed to where blue places was butted up agin pink ones. "What's happening—I can't prove it, but I know it's going on—is some of our neighbors here has been drilling slant holes...." he jabbed his finger at a angle under the pink places, "....right under your land. Sucking up oil from right under our feet here. And it ain't going into your tanks. It's going into theirs."

Slant holes?

"But that ain't legal!" I was so mad I coulda kicked a hole in the ground.

"Hate to say it, but there's lots that ain't legal in this business. Too much money in it. This one, well, it's like if you got a bunch of straws in a ice cream sodey, and you got a bunch of people sucking on it, and you ain't. It means we gotta get your straw stuck in there, and start sucking too."

"We oughta put the laws on them canker-eyed screwworms," Dock said. Then he thought about what he said. He didn't say no more.

I looked over at iron pipes stacked next to the lumber shack. "Poke 'em in, then! Poke 'em in! You gotta put on extra crews, do it."

I was starting to feel sick in my gut. All them dreams about being rich as John D. Rockefeller, or William Wrigley Jr.....

Right about then, something wet hit my face. Only it wasn't crude. Them black clouds'd been raining up west of us, and now they was right up on us. A wind was whipping up, and all of a sudden there come a big white flash and a KER-BOOM!

"Let's get you back in the car, honey," I said to Louise. "Little shower coming up."

I knowed better. One ear to that thunder boom, it wasn't gonna be no little shower. And sure enough, before we could get back into the car, them raindrops'd turned into sheets of water. Like somebody'd picked up the Gulf of Mexico and put it up in the sky, and pulled the plug.

We couldn't barely see the derricks.

"Dad-gum, it's Noah's flood!" Joe said. "We better get back to town 'fore the roads mud up."

"Yeah," said Dock. "We gotta get back there 'n sell some shares in this company. 'Fore ever'thing's sucked up 'n all."

That was one of the few bright things Dock ever said in his life.

It was too late. The road behind us was already muddied up. We couldn't have gone a hundred feet in that soup.

There was a knocking on the window. It was Clyde, all shook up.

"River's rising!" he hollered. "I'm moving my men up!" He pointed to the top of the rise. "Let's git y'all up there too!"

"What about the derricks?"

"We'll hitch your automobile to the mules."

"What about the derricks?"

"Gotta see how high the water gets..." He was breathing hard. "Lotta creeks feed this old gully...I've heard about flashfloods, these parts, but I dunno...it's all a risk...gotta drill where the oil is...and trust in the Good Lord, I guess."

Goddamn! I didn't know how the Good Lord was feeling about me right then. And I knowed all about flashfloods from back home in Texas. It's when the ground can't soak in no more water, and the creeks start rising fast, and they all start dumping water into the river, and you get a huge, tall wall that builds up and builds up and builds up—and then crashes downstream like nothing you ever seen in your life.

But what the hell could we do about it?

We all got out of the car, except for Louise, and stood soaked. Big mules was hitched to the Cadillac. And with them big mules pulling and all of us men pushing, we moved that big machine up the rise, through deep, thick mud.

I was too sick to my stomach to climb back into the car. I stood with Clyde looking down towards my derricks. Through them sheets of rain I could make out that the river was rising.

"Can't we tie 'em down?"

He shook his head. "They're down good as we can get 'em. Too risky, anyhow. If it's raining upstream near like it's raining here, best we can do is pray. Way that water's rising, only the Good Lord's gonna save 'em now."

"Oh no, He ain't," said Joe sticking his finger out from the front seat of the car. He was pointing upstream.

And there it was—a wall of water, high as a three-story building, coming right on down that river...churning, foaming, chewing up ever'thing in front of it. Carrying uprooted trees, dead mules, dead horses, a crashed-up farm wagon, ever'thing and anything you could think of. And before you could blink your eyes, that wall of water hit the derricks.

Over they went, one by one.

***

Nobody said nothing. What was there to say? It was like that wall of water'd knocked all the breath outa us. Except for Jess. He leaned down and pulled out a flask that was strapped to his calf. He opened it and then he opened his mouth.

"They're right," he said when he come up for air, "the ones that say water don't mix with oil. Water's nothing but the work of the devil. God knows, I'd never pollute no whiskey with it."

I didn't think it was funny. Neither did anybody else.

TWENTY-FIVE

We was setting in my room at the Loyal, back up in Omaha. Me and my three brothers. It was our last night there. We was switching over to a two-bit boarding house. I hadn't ordered up no thick-cut ribeyes. I couldna paid for 'em. My brothers all had long faces. You'da thought they was the family of a dead man at a funeral.

Joe lit into me. "We had ever'thing, Willis! Now we got nothing!"

"Oh, hell, Joe. Nobody'd get nowhere in life if they didn't take chances."

"Why you gotta take your chances with my money?"

"If it wasn't for me, you boys'd still be walking around in horse shit."

"Yeah, well, horse shit smells better'n bullshit, old man."

"What'cha saying, little brother?"

"I'm saying you're a thief, Willis. You took all my money, din'cha? I told you you could take $15,000 and you took thirty. Ain't one red cent left in my lockbox. I checked it."

Joe was right. I had took all his money. But I done it for his own good. I'd honestly thought them oil wells was a sure bet. Well, they wasn't. And so the talking went on, Joe throwing me the blame for ever'thing, me trying to tell 'em there was oil under our leases. And it was still there, even if some of it was getting drained off by them slant drillers.

I looked over at Jess and Dock. "You know, boys, this is a family business. How 'bout it?"

They knowed what I was saying, but they didn't say nothing back. Their faces was droopy. I seen Dock's Adam's apple go up and down as he gulped air.

"Look-it," I said, "that was what they call a 'hundred-year' flood.' Ain't gonna be another one 'til the year twenty and twenty-two. And we'll be dead as dogs by then. But we can be rich as

Rockefeller in three months if you help us out here. Me and Joe need $30,000, that's it. All we gotta do is pump the water outa them wells and build some new derricks. We'll give you fifty percent interest."

Dock 'n Jess still didn't answer. They just looked at each other with them droopy faces.

"What's your problem? Me 'n Joe was the ones that got busted, not you."

"Me 'n Jess 'r busted too," Dock said.

"What?"

"Reckon we went to the tables."

"You what?"

"Aw, don't give us that 'you what?'" That was Jess this time. "We wasn't doing nothing you wasn't doing, old man. You tell me the diff'rence between a bad hand and Noah's flood! Exact same thing!"

"It ain't nowhere near the same! Nowhere near it!" What fools! If it wouldna been for that hundred-year flood, me 'n Joe coulda been millionaires right then. But ain't no way you can beat professional gamblers.

Dock had a bright idea. "How 'bout we borrow some money from that gal of yours?"

"A widow with a kid? No, boys, this one we gotta figure out ourselves."

***

The one I most hated to talk to after the oil-bust thing was Louise. She'd been quiet all the way back from Smackover and I figured this time she was really gonna give me my walking papers.

I couldn't hardly believe it when she opened her door and run her hand over my forehead, like I was a kid with a skinned-up knee.

"You feeling any better?" she asked.

"Hell, no."

"Come upstairs."

Well, I'll tell you what, if I'd coulda knowed what was coming up next, I never woulda flopped on her bed like I done. But Smackover had sucked the starch outa me. So I flopped, my legs and arms throwed ever' which-a-way, my neck hanging off the edge like there wasn't no neckbone in it.

Louise walked over to the little desk she had in the corner. She opened up a drawer. She pulled some pieces of paper outa it. She come back over and laid them on the bed.

"What's that?" I asked.

"Newspaper stories. Read them."

"Last time you give me some newspaper clippings, honey, things ended up a little bit sour."

"Read them."

"I'd have to set up."

"Alright. Lay there then, but listen."

She picked the stories up and started reading 'em out loud.

They was about oil.

They was stories about oil strikes in this state and that state, about how oil companies was being set up in this place and that place, and about what kinda frauds to watch out for, and what kinda promotors to believe. They was stories about things like the Arkansas Oil Trust and about Burkburnett and about Mexia, even about the oil boom down in Eastland County in West Texas.

I set up.

"When you get interested in oil, Lou?"

She set the papers back on the bed, kneeled in front of me and said something that near knocked me back down: "You're not the only one who wants something out of life, Willis. I think if we put our heads together, we can get into it smarter next time."

"I'm busted, honey."

"You know how to get more money."

"What are you saying?"

"You remember when you told me to ask Lewis what he thought of you. Well, two times, I told Lewis I was leaving you, moving back to Wisconsin. And two times he told me that if I was leaving, he was staying. With you." She took my hand. "That's about all I have to say about it. I want to manage your money. I'll be your banker."

"I still don't know what you're saying here, Lou."

"Just keep it out of town."

***

You ever found out something you didn't know about somebody, and all of a sudden, that person looks completely diff'rent to you? Well, I looked at Louise while she was kneeling there, and she looked completely diff'rent to me. Like when it comes a six o'clock sun, and it's hitting a maize field, and it lights up the tassels on the stalks and makes 'em look like that whole field is on fire. That's just how Louise looked. Like she was lit up around the edges, and on fire.

And while I was setting there, looking at Louise, you know what else come to me?

My old Uncle Henry.

Uncle Henry was meaner'n dirt, but he was sharp, too, and something he always said stuck in my head: "I never had no trouble in my life figuring out dogs and cows and men. They usually act pretty much like you expect 'em to. But I give up, I give plumb up, when it come to cats and horses and women."

After a little bit, I give Louise a surprise of my own. "You know, honey, if you're gonna be messing with my money, I'm gonna have to keep a close eye on you. Let's get married."

I wasn't planning on asking her that when I come over that day. But I wasn't expecting none of what was happening.

What the hell? I asked it.

She smiled at me. "You can't make an honest woman out of me, Willis, until you're an honest man."

"Oh, I'm honest, honey. I just ain't straight."

"That's an interesting distinction."

"Well, how about we just play-act then? 'Til I get me a couple of them gushers."

"Play-act?"

"Set up house. Act like we're married."

"Wouldn't that be setting a bad example for your brothers?" She give me another smile.

"C'mon honey. It's a cupboard here. We'll get us a nice big house. You and me and Lewis. We'll be a family. We'll play-act it all the way. I'll get you a ring. I'll give you a name. Hell, we'll even take us a honeymoon."

"I don't know, Willis."

"I'll keep things outa town, honey."

"What would my name be?"

"I got lots of 'em. You get your pick."

TWENTY-SIX

Dock didn't know what a honeymoon was.

"Oh, Mother of God, what'll they come up with next?" he said, and he shook his head a few times like the whole thing wasn't nothing but a damn shame. "Back home, gal just packs up the wagon and moves her things from her folks' house to his folks' house, and it's all done. That's it. So don't you go spending none of my money on no honeymoon."

"Don't worry, Dock. You ain't got no money."

That was the truth. God's awful truth. He was broke. I was broke. All of us boys was broke.

We could barely buy us a hamburger. Much less me and Louise go on a honeymoon.

The week after me and Joe got smacked over at Smackover, and after Jess and Dock got smacked over by them dirty gamblers, my mind was racing helty-skelty: Ought we hit out farther West for fresh marks, maybe Oregon or Washington State? Could our tipster that was retired from the Texas Banker's Association maybe hook us up with crooked bank detectives, like him, but in other states? Was there any other tipsters who might could—

I hit on it.

Brentwood Glasscock.

***

Glasscock showed up at our boardinghouse in a nice suit with a fresh-brushed derby and fresh-shined Oxfords.

Bringing somebody new to our team wasn't something I'd counted on, or wanted. Particularly another ex-con that maybe you could count on, maybe you couldn't. That risk was why I'd got shed of Glasscock in the first place. But I also knowed he was a gold mine when it come to tipsters.

The boys was leery at first. They wasn't used to outsiders. But I told it to 'em this way:

"Glasscock's got a web of tipsters you can't beat. He can let us in on where the real money's at. The big hauls, not the scraps we'd been getting. Think about it this way: Do you get more meat cutting up a big fat hog into five pieces, or a scrawny little squirrel into fours?"

***

Glasscock joined the team.

Only problem: the first tips he give us was squirrels.

He thought we should try robbing trains for a little bit, that he could get tips on trains from his underworld friends, just like he could get tips on banks. And I knowed from robbing that train way on back with Red, that in some ways, they was easier than robbing banks, if you could get 'em way out in the country. Well, we did rob a few trains. Three of 'em, in fact. One in St. Joe, Missouri, and two down in Texas—Bells and Texarkana.

They was almost all busts.

Like in Texarkana, we had a tip that there was a big payment shipment on the Katy No. 34. Me and Jess hid out at one of the water stops, hopped onto the mail car, and throwed down on the clerks. I stuck a pistol in the back of one of the clerks—he was a short old boy, so squat he couldn't rare back up on me—and I made him take me to ever' one of them baggage cars. Our tipster said the money was in a big square chest in a baggage car. But there wasn't no box. Somebody'd switched the shipment day.

Outa all them three trains, all we got was $11,000. Total.

Then Glasscock said maybe we should go back to banks. He said long as we was in Texas, he had a good tip down on a bank in San Marcos, a little town about fifty miles outside of San Antone. His tipster'd told him the bank was flush up with extra cash for some reason or t'other.

So we lit on down to San Marcos and "Blooey!"

I used six ounces of grease on the vault door, it was so big and thick, and doggone if the whole thing—that whole door—didn't shoot straight through the bank window, crashing it into a thousand pieces, and skid all the way over to the other side of Main Street, kicking up white sparks the whole way!

217

Well, there was money inside the vault, all right, but not where we could get most of it. There was two safes: a square one we could blow, a round one we couldn't. It was the round one that musta had all the money; the one we could blow, a Steel Pete, had only a few bundles of greenbacks and a bag of loose bills.

Damn!

Meantime, that vault door'd made so much ruckus we didn't wanta waste no time on the loose bills that went a-flying. So we left thousands on the floor. (As we was running out, we seen two newsboys on a corner sacking their papers. "Don't mess with them nickel papers," I said. "There's money all over the floor in the bank. Go help yourself!")

On the way back to Omaha, we counted out what we'd got from that little Steel Pete.

It come up to about $30,000.

A fatter squirrel, but still a squirrel.

The boys was razzing me about "where the hell's the hogs?" and I was razzing Glasscock.

He barely blinked a eye. "I've got it this time. Canada. Small towns up there are twenty-five years behind the American banks. I know somebody who can give me a list of the square safes. Nearly all of 'em'll be marks."

"You sure?" My faith in Glasscock was draining fast.

"You don't believe me, we can go up there and case 'em first. We have plenty of dough to last us the summer. We can all headquarter in Toronto. Meantime, you and Louise can have your honeymoon. Go down to Ni'gra Falls. Whatever you want. If you have the right kind of wife, she won't mind if you have some company."

***

I can still see it clear as day, me and Louise driving to our honeymoon in a 1923 black Studebaker Light Six—with my three brothers in the back. Glasscock and his wife was behind us, in another car.

First thing we done in Toronto, we checked into the King Edward Hotel.

Being that it was my honeymoon, I wanted to slick it up.

That King Edward was the best hotel in that whole city, and the clerk put us in a brand-new part that shot up sixteen stories. None of us'd Newtons had ever been so high offa the ground and, right off,

Jess went to spitting juice from some Prince Albert tobacco outa a window to see it drop down all them sixteen stories.

"Rack up your umbrellas, folks!" he kept a-hollering down to the people on the street. "Prince Albert's raining down outa the King Edward!"

I give Jess five minutes to spit. Then I said why didn't we all go check out the city. Even back in them days, Toronto was a real busy, busy place. It's where a lot of the banking and other business was done for the whole country of Canada and so the downtown sidewalks was packed with people, most of 'em dressed in suits carrying briefcases, all of 'em hurrying somewheres.

I'd heard how Toronto had the longest street in the entire country—a street called Yonge—and I wanted to see it. Sure enough, that Yonge Street went on forever. The part we was at had buildings on both sides of it so tall it made you feel like you was walking in the alley of a canyon. Only it wasn't like no canyon that the Good Lord ever made. All up and down that street, there was slicked-up stores with ever'thing under the sun in their windows: beaver fur coats, big diamond rings, fancy ladies' hats with ostrich feathers.

Louise stopped at ever' window.

I told Louise it was bad luck if a lady didn't toss some silver on her honeymoon. She didn't want to at first, we was still so close to being broke, but I told her it was bad, bad luck if she didn't—and so she done it. She bought her a silver-colored hat with glittery beads on it from one of them shops, and, later on, she got herself a manicure at the King Edward's "lady's room."

And ever' night we was in Toronto, from that day on, we'd eat at some fancy restaurant.

The chef at the best one in town was a squat little Frenchman who got sweet on Louise, and he was always fussing over if we liked this or that. Some of it was pretty queer, but it all tasted good: a soup made out of ocean turtles; rolled-up French flapjacks; reindeer meat from Alaska; swordfish from somewhere. So we'd set there and eat all them things, and whilst we was a-chewing, we'd look around and watch all the other rich people chewing too.

I still couldn't get over watching how some rich people acted.

Watching rich people was like moving to some new part of the world and watching all the new animals you never seen before. Like camels or monkeys. They was all diff'rent from each other, of course, but there was some things I seen that was the same. They

219

preened a lot, and there's always some part of 'em puffed up—their chests; or their hair; or their lips. And most of 'em moved their arms and legs a little diff'rent than poor people, like their joints was oiled better.

Yeah, having money is a lot diff'rent than not having money. If you ain't but five feet tall, money'll give you a foot more. If you got a ugly face, money'll ease that face up. 'Course, if the folks looking at you ain't go no money, it works the other way. If you're ugly, you look uglier. If you're short, you look like a stump. But rich people don't know that. That's how come they put on airs. Well, hell! A lot of them folks didn't even earn their money. They got it from dead kin.

I can tell you this—me and Louise didn't put on airs.

Neither did my brothers.

We talked plain and we tipped big (except for Joe), and we enjoyed ourselves.

Only problem was, we was fast going back to dead broke.

TWENTY-SEVEN

"See that?" I said it low into Joe's ear.

Me and the boys was walking around the middle of Toronto marking time one afternoon while Louise was off getting her hair done, when I seen two men in light-gray topcoats and black-bill caps. They was standing on a corner, waiting to cross the street. Stretched between 'em was a leather bag so big and bulgy it looked like a pregnant sow.

"See what?" Joe said.

"Look-it. That bag."

"So what?"

"Look at what it says." You could just make out two words on the side — *Bank Property*.

"I know what you're thinking, old man." Joe shook his head. "But that ain't it. You think somebody'd be fool enough to take a bag fulla money down a street like this? There's a hundred people around."

"Canucks 'r dumb, little brother."

What me and my brothers and Glasscock done a week or so after we seen that bag is something that took more nerve than Jesse James, or the Dalton Boys, or any of them other Wild West outlaws ever had. I ain't bragging about what we done. We was crazy to do it.

But we done it anyhow.

And more'n fifty years later, I can still see them big, black head-lines.

***

When I first seen that bag, I poked Joe in the ribs.

"Let's trail 'em."

We started following 'em. And that's when I seen something that got me even more worked up: a third man, same light-gray overcoat, same black cap, walking close behind the ones with the bag. I suspicioned that third man was a guard.

We trailed 'em for three blocks 'til they come to a huge, bulky-looking granite building. It had stone letters on top: TORONTO CURRENCY CLEARING HOUSE. And just about the same time, from two other directions, come a bunch of other men. Some of 'em had big bags, some had little bags, some had briefcases. And each pair of men was followed by a third man.

There musta been twenty concrete steps leading up to the entrance of the building. And all them men marched up all them steps and disappeared through a big, heavy door.

"Whoa," I said to Joe. "Eleven bags. Four briefcases."

"Probably canceled checks."

"You don't need guards for canceled checks."

"It could be solid gold bullion, Willis, but we ain't gonna get it. Not in the middle of the business district in the middle of the day."

"Well, we can't bust in. Look at the building. It's solid granite. Only way we're gonna get that money is offa them messengers."

Joe give me one of his looks. "Bet they got a coupla six-shooters under ever' one of them coats."

"Naw, they got little short bulldog pistols. That one's coat flied open, I seen his gun. Won't hurt nothing."

"That's one of 'em. Maybe the rest of 'em got .45s."

I hardly heard what he said.

***

I spent the next four days with Louise to give her that honeymoon. Took her down to Ni'gra Falls. Even took her on a side trip over to a little Canuck town called Brantford. But during that whole little trip, my mind was in Toronto. When she was getting a manicure in Brantford, I bought me two automatic shotguns.

I wasn't gonna tell Louise what I was planning, not just then.

But I was getting more and more stirred up. The hell with all them little old country banks! This'd be just the deal we needed to get us a stake big enough to hit back into oil—and in one fast sweep.

I'd told Joe to do the casing. Ever' day, he was to go to a little café across the street from the Clearing House. He was to get there about seven o'clock in the morning. The café had a plate glass window, so he could watch ever'thing. I figured if them messengers was taking things into the Clearing House in the afternoon, they was bringing things *outa* the Clearing House in the morning.

Sure enough, I was dead right. Joe told me at 9:30 ever' morning, here come them messengers and the guards, walking with them bags and briefcases, outa the big building and down the steps. Then they'd split up. Some'd go down one street, some down another street. At about 4:45 in the afternoon, the same messengers and their guards'd come back from all them different directions.

He said it'd happened ever' day. Like the sun come up ever' morning and the sun went down ever' evening.

And why?

Joe'd found out. And it was the silliest thing you ever heard of! There was about eight or ten different banks in Toronto them days. And ever' bank had its own money with its own name on it. Like the Sterling Bank of Canada and the Union Bank. Ever' night all the different kinds of money that come into one of them banks during the day was sent in a bag to the Clearing House. That's where they separated it. Then, in the morning, each bank got its own money back.

'Course, it didn't make no diff'rence to us why.

Only thing we cared about was the money.

If we could grab just two or three of the big bags, we'd likely be setting high.

Inside my head, it was like I could see right straight through them bags—at all them bundles and bundles and bundles of money. At the edge of my head, I could see them Canuck fingers holding tight onto the handles of them bags. But them Canuck fingers wasn't gonna be no match for my fingers. My fingers always knowed just what to do and just how to move and just how fast to do it all. Snatch 'n grab, snatch 'n grab. Nobody ever beat my fingers.

***

I planned ever'thing down to the last detail.

We needed a diff'rent car, one that the laws couldn't trace, and I got one. A Studebaker Big-Six. Dark-red 1919 model. Four years old, but brand-new tires. Goodyear cord with fresh tread. I stole it right off a side street. Old boy that owned it had went into a store and left the keys behind. I just got in and drove off.

Drove it right to a garage I'd rented on the edge of town.

Me and Jess cased the business district three more times, to double-check what Joe told me. I come up with all kinds of excuses for Louise, how come I needed to be out and about them times. I seen the best place to hijack the messengers would be the corner of two streets—Melinda and Jordan. That's where about twelve of 'em headed after they come outa the Clearing House. Right before they split up.

I drawed a careful map.

When I was ready to lay it all out for the other boys, I called a meet in Glasscock's room.

I put the map on the bed. So ever' body'd know what to do and at what spot and at what time. I told 'em my plan: we was all gonna drive in one car to that corner. When the messengers come towards us, Jess and me was gonna jump out and each one of us was gonna grab one of the biggest bags. Glasscock and Dock was gonna be cover if we run into trouble. Joe was the driver.

"It's gonna be easy as snap, boys. Easy as snap."

Most times, Dock was ready to go along with anything I said, but this time he was hanging back.

"You sure the money's there, old man?"

Glasscock said he was for it, Jess said he'd go along even though he didn't like it, but Joe was even more agin it than Dock, even though he'd done the casing. "More I think about it, more I think it's the craziest thing you ever come up with, Willis. You was the one that said the Wild West was over. That daytime jobs are stupid."

"This is a diff'rent deal from a bank job," I said. "They're bringing the money to us. We don't gotta go to them to get it. And it's gonna be just five minutes work. Tops."

***

The morning come up gray and drizzly, but I didn't care nothing about the weather.

You don't need the sun to do a stickup.

At 8:30, I put Louise in the hotel limousine to take her to the Toronto race track. It was outside of the city limits. I told her I had a good tip on two horses—one named Blazing Glory, one named Jones Rich. I give her fifty dollars to bet on 'em. I told her me and the boys was going out to "case a job."

"I thought the little banks were out of town," she said.

"This is something diff'rent."

"Since when do you work in the morning?"

"Canucks do things diff'rent."

I was sorry I wasn't being altogether straight with her. But I knowed that this was our big chance to get some big money, and I knowed she'd try to talk me out of it if I'd told her about it. And I hadn't lied to her. We *was* gonna case the job. We was just gonna pull it, too.

We all got together in Joe's room at 8:45 sharp.

Joe give me a look when I handed him his box of bullets. They was buckshot. "What's this, Willis?"

"Could be a crowd of people around. I don't want birdshot spraying all over."

"And buckshot's better? Yeah, won't put your eye out. Just kill you."

"I know what I'm doing."

"Hell, yeah, we're gonna use some lead, Joe." That was Glasscock. "You sure *are* the baby of the family!"

Joe hopped to his feet and near hauled off at Glasscock for that one. But I told 'em to set down and shut up. I told 'em, if things got tough, to just shoot the hell outa a telephone pole.

***

At 9:35, exact, our car was parked right where it was supposed to be, at the corner of Melinda and Jordan streets. Five minutes before the messengers was to get there. But while we waited I said, "If we work fast, we can get 'em all."

All three of the boys' eyes went round. Glasscock's too. "What'd you mean, get 'em all?"

"We're gonna get 'em all." I'd come up with that while we was driving to the corner. "I'll grab two bags. Jess, you grab two. Dock, you get one. Glasscock, one. Watch me when they come. I'll point out who takes who. We just gotta work fast, is all."

"Aw shit, Willis!" Joe hollered. "You outa your mind! It's twelve messengers and six guards!"

"Ain't *your* problem, Joe. You got the car."

Glasscock started to say something else, but wasn't no time.

It was 9:40, on the nose, and here come the bags!

To this day, I can still see 'em, how they looked, near ever' detail. The messengers and guards was all walking fast, but easy, like wasn't nothing on their minds but getting from here to there. Several of 'em had big thick mustaches, and one of 'em kept raising his arm—the arm that wasn't holding the bag handle—and scratching his mustache, like it was full of fleas. I don't know how come I remember that one old boy so clear, scratching his bushy old mustache like that, except that I knowed with all that scratching going on, I might could catch him off-balance.

There they all was—right towards us, right towards us, right by us, starting to split up. Never even give us a glance.

I pointed quick: "Jess, those two'r yours. Dock, that one. Glasscock, there. I'll get the rest."

I shoved the shotgun under my coat and throwed open the car door.

Later on, the papers was gonna say that the whole thing only took five minutes. Just like I told the boys it would. But if you ever pulled a stickup agin a whole mess of Canucks, you'd find out that ever' minute feels like a week.

***

"Gimme that thing!" I run over to two of the messengers and yanked the bag outa their grips. Their heads spun around and their eyes turned to circles, but they musta been trained pretty good. Or they was just crazy. They wasn't about to give up that bag! They pulled it right back, right outa my hands! I spun around and BLAM!BLAM!, blasted the hell outa a telephone pole. I thought that'd scare 'em. It didn't. I reached over to grab a-hold of the bag again. And that's when one of 'em jumped on me.

Jumped right on my back!

He was a little guy, but I could feel a THUD! like somebody'd throwed a 150-pound sack of potatoes on my back....only that sack had arms and legs and his fingers was a-clawing around at my chest and one of his legs was crooking around down near my crotch.

Crazy Canuck!

Best as I could, I aimed my shotgun at the other messenger's feet to get him to let loose of the bag.

It didn't work! I pulled and pulled at the bolt. It was hung up.

It was hard for me to keep my balance with that little stumpy man hanging on my back. Made me stagger around like a drunk man. But somehow I got my arm down and grabbed onto my pistol. Had it in my waistband. Now one of the other messengers nearby—not one of my two—was starting to run off, but then he stopped and spun around. I tried to pull my pistol out, but the hammer caught on the inside lining of my pocket. Damn! To loose the pistol, I had let go my shotgun. But now the fella on my back hopped off and scrambled for my gun. "Drop it!" I hollered. He didn't do it. He come right at me. He started to raise the shotgun and I didn't know if that thing would shoot this time or not. I aimed my pistol high up on his right side. Pulled the trigger. That done it.

Drop goes that shotgun!

I didn't want to shoot him, but, hell, I didn't want him to shoot me either.

The first of my messengers still had a-hold of the bag. I banged him over the head with my gun. I figured he'd let go like any sane person would. But he held on like his fingers was glued to the handle and tried to jerk the bag away.

"C'mon, give it up," I hollered. "Let go!"

It was like one of them William S. Hart movies, pulling and tugging and shooting going on all over the place. And before any of us could get even one bag, one of the messengers was hollering at the top of his lungs, "Holdup! Holdup!"

Jesus Christ! All hell broke loose!

"Holdup! Holdup! Holdup!" come from all directions.

And where was my two messengers' guard during all this?

At the first, he was right behind me. He coulda shot me. He was armed. But I think he was boogered about hitting the messengers instead of me. So all he done was stick his pistol up in the air and fire: Powwwwww! Powwwwww! And then, can you believe it, he hit off running! Ain't it crazy how life is always throwing you surprises: The messengers was the brave ones, and the guard was the coward!

While all this was going on, outa the corner of my eye I seen Dock tussling with another messenger over a bag. That old boy wouldn't give it up either. He was coming out with his gun. BAM! Dock shot him. Shot him in the right shoulder. Down went that pistol. Where the guard for Dock's messenger was, I didn't know.

Finally, I got my bag loose.

I quick looked around to see if I could get some others. But by this time the other messengers was running helty-skelty down a alley with the rest of the bags. If I hadn't had all that trouble with my guns, I could've got at least one or two more.

Meantime, I figured Jess oughta have got a bag or two. But he was slow coming up, and the messengers and them guards was ready. They wasn't silly cowards like mine, and so it was four agin one when Jess tried to yank a bag from 'em. He finally give up when he seen Dock was in trouble.

As for Joe, he couldn't help much because he had to stay close to the getaway car, ready to git.

By this time I was back to the car with one bag. I was about to jump in when a big black sedan with some guards in it come squealing up to me. Stopped right there. On the passenger side there was a guy with a pistol. As he went to bring his gun up at me, I flipped mine up and shot right through that car door. Didn't have no time to think. Didn't have no time to aim. I didn't know where the hell I'd hit that old boy. But his door flied open, and out rolled his pistol.

It landed right at my feet.

We'd hardly noticed it 'til then but all sorts of stuff was raining down from the sky—flower pots, chairs, boxes, books. There was people upstairs in them tall buildings around the scuffling that'd seen ever'thing and heard ever'thing, and all during the tussle they was throwing ever'thing they could find in their offices, right down into the middle of us.

A big clay pot come crashing down to my left. Dirt and broke-up red flowers went flying all over. About twenty books come showering down to my right. And just in front of me, two heavy wood office chairs come barrelling down, spitting distance. They splintered into a million pieces.

I ducked and dodged best I could.

By now Dock and Jess was at the car with a second bag. And that was it. We only had two bags. And by that time the messengers and guards had all a-scattered.

Where was Glasscock while all this was going on? We didn't know. Except all of a sudden, when we was ready to take off, there he was.

"Let's go!" he hollered, and he jumped into the car with the rest of us.

Joe let out the clutch. The car took off with a screeching of rubber. It was a miracle none of us got killed. Joe, the Baptist preacher, said later that the good Lord musta had His arm around us. I doubt that. Them Canucks was just lousy shooters.

Our car was racing down that street—rocking and zig-zagging—when, sccrreeeeech! Joe had to slam on the brakes. There was a couple of cars in front of us that was hardly moving. We couldn't get around 'em, cars was parked on both sides of the street. Then we seen behind us a guard waving a pistol in his right hand, running after us. He seen we wasn't moving. Dock throwed his own pistol outa the window and, powww-www! powwww-wwww! shot the ground on both sides of that guard. Well, that set that old boy a-hopping. But he still kept coming. Crazy Canucks! I don't know why he didn't shoot instead of just run after us. Maybe he'd fired all his bullets. Maybe he thought if somehow he could catch up with our car he could stop us. All I know is that as we went on in the car he kept running on the sidewalk alongside of us and shouting, "Stop 'em! Stop 'em!"

We had to stop him somehow. Finally, Joe done it. We was passing a store with a big plate glass window. Joe pulled out his pistol with his right hand while he held on to the car wheel with his left. He fired direct in front of the guard into the window. SPLASH! Glass exploded ever'where.

That done it.

You never seen anybody turn-tail like that guard!

By this time we'd come to a intersection, King Street and Shaw Street. The one on my map where I'd marked "Turn right here." That's what Joe did. He squealed around that corner so fast we was near up on two wheels, and then we was hid pretty good in the middle of a whole bunch of other cars. We couldn't follow our getaway route exactly, there was just too many cars. But we headed kinda in the right direction.

In only a few minutes we was a mile or two from where we'd done the robbery . And, so far as we knowed, nobody who'd seen the stickup was anywhere near us. Once they got into all that traffic it'd be hard for them to keep on our tail.

Still, we couldn't be sure they wouldn't stop us somewhere along the way. Particularly if the police was sending out broadcasts about us and our car over the radio. So we wanted to get fast as we could to that garage on the outskirts of town.

But for the first time since the Battle of Toronto begun, I begun to breathe a little easier. "We was lucky to get outa there alive."

"You're damn right," Joe exploded. "This whole thing was

crazy...stupid, stupid!"

Meantime, the others kept looking back to see if there was anyone trailing us. Glasscock piped up: "Jesus Christ! Not a scratch on any of us! We showed 'em!"

Jess shot back: "Whatdaya saying, 'we' showed 'em?"

"We showed 'em. It means what it means."

Dock said to Glasscock, "Lemme see your gun."

He didn't answer. Dock reached over and pulled the pistol outa his pocket and smelled the barrel. "Ain't been fired."

"Willis said no killing. I hit 'em with the barrel. Beaned two or three of 'em."

Joe was breathing hard. "Hit 'em? Hit 'em, nothing! You *hid*, you yeller dog!"

"Shut up, all of you!" I said. "We got bigger problems here."

The traffic was getting even thicker. It was slow going. At one intersection a policeman was directing cars with hand signals, and we come to a dead stop. He kept waving the ones on the cross street along; it seemed like he wasn't ever gonna turn and wave us on. And if you never seen them Canuck policemen making signals with their hands, weaving 'em this way and that, it's quite a show.

Like their hands 'r dancing.

A couple minutes, I couldn't stand that show no more. I got out on the running board. I was gonna jump down on the pavement and poke my pistol at the officer and make him wave us on. But all of a sudden he turned on his own towards us, and he danced his hands up and down and sideways.

Off we went.

It wasn't five minutes more, we was out of that business district.

Just in case, when we passed a streetcar, Dock got outa the automobile and caught the trolley. And further along Jess done the same with another streetcar. Then Glasscock.

That left only me and Joe in the automobile. If the laws was looking for a car with five desperate bank robbers in it, it wouldn't be us.

For a minute or two after that, Joe didn't say nothing. But then I seen his fingers clamp down on the steering wheel so hard they turned white and out it come—all in a rush, even faster and harder than when that flash flood hit our derricks down in Smackover.

"Jesus, Willis, what the hell happened there?" Joe's whole body was shaking. "I don't wanta die just so's you can get your damn million dollars! We coulda all been killed! Hell, we coulda killed *them*! Hell, maybe we did kill 'em! Two of 'em was bloody as beef."

"Them Canucks was the stupid ones, Joe. They shoulda let go of the bags."

"They was doing their *job*, Willis!"

"And that's all we was doing."

"Our job ain't shooting people!"

"Shoulda let go of the bags then."

"If you was one of them messengers," he said, "would *you* a-let go?"

"Shut up, Joe. This ain't getting us nowhere."

A few minutes later the car was parked in the garage. I quick did a rough counting of the loot in them two bags. Come to right around $80,000. Better'n nothing. But not nearly what we coulda got, and after all the trouble! Hell. We hid the bags under the back seat and went to a picture show at a little theater around the corner. The show was about that trained wolf dog, Rin Tin Tin.

TWENTY-EIGHT

In my whole life I been really boogered only two times.

One time it happened in a watermelon patch when I was a little kid living near Cisco. I was hanging around with a bunch of older boys one night and they said why didn't we sneak into Old Man Rockwell's melon patch to get us a fat, ripe one. It was just coming a good dark. Well, there was a real tight old wire fence around the patch but we squeezed on through it. I was right behind a boy named Big Ears, and I'd just found me a nice big melon and I was going thump! thump! thump! to make sure it was ripe, when BLOOEY!, there blasts a gun, and all a sudden, Big Ears falls on the ground and starts a-hollering, "I'm kilt! I'm dead!" And then, BLOOEY! The gun blows again! And one of them other boys yells, "Oh my God, they kilt another!"

You talk about being scared!

I hit on back to that fence, my legs never run so fast in my life, but that wire, it's so tight I bounce right off it and get throwed back six feet. I pull myself up and charge at it again and, oh boy, I'm just a-clawing at it and my clothes is half ripped off and my skin is all scraped and bloody, but I don't care. At last I get through it and I'm just a-scrambling, looking back behind me one more time for the killer, when who do I see? Big Ears! He ain't shot a'tall. He's all bent over, just a-shaking. Laughing like a crazy man. See, that whole thing was just a trick. A boy named Roy was the one shooting off that gun, and he was shooting up into the air.

I'll tell you what, even if it was a trick, that fright stuck in my belly and wouldn't leave. It's like when you catch a chill and your teeth won't stop a-chattering. I just shook and shook for all the next day.

I never got another melon out of that patch.

After that I never was really boogered bad again 'til up in Toronto. On that bank messenger holdup. It didn't hit me full blast 'til it was completely over. 'Til I was going with Joe through the door for that Rin Tin Tin picture show. Yeah, I'd fought with Joe and got my back up over ever'thing. But when I really thought over what we done, I got scared inside of me more'n I'd ever been before. I still do. I will all my life. If them Canucks hadn't been such lousy shots, one of us—maybe all of us—coulda been killed. Or if they had caught us, they'd have stomped us to pieces. Or strung us up from that telephone post.

After the movie ended, Joe went to another theater down the street to watch a Tom Mix picture, and I caught a taxi back to the hotel. I wasn't there half a minute before a newsboy run up to me shouting, "EXTRA! EXTRA! Read all about the big bank messenger robbery!" He shoved a paper in front of my face with big black headlines, "SENSATIONAL HOLDUP DOWNTOWN!" I give him a nickel. It had a second headline: THREE BANK MESSENGERS SHOT DOWN. The story said one of the guards had got shot in the lung. And that all three was in the hospital in a "undetermined" condition. I'll never forget that word "undetermined." Good godamighty!

If we was murderers, them Canucks'd be after us 'til they caught us—and they'd likely kill us too.

In the hotel lobby, I throwed the newspaper away. All over the lobby people was reading that same paper with the same headlines. A few of 'em was crowded around a radio. I could hear 'em all a-yapping. That was probably happening all over Toronto, maybe all over Canada.

Maybe in Louise's room.

All I wanted right then was to get up the elevator, tell Louise what happened, and get it over with. She had to know. At the door to Room 1206—that's one number I'll never forget either—I stopped for a couple of minutes. I'd rather face all them bullets again than face her. But there was no way out.

I put the key in the door and turned it.

"You here, Lou?"

There wasn't no answer.

"You here, honey?"

The bathroom door creaked open.

She come out slow.

I froze. There was something in how she was looking at me I never seen in her eyes before.

233

"It was you, wasn't it?" she said.

"Whatdaya mean?"

"You know damn well what I mean."

She had a handkerchief in her hand. I seen she'd been crying. She wasn't crying no more, but her face was white and tight. And the way her eyes was moving, it was like she was trying to throw something outa her head, and it wasn't going.

I walked over to her. I put my hands on her shoulder. I looked her straight in the eye.

"When we come here, Lou, I didn't have no plans for this thing..."

"You shot them?" Her voice was so low I could hardly hear her.

"It wasn't nothing like you mighta heard. The way we planned it, nobody was gonna get hurt. We was gonna catch 'em off guard, by surprise...."

"You told me you were 'casing' a job, Willis. *Casing* a job? Three men and—"

"Listen to me, honey. Listen hard..."

"—and one is dying. A war veteran...with three children...."

"They was like crazy men, them Canucks. They wouldn't let go of the bags..."

She slumped to the floor. "It's gone too far, Willis. Too far."

"Lemme tell you how it happened, Lou..."

I crouched down in front of her. I put my hands on her shoulders again.

"We didn't shoot 'em to kill 'em..."

She threw her hands up and knocked my hands away. I never knowed a woman could have so much power in her arms. Her eyes was looking dead set again, only they wasn't seeing me.

Now she was hollering.

TWENTY-NINE

Next day, it was more big, black headlines—headlines so big and so black you'da thought the whole world had blowed up. Well, I don't know who in the devil them newspapers hired to write their stories, but could their reporters whoop and holler and kick up dust!

They wrote that we'd pulled off "the most cold-blooded and daring crime ever committed on the streets of Toronto."

They wrote that we musta been "schooled in the business of killing and maiming" and that our guns was "vomiting death."

They wrote we'd left one of them messengers "gasping in pain through blanched lips, a bullet buried in his lungs."

Like always, they got plenty wrong. One worse'n the other. One of 'em wrote: "It's quite possible that the mind that planned the robbery was not on the scene when the thing took place. It all smacks of a cunning that seldom goes with boldness and initiative."

Well, hell! They didn't know nothing!

I was hoping to God that Louise hadn't seen none of them papers. I figured she'd left in the night and took a train back to the States. All her clothes and bags was gone when I come back to our room in the morning. There wasn't nothing I coulda done. When she got something into her head, she was like Ma—stubborn as a gov'-ment mule.

I had a awful fear that I'd lost her forever.

And there was something else worrying me.

I wasn't scared, like the boys was, that she might snitch. It was something else. Right before the stickup, I'd hid a .45 pistol in her nightbag, the one where she kept her lady things. I'd put it there "just in case." And in all the ruckus, I'd forgot about that gun. And now that nightbag was gone with Louise, and God knows what was happening to her at the border of Canada, if they was to search her things.

Was Louise gonna get arrested for my pistol?

It made me sick with worry. But what could I do about it?

I gotta say something else quick, though. Not ever'thing we read in them papers that morning after that Toronto stickup was bad. The best thing, all three of them wounded messengers was still alive! Even the one hurt the worst, the one that'd took a bullet in the lung, was "moving out of danger," one paper said.

When I read that, I took my first full breath in twenty-four hours.

***

'Course, we still wasn't off the hook.

The papers said there was a $10,000 reward out for us and the laws had set up roadblocks on ever' highway going outa the city.

We knowed from the papers that the laws didn't have no hard descriptions of us, being that most of the witnesses was so rattled and ever'thing happened so fast. All they got was stuff like, "One bandit was wearing a brown suit and straw hat and witnesses described him as having a fat face." That was Jess. And "two witnesses said the getaway car was driven by a colored chauffeur." That was Joe. (He'd got hisself a dark hide from hanging out at a lake, looking at gals in bathing clothes.)

But there was probably hundreds of colored chauffeurs in Toronto, and thousands of white men with fat faces.

The laws did know we was driving that 1919 Studebaker; they called it a "red high-powered mystery car." Only that was parked in a secret garage.

Anyhow, me and Joe went out and bought us some wide cotton ducking, a few big sewing needles, and some thick thread. We took a taxi to the garage where we'd parked our getaway car. We took about $65,000 of the loot and sewed it in layers into that tape. Then we wrapped it around our chests, like it was a vest.

We put our shirts over them belts, and when we was done, we looked like burly muscle-men with barrel chests.

We took another taxi to the garage where we'd parked the car we'd drove up to Toronto in. In that one, we headed outa town. Sure enough, we passed a couple of roadblocks, but the laws was looking for a 1919 dark-red Studebaker—not our 1923 black one. We went about thirty miles outside of town, and buried the money in some old sandy country. Then we went back into Toronto, split up the rest of the money into fives—and all five of us sewed it into that ducking, same way, and wrapped it around our chests.

When we cut outa town, in our car and Glasscock's, the laws was still posted all over the sides of the roads. But we was split up and driving in two cars—neither one of 'em a 1919 Studebaker—and nobody blinked a eye.

Even with how bad things had gone in Toronto, they was beginning to look up.

Except the boys was still mad at me. And Louise was gone.

***

First thing I done when I got to Detroit, I checked by telephone with a friend of Louise's in Omaha. She said Louise had left town, took Lewis to her folks in Wisconsin. The good part of that was, she'd got across the border, even with that .45 in her lady's things; the bad news was, she'd left me.

I wasn't gonna give up in trying to get her back, I wasn't ever gonna give up. But like as not, I was gonna have to do it a diff'rent way. The last time I did it, it was by trying to go legitimate, to get into oil. Now I was gonna have to drop the trying and just *do* it. 'Course, the only way I knowed how to get enough money to go straight was to stay crooked a while longer.

First off, I found a fence for the money we'd brung with us; he give us 90 cents on the dollar.

Then, two weeks later, me and Joe drove back up to Canada and dug up that $65,000. We planted it all under the cushions of the car, stuffed it in there with them springs, and headed back. Joe did the driving. He was still mad at me, so we didn't say much of nothing the whole trip.

But we done what we went to do.

When we come to the border, I got outa the car and went to walking across the bridge, casual-like. Outa the corner of my eye, I seen the border inspector walk over to Joe. I never did turn my head, just slid my eyeball way to the corner of my eye socket. The old boy asked Joe a coupla questions, I seen Joe's head moving around, and the inspector waved him on.

Yessir! We'd got away with it!

All them Canuck messengers was alive! And not a nick or scratch on any of us!

Still, I felt like somebody'd stuck a thumb-buster in my chest and pulled the trigger. There was a big empty hole there, right in my middle. I wanted to get as close to Louise as I could. And I wasn't ever gonna give up on that gal. Even if the chances of her coming back to me was a million to one.

Soon as we got back to the States, I told the boys and Glasscock we was gonna switch headquarters. To Chicago. That was the closest big city to where Louise was at.

"Why Chicago?" Joe asked.

"'Cause it's the wickedest city in the United States. We get picked up for anything, there's fixers ever'where."

THIRTY

"She's not talking to you. Don't call anymore." Louise's Pa and Ma told me that ever' time I called up to their house from Chicago. Louise was there, all right, with Lewis, but she wouldn't come to the phone. And if I went up there, they told me, she wouldn't see me.

Oh, Chicago was a wide-open place back then!

Folks called it "the hub of the nation" because it had trains running from it north, south, east, west. And it was filled with honest, hard-working people—lots of 'em immigrants that sweated their hind-ends off at the factories and packing houses. But Chicago was rotten at the core. It was run by crooked thugs—the newspapers called 'em gangsters—and by crooked police and politicians.

Them days, the gangsters made their money mostly from bootlegging.

It was that Prohibition law that made it a crime to sell hooch, or even to drink it. But all that law done was make people wanta drink it even more. One of the songs ever'body was singing went, "You Cannot Make Your Shimmy Shake on Tea." Well, there musta been shimmies shaking all over Chicago 'cause the papers said bootleggers sold more'n $60 million of beer ever' year. Sixty million dollars!

And that was just beer.

I hadn't been in Chicago one week before I seen one of the city's biggest, meanest gangsters, Deany O'Banion. It was when me and Glasscock was walking down North Street. Ever'body in town knowed about O'Banion. He run a flower shop across from a Catholic cathedral, but flowers was just his front. When it come to ruling Chicago's underworld, O'Banion was one of the Big Ones. Johnny Torrio and Al Capone had their fists on the south side; O'Banion had most of the north.

"That's O'Banion," Glasscock whispered, and he poked me in the side. "White suit."

I couldn't keep my eyes offa that old boy. He had a round face, like a lump of Ma's biscuit dough, and his mouth and his eyes was like the way a knife slits into dough. You couldn't see no lips, couldn't hardly see no eyelids. And he was limping, his right leg was shorter'n his left. But even with that dough head, and that ker-thump of a walk, his chest was puffed out like he was the king of Chicago. He had on a snow-white suit, double-breasted, with a red rose stuck in the lapel, and he was shaking hands and slapping backs on half the people that walked past him.

"See how he keeps his left hand in his pocket?" Glasscock whispered.

"Yeah."

"I hear he's got three secret pockets for his guns."

Lemme tell you what: If I coulda knowed that the Newton Boys was gonna cross paths with that O'Banion one day, I woulda give that gimpy old son-of-a-bitch a even harder look. But something like that didn't even come into my mind.

I didn't have no plans to do any jobs inside the city.

It woulda been a good deal if me and my brothers coulda figured out a way to dip into all them bootleg profits. But we wasn't fools. I knowed how jealous them Chicago gangsters was of their territories, and they was cold-blooded thugs. They said they had a code, but it wasn't no code of the West. Hell, they didn't even have the manners of a rattlesnake. Didn't even buzz before they bit. If somebody was trying to do business in their part of town, you was likely to find that person slumped over the steering wheel of his car, with a bullet in the back of his head, or shot up with bullets on the sidewalk.

But I'm getting ahead of my story here. Because for a long while nobody messed with us. In fact, most of the time I wasn't even in Chicago.

I was out on the road hunting for marks.

And I liked being on the road, a-moving. The boys liked me being on the road, too. They stayed in Chicago and lived it up! They was all so hacked at me over Toronto, particularly Joe, that I told 'em I'd pay their hotel bills for a month while I was off doing the scout-ing work. I figured that'd give time for the "hot coffee to cool," and that's just what it done. 'Course we was all hacked at Glasscock, for being such a yeller-dog. But I didn't want to lose out on his tipsters. So I just let him be.

Anyhow, while I was on the road, there was plenty of things for the boys to do in Chicago, particularly Joe and Jess. They was free to roam around more'n Dock was. They become big White Sox baseball fans and started going to ever' home game there was. Joe even kept a list of ever' player's hitting and batting averages. Other times, they'd go out to the Union Stockyards to visit with live animals, or to the meat-packing plants where they could watch the big, bloody carcasses being cut up into steaks, roasts, and chops. They liked to ride around the city on that elevated Railway, called "the El."

And, of course, they chased after gals. Jess was still the worst of 'em when it come to that. He'd hit a café and take out ever' gal in it—starting with the head waitresses and then going down to the lower waitresses, the cooks, the dishwashers, and finally the scrub girls.

Dock was the one that had the most trouble keeping his spirits up. I'd warned him to lay low, so I bought him a radio for his room. Back then the radio was a pretty new invention, and I bought Dock something called a "crystal set." It had a little thin wire called a "cat whisker" that you put down on different places on a little round silver "crystal" to find different stations. You listened with a headset over your ears. Most of the programs was music—Dock 'specially liked country music, the polkas and waltzes that was the favorite of all them Germans and Polacks that lived in Chicago.

Still, before too long Dock got tired of laying low. And after a while, Jess and Joe was starting to get restless too. Whenever the boys started to complain, I'd remind 'em they was living better than millionaires. "Millionaires can't take time off whenever they want. Or do whatever they want," I said. But Jess was starting to do some thick drinking again, I could smell it. You ever got a whiff of a rotted orange? That's how hooch stinks when it's stale on your breath.

Well, I gotta be straight here—I was getting itchy too. It was driving me crazy not to be with Louise; she was always in my head. It woulda been real easy for me to hook up with another gal there in Chicago, or any of them big cities I was passing through looking for marks. Women was swarming all over them days—good-looking gals that didn't just show their knees, they showed their arms too. I seen in the paper how Mister Henry Ford's wife hated it that the city gals was wearing skirts that "left the knees open to public gaze and showed their bare limbs." But that Missus Henry Ford didn't know the half of it! Lots of them city gals'd do things with a man you could only get from a whore back in the old days. You can't believe how forward some of the women was in the 1920s.

Only I didn't have a lick of interest in any of 'em. Not a lick. Just Louise.

Most thieves I knowed hopped from one skirt to the other like they hopped from one mark to another. One woman's just about the same as the next, long as she's got the goods. But that's where I was diff'rent. When a woman got under my skin, she was in there for good, even if she wasn't there. It'd happened with Vela way on back. And now with Louise. What was it about that little Jew lady that drove me crazy, just plumb crazy, when she wasn't around? I was missing ever'thing there was to miss about her. Ever'thing! How she pushed her hair outa her eyes, how her leg twitched when she'd had a Scotch, how she winked when I let her trump me playing cards.

Still, I had to keep going.

Glasscock had good tipster friends in Chicago, and it wasn't long before I'd got me a new list of out-of-the-way towns that still had them old-fashioned square safes. When September come around, me and the boys started back to work. But once we got things rolling, I seen that it was gonna be hard to keep 'em rolling. Even if a town had a square safe in August, there wasn't no promise it'd have a square safe in October. Marks was drying up. And more banks was getting slicked-up burglar alarms that was hard to trip.

And where'd that leave us?

In the middle of drought, that's where.

I thought about hitting Canada again, checking out the little towns in the east, where we'd been heading when we got hung up in Toronto. But then I seen in the paper where the banks up there was getting wise, too. "Many vaults," that story said, "when opened by explosives, will contain an unpleasant surprise for the bandits. The breaking of the vaults will explode bombs."

Crazy Canucks!

All this was getting me more and more edgy. Where was I going from here? What now?

***

Then, one Sunday afternoon, I got a call from Glasscock.

"I have a different kind of tip this time," he said. "This one can throw us right down onto Easy Street—forever. If this job goes down, you can drill a thousand oil wells! I'm telling you, Willis, this is it. My tipster's a Chicago big shot. He's rich. He's politically-connected. And he wants to talk."

Well, I thought, what the hell?

You put a cowboy in a drought, he'll drink horse piss if he has to.

THIRTY-ONE

The big shot was big all over.

Him and Glasscock showed up at our meeting place—a dock off Lake Shore Drive—in the fella's long black Peerless. And when the fella got outa the car, the whole thing rocked.

His name was Jimmy Murray.

Murray looked just about how you'd think a Chicago big shot would look. Lots of gold rings and coal-black hair oiled on top of his head. Even with a strong wind a-blowing offa the lake, his hair wasn't moving a mite. And he had two chins, the bottom one bigger'n the top one. When he talked, his voice was kinda muffled, like it was pushing up through both them chins, up into his mouth.

But what he had to say made me set up straight as I ever set up in my life.

"I run booze," he told me. "That's my bread and butter. Along with a few other things. But this job, what I'm proposing here, is something real different. And real big. I think you boys are just the eggs to do it. We don't want any killing, see. And the Chicago boys don't know how to do anything if somebody doesn't bleed." He lowered his voice like he was afraid somebody'd hear him, even though we was setting on benches at the end of the dock and wasn't nobody around but some birds.

"My inside man's an ace U.S. postal inspector..."

I near blowed off the dock.

A U.S. postal inspector!

Murray seen my jaw drop. He give me a smile.

"Me and this bird, we go way back," he went on. "We both grew up on the south side—same block. We're tight. Stayed that way. Only now my pal's pants are tight, if you know what I mean. He likes gin too much. The girls too much. The ponies too much. And all that 'too much' means

Jimmy Murray, Chicago politician and beer runner.

too little right here." Murray stuck his hand in his pocket. "He's in deep. He needs fast dough, and he knows how to get it. He just can't do it himself. And when I say fast dough, boys, that's what I mean. One night's work. And you'll wet your pants when you hear how much we're talking about."

This was the idea. Chicago was such a big, rich city there was always big mail trains going in and outa town filled with treasures— U.S. currency, negotiable bonds, jewelry, all sorts of other loot. Because Murray's pal was a U.S. postal inspector, he knowed exactly which of them mail trains carried what, where and when. If somebody wanted to tap into one of them treasures, all they had to do was to stop the train out in the country and rob it.

The best part of it: Murray's pal wasn't just any old corn pone postal inspector. He was a top ace that some folks called "Old Incorruptible." He'd put the screws on some of the biggest mail-train thieves in Chicago, like "Big Tim" Murphy. Story was, that inspector had spit in Big Tim's face when Big Tim'd tried to bribe him with $100,000.

Who would ever suspicion the top ace inspector of the U.S. Postal Service, a man who'd cracked open the last five big mail-train robberies, and spit in Big Tim's face, would ever be on the inside of a job?

"I wanta meet him," I said.

***

I met the "inside man" on a chilly day at the back of Jacobsen's Restaurant at 11th Street and Michigan Avenue. I was alone. Glasscock and me agreed it'd be better if the fella only seen one of our faces, "just in case." The "just in case" was if we run into trouble with the laws later on, or if it was some kind of a double-cross.

We set on a box in the alley where nobody could hear us. I told the man my name was James H. Watson.

First thing the fella said to me: "I'm going to indulge you in some strong talk here, Watson. Hear me out. I know my groceries. I can tip you off to just about anything that goes into the mail trains. The one I like best goes from Chicago to Milwaukee to St. Paul. It's short, it's fast, it's loaded."

I wasn't sure I much liked how he looked or how he talked. He was a skinny thing, jug-headed, and he only used one side of his mouth. And he was one of them "smart-guys." Used big words and mixed 'em up with street talk. But when it come to the job and the money, I liked what he had to say.

The inside man said his plan was: The robbers would take one share each while him and Murray would divide one.

"I'm not one to toot my own pipe, Watson," he went on, "but I can tell you this—nobody plays me for the chump. Some of these postal inspectors are the dumbest Caucasians you've ever seen. They don't even know there's enough in just one of those cars for all of us to be sitting pretty the rest of everybody's lives."

"How much you need to set pretty?" I asked.

"My needs are modest. Sometimes there's seven or eight on these trains."

"Seven or eight what?"

"Mil."

Jesus Christ! A jolt shot from my ears to the ends of my toes!

'Course, I knowed nobody was gonna just hand that kinda money over to a band of robbers without a fight.

"That much money," I said back, "somebody's gonna be keeping a close eye on it."

"Oh, yes. The clerks on the train have guns. I'll be clear with you about that. But they won't shoot 'em. They don't know how. I know. I'm in charge of gun training."

I laughed. I don't know if I was laughing with that old boy, or at him. But I laughed anyhow.

"How 'bout the gangsters?" I asked next. "It's their backyard."

"Oh, their minds are on other things right now, like the new mayor and the new police chief. Mayor and the chief are talking about 'reforming' this town. But what happens when you clean out a toilet, Watson? That's right. You have to slop out a lot of crap first. The gangsters are all too busy protecting their own turfs to pay attention to us. Besides, you can pull this job way outside of the city. Out in the country. That's nobody's turf."

He nudged me like we was already partners.

"If I didn't love my wife and kids so much, Watson, I'd go to California after this job goes down and buy me one of those pink mansions; you know, the ones with a swimming pool shaped like a kidney bean. And I'd live just like Fairbanks. Or who's that pouty-mouthed one? Rudolph Valentino. I'd live like Valentino."

Hell, I didn't care nothing about moving to California and living like no movie star. I didn't even care about living like one of them Chicago millionaires in the big mansions that set along the edge of that Lake Michigan. I seen a few of them millionaires, and they all looked like they was dead men a-walking. Just bored silly. But the sound of them millions, that I loved! Yeah, this'd be it! *The* job. And it would get me back *the* woman.

It's true me and my brothers'd never made much outa robbing trains before. But we'd never had the right inside man.

***

I wanted to be sure.

For three whole months, I watched that inspector. He let me do it. I went to the postal station and into a big office that had his name on the door in black letters: "Inspector Frank Fahy." He had a peep-hole that looked out onto the loading dock, and I'd look through that little hole at all the Irish and Polack mail-handlers, big sweaty men with big bulgy muscles, piling bags into mail trucks. Bag after bag after bag. Then I'd hit on over to the depot and watch 'em take them bags outa them trucks and load 'em onto the trains. Bag after bag after bag.

I checked times and dates and schedules.

Ever'thing checked out. Fahy was on the square.

'Course, that jug-headed postal inspector was a odd one, lemme tell you what. That first time I'd talked to him, he was cocky as a jay-bird. But as the weeks was going by, he was getting more and more jittery. He'd bit up his bottom lip so much it was scabby. And the sleep circles under his eyes was getting blacker and blacker, 'til he was looking like a raccoon.

Me, it was the other way around. I didn't sleep a wink after our first meet. Hearing about all them mail trains sent my mind going helty-skelty. But the more I was working out the plan, the calmer I was getting. Fact is, I was starting to get that "old slow feeling," like how I felt about Louise. Where things just felt right. Hell, ever'thing about this job felt right. There I'd been wanting to make me a million dollars, and here it was.

I just had to work a few things out.

We knowed we wanted to do the job out in the country, at night. But where, and how, and what then?

One afternoon, I got in my Studebaker and drove northwest,

248

outa Chicago. I went the same direction as the tracks used by the Milwaukee-St. Paul mail train. And about thirty-five miles up, a couple of miles past a little town called Rondout, I found the perfect spot.

It was where a country road called Buckley crossed the tracks.

It was very, very lonely. At night, it'd be very, very dark.

I stood at that spot, and I closed my eyes, and I went over the whole job in my head—from beginning to end.

How was we gonna get the train to stop?

I come up with a plan.

How would we deal with all them mail clerks without nobody getting hurt?

I come up with a plan.

Where was we gonna take all them mail bags, and how was we gonna get them there?

I come up with a plan.

How was we gonna deal with the laws that was gonna come after us and the Chicago gangsters that was gonna get jealous?

We was gonna hightail it to Mexico!

***

That whole time I was studying up for the big train job, I never said a word about it to my brothers. I didn't want 'em giving me no mouthing if things didn't work out. But after I'd watched enough, and seen enough, and thought about it all enough, I was ready to tell 'em.

I called a special meet at the hotel. And ever'body showed up but Jess. Jess'd been sharing a room with Joe, so I asked Joe "where's Jess?"

"He's on a drunk, I reckon. Ain't seen him for a week. But you ain't been around much to rein him in, old man."

Rein him in?

What I wanted to do was strangle that old boy! A good business team is like a machine, see, and you can't just yank out one of the parts when the whole thing is oiled and humming. Even if that one part is getting itself oiled with ninety-proof hooch.

I had to find Jess, and I had to find him right off. So I done what any good detective woulda done: I hunted down his skirts. Joe helped me. We talked to maybe six or seven of the café gals Jess'd been messing with. And number seven, a brawny, busty waitress, give us the goods. "He said he was tired of cities," she said. "He was going to Nebraska to join up with Booger Red's Wild West Show."

Booger Red's Wild West Show?

THIRTY-TWO

"BOOGER RED'S—The Last of the REAL Wild West!"

We seen the first poster on a outhouse.

We'd just crossed over the Nebraska state line, and Booger Red posters was ever'where. On outhouses. Sides of barns. Tacked up on fences. We followed 'em to a little town called Tekamah, me and Glasscock in one of our getaway cars. (I'd left Joe in Chicago so he wouldn't get a whiff of horse again; left Dock, too, to keep him laying low.)

There was a big banner stretched across the main street in Tekamah: "Come and See Booger Red Ride—the Ugliest Man Living or Dead. A $100 Prize for any Person who brings in Anything that Can't be Rode. Anything you can Lead, Ship, or Drag in."

We didn't even need to ask where the show was. Just followed the trail of horses and buggies and automobiles.

The show was all set up in a field about a mile out of town. There was a big tent puffed out like a giant balloon with a ticket booth out front. And not far away was a smaller tent that had a sign: "Performers and Contest Animals." That's where I hit to right off.

I blowed past a line of people bringing in rowdy animals— broncs and bulls and a coupla crazy-eyed burros—for the $100 prize, and started to walk in through a flap in the tent. But a big hand come down on my shoulder.

"Can't go in there, pal," said a big deputy sheriff.

"My brother's in there. Our pa's bad sick."

The law shook his head. "Yeah, I heard it all. Ever'body wants to get a peek at Mister Booger Red's booger face has either got a lost dog or a sick somebody. Sorry, pal. Gotta buy a ticket like ever'body else."

Well, I didn't know nothing about no booger face, and I didn't care; all I wanted to see was a fat one—Jess'.

Me and Glasscock bought tickets.

We got inside the grandstand just in time for the start of the three o'clock show. A little band with a couple of shiny trumpets begun to play, and there was drums sounding like Injin tom-toms, and then, whooping and hollering, ten cowboys and ten Injins come galloping out of a slit and went around in circles. You didn't know if the cowboys was chasing the Injins, or the Injins was chasing the cowboys, but it really didn't make no diff'rence. The idea was to get the crowd all stirred up, and that's just what it done. The people was cheering and whooping and hollering.

I peeled my eyes for Jess. But I didn't see him.

Then out come Booger Red!

He was on a huge black stallion, had his thumbs tucked in his suspenders, was a-smiling and a-crowing. And ever' now and then he'd yank off his big old high-crown hat and flap it around in the air. And that's when you seen the hair that give him his name; wasn't a whole lot of it, but it was bright red. And the "booger face"? I found out later what that was about: When he was a kid, some gunpowder'd blowed up right in front of his face, knocking out a eye and scarring up his mug. But if Booger Red had a ugly face, you couldn't hardly tell it, that old boy was moving so fast.

***

That show went on for hours.

There was cowboys bulldogging steers; pigs balancing apples; men throwing Bowie knives at ladies, knocking cigarettes outa their mouths.

But no Jess.

Then, about two hours in, the announcer climbed up on a platform and started hollering into a cone: "Alright, now, ladies and gentlemen, the famous Booger Red riding contest! Hundred-dollar prize for anything that cain't be rode, folks! They been led in, they been shipped in, they been drug in. Time'ta watch the dust fly!"

I throwed my eyes back to the arena. "If he's here, this is it."

"If he's not too drunk to stand up," Glasscock said back.

I kept my eyes glued on the chutes. One after another, out they come—a couple of them grouch-ass little burros and a lot of wild-eyed broncs and kicking bulls: only problem for us, it was Booger Red hisself atop most of 'em. God, them animals was packed with mean, humping up and circle-bucking and splaying their legs and doing ever'thing else you could think of to throw that old boy offa their backs. He rode 'em all right down to sweat.

But no Jess.

Then, right when I was thinking my brother'd led me on some wild goose chase, the announcer come back:

"You all ready for some real dust to fly?"

The crowd whooped and hollered.

"Well, we got coming up a real outlaw, one that Mister Booger Red *knows* ain't never been rode. Last old boy that tried to do it is pushing up weeds at the Sweet Home Cemetery. This bronc's name is Paydirt. Nobody's ever rid him, and the gamblers are giving ten to one nobody ever will. Like you know, most times, it's Mister Booger Red hisself that rides the wildest of the wild. But we got a cowboy here today, name of 'Jesse James' Wayne, who begged Mister Booger to let him try. Ladies, if you don't wanta watch this contest between a man-killer and a champeen cowboy, put a handkerchief over your face. This could all be over in two or three seconds."

Glasscock punched me. "It's him."

"Yeah, and if Paydirt don't kill 'em, I will."

Why the hell did my brother have'ta pick the worst bronc in the world? Particularly if he'd been drinking? If he only got a broke arm, or a broke leg, he'd still be no use to us on our big job. Damn him!

"I wouldn't worry," Glasscock said. "I'll bet that 'killer stuff' is just pump-up. Probably some old farm plug."

The gate to the chute swung open and out it come.

It wasn't no plug.

Paydirt raced out squealing—a bald-faced, bawling man-killer that seemed to know ever' trick in the world for turning a human being into jelly. That animal took Jess all over that arena, snapping him back and forth like you'd pop a whip. Moving so fast it wasn't nothing but a blur: a blur up and down, sideways, around and around, spinning, cat-backing, crawdadding, sunfishing, even standing up on his hind legs.

Well, I'll tell you what, I'd got to where I could blow a safe or a vault with six ounces of grease and not feel one ounce of jitter. But when I seen Jess on that bronc, blood squirting outa his nose, his neck whipping back and fro, my stomach hopped into my throat.

Still, through it all, Jess was sticking on.

For a flash, but only for a flash, I was right proud of my brother. Riding broncs, the worst of 'em—that was the one thing Jess could do just about as perfect as it could be done.

The crowd knowed it too, how perfect that old boy was riding that bronc.

Ever'body in the stands was jumping up to their feet and they was a-whooping and a-whistling and the ladies was waving their hankies. And when Jess' three minutes was up, and another rider come racing in and dragged Jess offa Paydirt's back, you couldn't hear yourself think for how that crowd was a-hollering. The judge give Jess a blue ribbon and a hundred dollar prize, and then that fool old brother of mine went to strutting around that arena, fanning his hat and waving to the crowd, just like he won hisself a *million*.

***

Together, me and Glasscock walked to the back of the tent. It didn't take us more'n a minute to find Jess. He was setting on a bale of hay pouring whiskey outa a bottle and into his mouth. After he'd poured five or six times, he'd hand the bottle to a Injin standing next to him. The Injin was wearing a long feather head-dress that come all the way down to his heels.

"Hoddy, Jess."

Jess didn't look over. He didn't know it was me. He just smiled and raised his bottle, like he was giving some old boy a friendly salute. Only this old boy wasn't feeling friendly. I grabbed the bottle outa his hand and turned it over.

For a little bit Jess stood there looking at the wet spot on the ground. He blinked his eyes and swayed a little. Then he looked up.

"Willis!"

"Good ride, boy. Now get your stuff. Let's go."

"What the hell you doing here, old man?"

"I need you in Chicago, Jess."

"Kiss a pig's nose, Willis. I ain't going one red inch but sideways here." And he moved a inch sideways and near tipped over.

The Injin with the feathers was standing there next to Jess like *he* was Jess' brother. I told him to scoot on, that I had some business to do with this cowboy. He walked off with the droopiest look you ever seen. Like he just couldn't get over how anybody'd waste all that good firewater on a bale of hay.

When he left, I said to Jess, "Look, it don't make no sense, you riding in some Wild West show for a coupla lousy dollars a day. You can make a thousand *thousand* times that on this next job."

"What I want in my life, old man, is hog legs." And he coughed a coupla times. "Legs so goddamned bowed you c'n run a 300-pound hog through 'em."

"Well, you'll get you them hog legs a lot faster if you listen to me. You want a big ranch or not?"

"That question's getting smelly, old man. You think you're so smart? I say you ain't. Where's all them millions you was gonna make offa oil? Huh? And what the hell happened up there in Toronto? Huh? And how good you been doing at filling up the well, old man? Naw, Willis, the modern world is catching up with us and I don't much care for the modern world."

"All you're gonna get working here is a broke neck, Jess. And listen to me...."

I caught myself. I looked around ever'where to make sure nobody had their ears out. I said in a low voice, "You go down South with this show, the laws'll get you for sure. They got arrest warrants out agin us for New Braunfels and San Marcos."

I wasn't giving Jess no bull. According to what I'd been hearing through the underground, there was a mess of warrants out in Texas for all four of us Newton Boys, not just Dock. There was even a murder warrant out for me, for what I didn't know.

It wasn't that they had any evidence on us. It's because—sure enough—we'd been double-crossed by that dirty-rat ex-detective for the Texas Bankers Association. He'd found out he could get even more money for his retirement if he played both ends agin the middle.

"Aw shit!" Jess said. I think that news had shook him outa his drunk. "You're telling me that *now*?"

"Now's when you need to know it."

"Goddammit, old man! You never give nobody the full story. I can't believe I was ever lame-brained enough to hook up with you, Willis. Sometimes I think the only thing I got under this hat here is hair, and that ain't what it used to be neither."

***

Wouldn't you know it, after all that trouble to get Jess back, when I finally got all three boys together for the meet in my hotel room, to give 'em the particulars about the big job that was gonna make us millionaires, ever' one of 'em balked.

"We ain't never hit a train that wasn't no bust, Willis. How you know the money's gonna be there this time?" That was Dock.

"*Millions?* You never did say it was *millions*! Nobody's gonna give up all that money without one son-of-a-bitch battle!" That was Jess.

The biggest trouble was with Joe. He'd been reading too many of them old Wild West story books.

"You got a holdup that amounts to a whole lot of money," Joe said, "something *always* goes wrong. And did'ya know that if they hang you, they gotta weigh you first to figure out how long the rope's gotta be? They figured it wrong with old Black Jack Ketchum, yeah, when they got him for that train job out in Twin Mountain, New Mexico. His head popped plumb off his body."

"Hey! I weigh the most of any of us," Dock said. "I get the shortest rope, or the longest rope?"

"Shortest," Joe said. "If they use a rope. They got them electrocutions, now, some places. Willis, you know if they use ropes or electric chairs in Illinois?"

"Yeah, electric chairs!" Jess cut in before I could talk. "I hear they strap you up and they flip on a switch, and wham! Fried!"

"And they say if you got a bald spot on your head, that when they jolt you, a big old puff of smoke comes off." That was Joe again.

"Hey, Jess!" That was Dock. "With that patch of yours, that means you're gonna smoke when you fry."

"Shut up!" Jess was hot.

"Oh, what're you crazy boys so boogered over?" I said. "Hell, I could go out and rob this thing with three fifteen-year-old boys."

Then I rolled over and went to sleep.

THIRTY-THREE

Two weeks before *the* job, there come a surprise.

I'd quit trying to call Louise at her folks' house, but I'd been sending her letters. With my return address marked on 'em, a downtown post office box in Chicago. I'd sent ten of 'em. And all ten'd come back. The first nine was still glued, just like I'd glued 'em. But the last one looked like it'd been steamed open and glued shut.

Then come a telephone call about eleven at night.

Most times when I got a phone call that late, it was a man's voice on the other end. Most times, it was a croaky voice, or a snarly voice, or a sour voice. But this voice was soft. Soft and kinda shaky. It said it wanted me to come up to New London the next Saturday and meet up at a place called Rainey's Dairy Farm. It was about a mile outside of the town.

"You coming back to me, Lou?" I said into the phone.

"I want to see you, Willis." That's all she said back.

***

I got there early. It was a moonshiny night, and I seen a whole herd of dairy cows bedded down. I could hear 'em a-lowing. I don't know what it is about me and cows, but something about looking at cows in a pasture always made me feel good. And all that lowing made me feel like, somehow, ever'thing was gonna be all right. Only my stomach was balled up in a knot. And that knot got tighter and harder when I seen headlights, bouncing up and down.

When she got outa the car and started to walk towards me, the moon was throwing a milky light on the top of her head. There wasn't nothing I wanted more'n to run up to her and throw my arms around her and kiss her. I'd been seeing her in my mind for months, ever since that mess in Toronto. And that whole way driving from Chicago to New London, I'd been seeing her in my head.

I'd been thinking how she was gonna look, how she was gonna feel, how I was gonna wrap her all up in my arms.

Only now that the time come, it was like too much water'd gone under the bridge to make out like ever'thing was okay.

She stopped when she was about five feet away. She stood there and didn't say nothing.

"God, you're looking good, Louise. You don't know how much I been missing you."

She still didn't say nothing.

"How'd you get my number, honey?"

Nothing.

"Lou, say something! You was the one that called me!"

She looked down and snapped open the handbag she was holding. She reached inside it and pulled out something that was wrapped in brown paper. She took the paper off. The paper crackled.

"I think this is yours, Willis."

The .45 looked big and shiny under that old moon.

"You gonna use that on me, Lou?"

"If they'd found this on me when I crossed the border, Willis, I could have been arrested."

"I know that, honey. That whole thing was worrying me sick. How'd you get it across?"

"I did what most women do when they go into their nightbags and find a loaded pistol."

"What's that?"

"I hid it under my douche bag."

That done it. I walked over to her and took the .45 outa her hand and laid it down careful and I throwed my arms tight around her and kissed her all over the top of that little head. Her body felt like a tight, little bundle, and that tight, little bundle was trembly, and I could feel the wet on my arms.

"I'm sorry, Lou. You don't know how sorry I am."

She pulled her head out from my arms. She looked up at me. I seen the moon in both of her eyes, two little white balls, and it looked like there was about a half dozen other things in there too—some sad, some scared, some mad, some tired, some a-wondering...And what else? I wasn't sure.

I cupped her chin in my hand. "None of 'em died up there, honey. You heard that, didn't you? Not-a one."

"That was luck, Willis. That's all that was."

"Joe says it was the Good Lord that had His arm around our necks."

"I doubt that, Willis."

"Look, Lou. That whole thing in Toronto, I just got reckless. Same old story. I ain't a bad man, you know that. I just wanted something bad. I wanted it so bad I didn't think it all through. I just gotta learn how to rein that old horse in that wants to get there, that wants to get there right now."

"That's what you've learned?"

"What I learned is, I ain't got much of a life if you ain't in it, Louise. You coming back to me, ain't you? I hope that's why I'm here."

She didn't say nothing right off. Then she looked away.

I pulled her chin back, gentle-like, so she was looking at me again. "I want you back, Lou. You coming back to me?"

Now there was tears spilling outa her eyes, and them two moons was sliding all over. "I've thought about it a lot, and I've decided there aren't any 'whys' to love, Willis. It just is. It just is, and that's it. But there's also lines a person can cross, and lines a person can't cross."

"No more crossing, honey."

"You promise me that?"

"Look, Lou..." My mouth was dry. "I only got one more job left. I ain't gonna give you the details, but it's a diff'rent thing. It's at night, no shooting. It's more a nerve deal. I been studying this thing for months to make sure I get it right. And it's gonna be the last one. The last job. That'll be it."

She didn't say nothing. I seen her jaw tighten up.

"I gotta do it, Lou. I can't back out now, that'd be worse. But I got something to show you I ain't blowing bubbles this time, that things 'r gonna be diff'rent after this."

I reached down and picked up a brown package I had with me. "Take this home. Count it out where nobody can see you. Then rent you a safe deposit box. I want you to know I'm serious, Lou. Think of this as a down payment on a new life—a house, a oil lease, whatever you want."

"How much is it?"

"$20,000."

"Is there any possibility I'll need this to bury you, Willis?"

"You ain't gonna be burying nothing but the hatchet, honey."

THIRTY-FOUR

We knowed all the numbers and the names and the places and the times.

We knowed 'em all by heart.

The train was the No. 57, Chicago Milwaukee & St. Paul Railway. It was due to leave Union Station at 9:10 p.m. It was a short train, only ten cars: two express and eight mail coaches. Like a weasel without a tail. But being short helped make it fast. Hell, it was the second fastest train in the country. Blowed down them tracks at sixty miles a hour.

The car we was gonna hit was the second one behind the engine. That was the one that carried all the registered mail. But it was gonna be the toughest one to crack. There'd be seventeen postal clerks inside it. And a boxful of pistols right in there with 'em. 'Course the pistols was only there "just in case." Nobody'd ever tried to rob that train before.

Who in the hell'd have guts enough to try to hold up a train with seventeen armed clerks? In the middle of the night?

Going outa Chicago, the clerks inside that car would be busy sorting mail and yapping to each other. All around 'em would be seventy big leather bags, and most of them bags'd be filled with special delivery mail, registered mail, greenbacks in diff'rent denominations, stocks and bonds. A few of 'em would be filled with jewelry heading to shopkeepers—gold pocketwatches and rings and loose diamonds and such like.

We knowed all this from our inside man.

At 7:30 on the night of June 12, 1924, our inside man was at home having dinner and drinking gin martinis with his wife and three friends.

***

260

At 7:30 on the night of June 12, 1924, I was asleep. I'd took a nap.

Jess had to wake me up.

The other boys had already left for where they needed to go, so me and Jess hit over to the railroad yards.

Nobody looking at the two of us woulda ever thought we was robbers getting ready to hold up that No. 57. We looked exactly like the other railroad workers wandering around that station. We was wearing dirty blue coveralls, and brown caps with visors, and big heavy work boots.

We kept on walking 'til we come to the blinds, right between the coal tender and that first express car. Five or six dirty hobos was standing on the little platform, waiting for the train to take off.

"C'mon, you bums, beat it! We're the laws!" I kicked one of 'em in the shin with my work boot and it was like I'd throwed a flash-light on a bunch of cockroaches. They all went a-hopping, in ever' direction.

I looked at Jess and laughed.

We reached up and grabbed onto one of them metal bars that's hooked onto the coal tender and we pulled ourselves up onto the blinds, taking the place of them hobos. We leaned ourselves up agin the cold steel of the mail car and waited for the engineer to blast the high-ball.

I looked at my pocket watch. It said 9:06.

The high-ball come a coupla minutes later.

TOOOOOOOT! TOOOOOOOOOT!

The couplings started rattling. The cars begun to shake. The train started hissing steam and puffing out clouds of smoke.

Before long, we was moving outa the station. The train rattled along pretty slow for a while, 'til it got outa the downtown part of Chicago. Then, when the tracks lined up straight as rulers, it started speeding up. I was used to riding trains on the blinds. Still, it was rough going.

The cars went bumpety-bump, clackety-clack over the joints of the track, and when them cars went bumpety-bump, so did me and Jess.

We held on best we could.

Before long, we'd hit the country, and it was pitch-black. Dark as the devil. There wasn't no lights on the coal tender in the front of us. There wasn't no lights on the car in the back of us. We couldn't see a thing. But in my mind, I was seeing things. I was going over and over what we was gonna do, and how we was gonna do it.

I didn't see how nothing could go wrong.

***

Joe, and Dock, and Glasscock was gonna be waiting for the train at the Buckley Road Crossing, out of sight. It'd be dark as pitch there.

They was gonna have driven there in two Cadillacs. We knowed we was gonna need big cars to load all them the mail bags in, and so one day we went up and down a bunch of streets in a rich section of Chicago 'til we found the Cadillacs. We hooked chains to 'em and towed 'em off to where we had rented some garages.

The boys was gonna park the cars about a hundred yards from the tracks.

When me and Jess got the train stopped, Joe and Glasscock'd be on the left side, ready to help me get in the main mail car. Dock'd be on the far side, making sure nobody come out a door. Later, when we was taking bags off the trains, Dock was supposed to go get the Cadillacs and bring 'em up to where the train was stopped.

My brothers was gonna be armed with pistols, like all of us was. But they was also gonna be carrying what we was gonna need to deal with them seventeen armed clerks—gas masks and quart bottles of a poison gas called formaldehyde. All that stink'd get them clerks outa that mail car easy as snap. And just in case it didn't, my brothers was gonna have a little bottle of nitro to blow off the damn door.

***

About forty minutes after me and Jess last seen the lights of Chicago, the train's whistle blowed—loud and clear and pretty. It was the signal we was coming up on Rondout, that little town a coupla miles before the Buckley Road Crossing.

Me and Jess give each other looks.

Both of us hooked our hands onto the bars of the coal car. We was a-rattling and a-shaking as hard as that train, but we took it a inch at a time, and we cooned our way up—one inch, one inch, one inch—onto the top of the tender.

It was ever'thing we could do to keep our balance. Damn, that train was fast! Once we got on top, we crouched down on our hands and knees, on all that bumpy black coal, and crawled like tomcats. Our hind-ends was sticking up in the air, and they was a-shaking and a-swaying.

We couldn't see much of nothing around us, in front of us, behind us, but black.

Down below, the wheels was going clackety-clack, clackety-clack.

When we come closer to the engine I give Jess a signal to duck down, and I peeped over the rim into the cab. And there they was, calm as they could be, not a care in the world! The engineer was setting in his chair, his long legs stuck out in front, watching the track. One hand on the throttle. One hand eating a apple. The fireman was shoveling coal into the firebox, slow and easy, stopping ever' so often to look at it. I could see them coals a-glowing in that fire-box, red, red, red.

I looked at Jess. He looked back at me.

I give him a nod.

***

When you're blowing a bank, the thing that sets it off is when you put the match to the string. This time, what set ever'thing off was that nod. It was a one-inch nod, I'd say. My chin went down one inch, it come up one inch, and that was it. That was it. Just a little nod. But that little nod's what set off the biggest train robbery in the whole history of the United States of America!

Me and Jess hopped down into the engine.

"Okay, men! It's a stickup!"

We hollered it at the same tme.

Both their heads come spinning around, the engineer's and the fireman's. And their eyes throwed right into the muzzle of our .45s. The fireman let out a yelp and dropped his shovel and throwed up his hands. And the engineer throwed up his hands too and started a-hollering: "Don't shoot! Don't shoot!"

"Get back on that throttle!" I told the engineer.

He was so boogered he couldn't move. He was froze stiff, hands in the air.

"You hear me?" I hollered. "Get your hands on the trottle! I want you to stop this thing on the two-mile crossing."

263

"Don't hurt me! Don't shoot! Don't shoot!" His hands was still in the air.

Crazy engineer! I pushed my gun in my pocket and grabbed his hands and I pulled 'em down and set 'em on the throttle.

"Get it stopped, mister! I want the first express car right on the crossing."

His hands was on the throttle now, but they was still froze. Not moving. And I could see through the window the headlights of the train cutting into the dark. And now they was hitting the crossbars of the Buckley Road Crossing.

"Jerk it!" I yelled.

Finally, he come unfroze. He shoved the throttle in and throwed the air brake under it. There come a great blast of steam and a grinding of wheels and a banging of couplings. The train lunged and jerked and jolted. But shit! When it finally come to a dead stop, we'd went way too far. We was at least three car lengths past the Crossing.

"Goddammit! Back her up!"

"A train ain't easy to stop, mister." He pulled on the throttle to back up. There was a crashing of couplings down the cars and the train lunged backwards. It jerked and it lurched, and it stopped and started, about five times over before it made it to the right spot.

I turned to Jess. He still had his gun on the fireman. Both of 'em looked scared, the fireman *and* Jess. The fireman was shaking and telling Jess, "Mister, don't point that gun right at me. I'm scared to death!" And Jess was saying back, "Byyyyyy God, you ain't scared no worse'n I am!"

It was hard to believe it, after all the jobs I'd pulled with Jess, that he'd be boogered like he was. But he was. I kept my gun on the engineer but I throwed my other arm around Jess' shoulder.

"Tell 'em a couple of windies. Gimme ten minutes. Then bring 'em down."

"Got 'em covered." His voice was trembly.

With that, I turned around and climbed down the metal ladder that went eight feet down to the ground. I hopped the last three feet and headed down the line. It was so dark I couldn't see yet whether the other boys was there or not.

***

It wasn't 'til the next day, when I read it in the papers, that I learned what was happening in the armored mail car when the train jolted to a stop. All the clerks was puzzled. Why was the train stopping in the middle of nowhere? Only a hour outa Chicago?

"Something's wrong," the chief clerk said. "Maybe we hit a cow." About the last thing on his mind was a holdup. Who'd be crazy enough to try to hold up No. 57?

"You want us to get out the guns?" one of the other clerks asked him.

The chief clerk laughed. "Not unless you wanta shoot a dead cow." Then, when the train started backing up, he quit his laughing. "Holy Jesus. We really musta hit something."

***

I was heading quick down the line to find the boys. I hoped like hell they was there and doing their job. It was too dark for me to see much, so I still hadn't seen none of 'em, or the Cadillacs either.

I kept on and before long I seen a dark shadow crouching up close to the second mail car. I knowed it had to be one of us. I was walking as light on my feet as I could, but the shadow heard my boots on that rocky roadbed.

It spun around, gun out. It was Joe. When he seen that the noise was me, he motioned me on.

In a few seconds, Glasscock showed up from behind. He'd come from the other side, between two cars.

My mind was so much on one thing I didn't give him a second look. If I had, I mighta seen he was looking strange. I shoulda heard it in his voice. I shoulda knowed that something was wrong. Only I didn't. My mind was so much on one thing.

"Where's Dock?"

"Other side, I guess. He knows what to do."

"So far so good." I whispered loud enough so both Joe and Glasscock could hear me. "Now we gotta get the bags. Glasscock, cover me. Joe, punch them windows in."

Joe went up to the armored car and hit the windows with the barrel of his shotgun. Smashed 'em right in. Glass went flying ever'where. I crawled up right below the broke window and shouted to 'em inside: "This is a holdup! I got twenty-five men with guns out here, all around this train! You ain't got a chance! Come on out! Hands up!"

Nobody answered.

I hollered again. "Come on out with your hands up! You don't do what I say, we're gonna blow you all to hell!"

Nothing.

I tried the door to the car and it was locked tight. Locked from the inside.

"Gimme the formaldehyde," I whispered to the boys. "Get your masks on."

We all quick put on our gas masks. They was from the World War. We'd bought 'em at a army surplus store. They made us look like some kinda animal with big round snouts. Joe handed me the bottles of formaldehyde and I throwed the first one, hard as I could, through the broke window. Then another, and another.

The car door flied open. Out come the clerks. Gasping. Choking. Struggling for breath. All pushing and shoving.

Their hands was up high in the air. All seventeen of 'em.

I trained my pistol on 'em. So did Joe and Glasscock.

"Which one of you's the chief clerk?" I asked.

A tall, skinny guy raised his hand, kinda slow-like.

I motioned to Joe, "Give him your mask." Joe pulled it off and give it to the clerk. I hopped up on the car. "Put it on," I said to the skinny old boy, "and get up here."

I kept a bead on him while he put on Joe's mask, and climbed on up. I was still wearing my mask. Inside, even with them masks, we could smell that gas stink. God, what a awful stink! But I didn't care because there they was!

Dozens and dozens of pretty, pretty mail skins!

"Alright," I said to the clerk. "All I want is the registered. But I want ever' damn sack of it. I know what's on here. You miss one...even one...I don't want to even think about it."

The fella begun digging through 'em, and tossing 'em in a pile. One by one, I checked the labels, and one by one, I throwed 'em out the door. One by one, THUD. A pretty, pretty THUD!

Soon there was a big pile of 'em. More'n sixty sacks. Ever'thing we wanted. "Good job." I stuck my pistol into the chief clerk's back. "Let's go." He hopped outa the car, I followed him, and we went up to where them other clerks was standing. Their hands was still up, and you never seen such looks. They had them round eyes and tight lips and some of 'em seemed like they wasn't even breathing. Yeah, most of 'em was scared to death. Like all they wanted was for us to

266

take them sacks and blow away. Like they'd be completely happy if only they was left with their lives.

"All right," I barked at 'em, "each one of you pick up two or three of them sacks."

Each one did.

"Now, march that-a-way." I waved with my pistol toward the road.

They marched in single file, each one carrying sacks. Joe was on one side carrying a sack. Glasscock was on the other side. I brung up the rear. It was a sight you can't hardly imagine unless you was there—a long line of mail clerks, carrying dozens of sacks of loot, for a short line of robbers.

I watched the backs of all them clerks, with them flapping sacks, and all I could think was:

How many millions? How many millions!

***

That's when things begun to go wrong.

When we got to the road, there wasn't no Cadillacs waiting. My stomach hopped back into my throat again. "Goddammit, where's Dock? He was gonna get the cars right here, this spot. Joe, you seen Dock?"

Joe shook his head.

"Hey, Dock," he called up the far side of the train. "You there, Dock?"

Wasn't no answer.

"Goddamn crazy Dock!" I couldn't believe he'd screw this one up. I knowed Dock didn't have good judgment, but I'd give him the easiest job in the whole deal. How hard was it to bring the cars to the road?

"Go find him, Joe!"

I watched Joe run down towards the end of the train and disappear around the caboose. I could hear him hollering on the other side, "Dock! Where the hell 'r you?"

I didn't hear no answer back.

"Dock! Where the hell 'r you?"

Nothing.

I seen the clerks looking at each other. Me and Glasscock kept our bead on 'em tight.

In the middle of all this, Jess had brung the engineer and the fire-man up to where the clerks was.

Then I heard it. Somebody way off, a-hollering: "Oh my God! Oh my God!"

Ten seconds later, Joe's shadow come whipping from around the caboose and running, helty-skelty. He was racing so fast and panting so hard I couldn't hardly make out what he was saying.

"It's Dock! It's Dock!"

In them two seconds, a thousand pictures run through my head...then Joe was up on me.

"He's shot! Dock's shot!"

"How the hell....?"

"He's hurt bad, Willis!"

"Where 'r the cars?"

"Up the road."

"Get 'em!"

I felt sick all over. There shouldna been no shooting. None a'tall! I left Glasscock to guard the clerks and me and Jess run back to where Dock was laying.

About mid-way up the line I seen a dark shape a-lying on the ground.

I run up to it.

"Aymmmmm......sho-ooooo.........awwwwwm......hur-rrrr...." He was moaning, moaning.

Godamight! Blood was spilling outa his mouth like a river. There was blood all over his face. Blood all over one of his shoulders. Blood all over his right hand.

Me and Jess crouched down.

I don't know how we done it, the two of us, Dock was so big, but we picked him up and carried him to the road. Blood was still spilling outa his mouth. There was near as much blood on me and Jess as on Dock.

We laid Dock on the ground by the side of the road. He was still moaning, moaning. I turned to the clerks. I was mad like I never been before in my life. I asked if any of 'em had shot Dock.

Nobody said a word.

"One more time! I'm gonna ask you all one more goddamn time! Who shot this man?"

Finally the chief clerk spoke up. "It weren't none of us. We all thought we heard something. Shots. Or something. Other side of the

268

car. Only the train was backing up. Couldn't tell if that's what it was, 'r what."

By this time Joe come up with one of the Cadillacs. We started throwing in as many sacks as we could. We pushed some of 'em down and around so they could be a soft bed for Dock; so we could lay him on 'em. While we was doing that, I seen how nervous Glasscock was. How he wouldn't look me in the eye.

"Lemme see your gun."

"What d'ya doing?" he said.

I grabbed it out of his hand. I opened the chamber. The stink went up my nose.

"You fire this thing?"

"So what?" he said. "Shot a Hoosier, coming at me with a gun."

"That wasn't no Hoosier, you goddamn, fool son-of-a-bitch!"

THIRTY-FIVE

That's when come the slide. That's what I call it, the slide.

It wasn't a slow slide. It wasn't a fast slide. It was both of 'em, fast and slow, both at the same time.

Ever'thing that happened after Dock got shot went by so fast and so slow, both, that when I think back on it, ever'thing's a blur, and ever'thing's burned in my mind, ever' detail. It's hard to tell it exact, how things can happen strange like that, but that's the way they was.

Right then, what was going fast in my head was what I was seeing, and what was going slow was what was in my ears. Godamight, the noises coming outa Dock, a-laying. Moaning, awful moaning. But the worst of it was how he was breathing. I never heard sounds like that before, other'n when I was hunting, and I'd shot something, and the animal didn't die right off.

Gasps and gurgles, gasps and gurgles. Horrible, horrible sounds.

Me and Joe and Jess picked him up, careful, like he was a fresh baby, and we laid him in the back of one of them Cadillacs, where we'd made that soft bed outa some of the mail sacks.

His blood was dripping down onto the leather.

We jumped in the cars and peeled out. Glasscock was driving the car with Dock, with me in the front seat and Joe in the back, taking care of Dock. Jess was driving the second car, behind us.

It was back country we was flying through, with a back-country road: dirt, ruts, humps, bumps. Our headlights was slicing into the black, but all you could see was more black, and dust. We hit a rut. Dock moaned. We hit a bump. Dock moaned louder. A little dark shadow was up ahead. It got bigger. Two eyes was glittering like diamonds. Coon. We was on it. Ker-plunk! We hit it. Dock cried out. One of the bags on one of the piles slid off onto the road.

We kept going.

It was damn odd, how ever'thing that happened right then was a blur in my head, and yet I can recollect ever' detail. Things was

270

going fast, and things was going slow, both at the same time. Now Dock's breathing was getting weird. Like it was getting stuck in his throat.

I reached over to him and run my fingers over his forehead.

"It ain't your time, Dock. Hang in there, old boy."

When I done that, his mouth fell open. Blood come glumping out.

That's when I seen that the bullet in his jaw had near sliced his tongue in half.

Goddammit! I'd planned the robbery foolproof. It seemed like no matter how hard I tried, there wasn't no way of getting rid of foolishness.

Joe was holding both of Dock's hands. We was heading toward our hideout, about a hundred miles southwest from Rondout, near the little town of Ottawa. We'd arranged for it weeks before. It was a old cotton gin that'd been turned into a paint factory. It belonged to a kin of Jimmy Murray's. It was big enough you could drive a car into it.

Glasscock wasn't looking right or left. His fingers was clenched onto that wheel like if he let go, the wind'd blow him clear outa the car. He was looking straight dead ahead. He didn't look at me once or say nothing. He knowed what I was thinking. He knowed it.

***

It took us seven hours to the hideout. Seven long, long, long hours.

Ever' twenty minutes or so, we'd stop and give Dock a break from all them bumps and humps. He was still awake, he hadn't passed out, but he seemed like he was just on the edge of it. We'd wrapped cloth over wherever we thought he'd been shot, it looked like five or six places, but it was so wet with blood it was like you'd drenched it in a river.

When we finally got to Ottawa, Murray was waiting for us in that big Peerless. I can still see that big fat white face getting outa that long car and coming towards us. He was wearing a black suit and in all that dark, it looked like just his head was bobbing towards us, all by itself, a big round moon without nothing holding it up.

"Did'ja get it?" That was his first question.

"We need a doctor!" I said. "Man's hurt here!"

Murray looked at Dock. His mouth dropped open. He hadn't seen Dock at first. And when he did, I guessed what was going through his mind. I was right. He shook his head. "Forget it. Chicago, maybe. But it's too risky."

"Nobody gets nothing if he dies, Murray!" I hollered. "We gotta get a doctor! Fast!"

"It'll blow up the deal."

"He needs a doctor!"

"Sorry."

A big hand come down and clamped down on Murray's shoulder.

It was Joe's hand.

"We're taking him to a doctor. That's it." Joe'd stuck his face right down in front of Murray's face. In fact, Joe's whole body was pulled up agin Murray. Joe'd filled out a lot since he first come to me. I never seen him look so big, or so solid. He looked like a mountain.

Murray didn't care. He craned his neck over to my ear and said low, "Dock isn't gonna make it that far, Willis." He was trying to sound sad. "I know you wanta save him. I wanta save him too." He shook his head. "It's too late."

I knowed Glasscock was thinking the same thing. Only he knowed better'n to say nothing. He just stood off from the rest of us, his cheeks sucked in.

I yanked the .38 outa my waist holster and punched it up agin Murray's nose. "You know the works in Chicago, Murray. Get him a doctor!"

With my other hand, I pulled a bunch of big bills outa my pocket—it was all old money—and I threwed it down on the running board of the Cadillac. "Here's two thousand. Use it for a doctor. You 'n Joe take him in. Ever'body'll get their share. You got my word."

Murray was still dragging his feet. "You gonna leave all that money here?"

"Get going!"

THIRTY-SIX

Our shadows was flickering and fluttering all over the inside walls of that big, hollow warehouse. My shadow, and Jess' shadow, and Glassock's shadow.

We'd set up oil lamps on two sides, and the lamps was kicking up black, fast shadows. You could see our knives in them shadows, they was long as swords, and you could see the shadows of our arms flying up and down, up and down—stabbing, stabbing, stabbing.

If you was just watching the shadows, you mighta thought we was stabbing somebody to death.

We wasn't. We was slicing open all them dozens of thick, leather bags, and pulling out all the loot.

The loot, my God, the loot! Piles and piles of it.

All over.

If Dock hadn't a-got shot, we'da all been whooping it up and dancing all around that loot, whooping and dancing all over that warehouse. I never seen so much loot in my life: Liberty Bonds, stacks and stacks of 'em. Greenbacks, stacks and stacks of 'em. Stock certificates, stacks and stacks of 'em. And bags. Bags filled with loose diamonds and rubies. Bags filled with gold chains. Bags filled with gold ring settings. Bags filled with silver coins.

We was millionaires!

Only nobody was dancing. Nobody was whooping.

All you could hear was the sound of leather ripping, and breathing. Ever' so often, Glasscock'd suck in a extra-big breath and start to open his mouth, like he was gonna say something. He never said nothing. Ever' time, he'd just let that breath out and close his mouth again. One time, he pulled out a little glass bottle from his pocket and swallowed some of his pills.

I could hardly stand to look at him. To be honest, there was part of me that wanted to do him like they do a hog at hog-killing time— throw down on him, hang him from a tree limb, chop off his snout

273

and his ears, drain out his blood, yank all his lousy guts out.

When Glasscock seen he shot Dock, did he just keep shooting so we wouldn't have to mess with a hurt man?

Or maybe did he shoot Dock on purpose?

One less man meant more loot to split.

***

If Dock'd died on our way to that warehouse, we woulda buried him and kept on going. But he didn't die. And I never one time, not one time, thought about letting him die to cut down on the risk of blowing up the job.

That thought just never come to me. Brothers do that for brothers.

When the Dalton gang pulled that two-bank job in Coffeyville, Kansas, back in eighteen and ninety-two, Emmett Dalton was galloping off, making a getaway, when he turned around and seen his brother Bob'd get shot offa his horse. Emmett didn't think twice. He wheeled around and charged right back through all them blazing guns.

There was only one thing I didn't like about that story. Bob Dalton died anyhow. And Emmett went down with twenty-one slugs of buckshot, and ended up in the penitentiary for fourteen years.

So I wasn't thinking about the end of it.

That picture of Dock all shot up kept blowing back into my head that whole time: while we was dividing up the loot into shares; while we was putting it in the Cadillacs and driving to a barn of somebody we knowed nearby; while we was pulling off ten bales of hay and digging a big hole and burying most of that loot; while we was back on them country roads driving in the general direction of Chicago; while we was turning off into a deserted field southwest of Joliet and shucking one of our cars and the empty pouches; while we was back on the roads to Chicago.

Was Glasscock just a idiot yeller-belly—or was he a murderer?

No sooner we hit Chicago, we could see the whole town was worked up over the train robbery. Newsboys was running all over the city shouting, "Read all about it! Read all about it! BIGGEST TRAIN ROBBERY EVER!" My stomach flied into my throat when I seen them newsboys running around waving them papers. Had they found Dock? Was they gonna say that one of the robbers was dead, and a search was on for the rest?

After we'd dropped the car at the garage, I told Jess and Glasscock to wait. Then I walked outa that garage like I was just a ordinary man. The first newsboy I seen, I walked over to him and give him a nickel. I sucked in a breath. I read it. Jesus Christ! We'd got $3 million! It wasn't eight, like Fahy'd said it might run to, but it was still a helluva lot. Yeah, three million dollars!

And the laws didn't have nobody.

The story said they'd only found a few clues—blood where one of the robbers had been shot, two gas masks, some broke formaldehyde bottles, a little bottle of nitro, and one mail sack that had dropped off the getaway car. The story said half the city's detectives was working on the case. Others was coming into Chicago from all over the country. The Chicago police chief told the reporters: "I assure you that we'll have the culprits within a few days."

I quick went back to the garage. I told Jess to find hisself a out-of-the-way hotel and to spend the night there and in the morning to catch a train to Texas. I told Glasscock he better get outa town too. I told 'em both to take some of the money: $35,000 for Jess; the same for Glasscock. I give 'em both the address and phone number for where I was gonna go: the apartment of one of Murray's friends.

"Call me right before you leave. Somebody else answers, not me, hang up."

***

"How's Dock?" First thing I asked Murray's pal.

"Not good."

"Murray get a doctor?"

"Yeah."

He wrote out the address where Dock was at on the back of a old envelope. Fifty-three North Washtenaw Avenue, I'll never forget it. It was the apartment of another one of Murray's boys, a booze-runner.

I didn't waste no time. I caught a cab to go there. I'd borrowed a Panama hat with a big wide brim and it was low over my face. I got outa the taxi about four blocks off from that address. No sooner I got out I tucked up in a alcove of a building. I wanted to see if any suspicious cars'd been trailing us. I didn't see none. I come outa the alcove and walked slow towards the apartment.

It was a two-story building, square brick, a lot of weeds poking up in front, paint peeling on the window shutters. Before I went in I walked past it for half a block. Then I turned and come back, looking in ever' direction to make sure nobody was behind me. I didn't see nobody.

I walked up some creaky steps to the second floor. I went to the apartment number, Number 5. What if Dock was dead in there? I sucked in some gulps of air. Ever'thing seemed like it was in a dream, or like it was happening to somebody else, not me. Not Dock. Not any of us.

I knocked on the door. It opened a crack.

"It's me, Willis. Lemme in."

The door swung wide open.

A dozen arms come out and grabbed me.

THIRTY-SEVEN

The Chicago police throwed me into a "death cell."

No windows. Nothing except plain cement walls. Nobody talks to you.

You're alone, a hundred percent alone, like you never been alone in your life.

They wanted me to spill the beans, give 'em the names of ever'-body that was in on the train job, and I wasn't gonna do it. No matter what they done to me, I wasn't gonna snitch. That was one of my rules. And I had a few of 'em—no drinking, no whoring, no killing, no lying to people you did business with. And no snitching. The only way I mighta talked was if I thought it was gonna help Dock in some way. But I knowed the less I talked, the more they was gonna wanta keep Dock alive. If Dock *was* alive. I didn't know.

And so they throwed me in solitary, in a little cell in the town of Rockford on the outskirts of Chicago.

Well, you ever seen a field rat, or even a field rabbit, after it's been caught and penned up in a little cage? Most of 'em 'll run round and round that cage like crazy, trying to find a way to break out, and when that don't work, if it's a wood cage, they'll gnaw and gnaw that wood 'til their teeth wear down or break off. After that happens they'll crawl off into a corner and they'll just lay there like that, their eyes all kind of glassy, like the eyes of the crazy man, 'til they die.

I wasn't a rat. I was a man. Only I was caged up like a rat. And the first few days I was in that cell, I went round and round that cage like crazy, too, trying to figure a way to break out. Only it was my thoughts, more'n my feet, that was going around, going over what'd gone wrong, and how I could turn it all around before the teeth in my mind broke off, and my eyes got glassy...

***

277

For the first few weeks in that death cell, ever'thing that went through my mind was clear. And I kept thinking about how things'd went down. The Chicago police grabbing me through the door of that apartment. Cuffing me. Throwing me into a chair. Hollering at me to "Start talking."

Me looking all around for Dock. But no Dock. No Joe. No Murray.

Nobody but them big, hollering laws.

Though a open door, I could see into the next room. I seen a messed-up bed with dark spots on the sheets. But I couldn't tell if they was shadows, or stains of blood. I'd told the laws that I was a oil man from Texas that'd come there looking to buy me some beer, and that my name was James H. Watson. "Yeah," they'd said, "well, you was 'Willis' when you knocked on the door."

They'd knowed I was lying. But I knowed the Chicago police was the crookedest in the world. I'd told 'em I'd give 'em $20,000 if they'd give me the air, and they acted like they was going along with it. Was they playing me for a sucker? I didn't know, but I'd got 'em to let me call Louise.

Her voice'd went low. She'd knowed something was up, but she hadn't asked me no questions. She'd quick got on the train and brung that money from New London—the $20,000 I give her as a down payment on the future—and we'd all met her at the depot. She didn't ask me no questions, just handed me a brown package. I'd handed the package to the dicks and took her arm and started to walk off.

That's when a gnarly old hand'd come down on my shoulder.

It was Captain William Schoemaker, the new chief of the Chicago police detectives. Sharp little nose, watery eyes. He'd showed up from God knows where.

The last I seen of Louise, she was like in shock, holding her handkerchief to her mouth.

They'd took me straight to their station downtown, and that's when they let it out they'd got Joe and Dock too. They wouldn't tell me who'd tipped 'em off to Dock being in that apartment on Washtenaw, only that it was a "informant."

I'd strung 'em a line; told 'em my partners was two St. Louis mobsters named Blackie Wilcox and Sam Grant.

But they'd figured out—soon enough—I was lying.

And none of us three—Joe or Dock or me—was talking.

The Chicago laws'd thought Joe'd give in the easiest, being he

William Schoemaker, chief of Chicago detectives.

was the youngest. When he didn't say nothing, they'd beat him black and blue. Broke his nose and put lumps on his face and head. They walked me past the room he was in. They was still working on him. I seen the marks all over his face, and blood pouring outa his nose. And Captain Schoemaker was acting like he was gonna poke Joe's eyes out with his two long fingers.

Joe still wasn't talking.

They wouldn't tell me much about Dock, only that he'd been took to the Cook County hospital. I didn't think he was gonna talk either, no matter how bad off he was. Still, that Schoemaker'd wanted to make me sweat. He'd put his mouth close up agin my ear: "Most men crack when they're about to make the acquaintance of Saint Peter at the pearly gates."

It didn't do no good.

Oh, did they want me to talk! They didn't beat me up, like they did Joe, but they done ever'thing else—they'd shouted at me, and shook their fists, and Schoemaker'd kept sticking that needle nose in my face. So close I could smell his breakfast, or his supper, or his dinner, or his coffee. Said he was gonna send me and ever'body else that was in on the robbery up for twenty-five years. Or maybe more, if they could stack up a bunch of counts.

It hadn't done no good.

Finally, they'd throwed me in that death cell.

There wasn't no bed, no chairs, no nothing. There was a drain in the floor for pissing, and in one corner, a "sugar pot" for the other. They handed you your food, or what they called food, through a trap window but they didn't give you no fork or knife or even a spoon. They didn't want you to have nothing you could stab a guard with, or yourself, if you went crazy. You ate with your fingers, and at night, when you was sleeping on the floor, you could feel the cockroaches crawling all over you to get at whatever was left on your fingers—crumbs, juice, mush.

Like I said, all you can do when you're ain't sleeping is pace round and round and round and round, like them trapped rats and rabbits, 'til you feel you're going crazy, 'cause no matter how many times you go round and round and round, you're not really going nowhere. There's nowhere to go.

I didn't have no money. No diamond rings or stickpins, to bribe a guard. And even if I had some, it likely wouldn't have worked. Not this time. It had to be another way.

The only way outa that hell-hole was in my head, but after a while, after nobody was talking to me no more, or even asking me if I was ready to talk, after the days slid into weeks, it was all I could do to keep my thoughts from getting all scrambled up and tossed around in ways that didn't make no sense at all....

***

You see people you know—Ma, Pa, Jess, Dock, Joe, Louise— and they're all standing in some room, and that room looks like you been there before, but you don't know where it is...and all the people you know 'r talking to each other, but the things that's coming outa their mouths don't sound like human words, it's more like a bunch of mockingbirds a-chattering...

...*tck, tck, tck...achaw, achaw, achaw...*

I'm standing in the middle of 'em, and I'm telling 'em I'm gonna escape, just like I done offa Pa's cotton patch back in Rising Star, and just like I done offa the prison farm at Imperial, but now they ain't mockingbirds no more, 'cause they all got their heads thrown back and they're laughing like they're about to choke.

"Ain't no way out this time, old boy," they're saying.

I walk from side to side of that cell, like I'm in a cage, only there ain't no wires for me to look through to the outside, not even one hole. Just cement walls. I walk right to the left, left to the right, up and down, down and up. I wanta get the kinks outa my legs and pump the blood up into my head to figure things out...but ever'where I look there's only a cement wall.

Pork-fat hash....

Pork-fat hash, that's what's on the plate that gets slipped through the slit into my death cell. Brown and lumpy. Like dung. And some peas. I count ever' pea on my plate—one pea, two pea, three pea, four pea, five pea, six pea, seven pea, eight pea, nine pea, ten pea, eleven pea, twelve pea, thirteen pea. That's all. Thirteen peas.

All a sudden, the devil shows up in my cell, and he's crooking his finger at me and he's laughing too, and for a few minutes it's like I'm the one—not Dock—that's got them five bullet holes...the pain's like to kill me...like it's my tongue that's near shot in half, and when I wipe my mouth, I'm ready to see it's blood that's making it wet, not spit. I'm ready for seeing red blood, I'm all tensed up for it. But what's there is just plain old yeller spit.

I recollect it's Glasscock's the one that caused it all. Glasscock, with them sucked-in cheeks that's yeller too.

My mind snaps back. The devil ain't in my cell no more. It ain't nobody in this death cell. There's nobody else, nobody, nobody, not a single person to talk to, and not even one piece of light to hold onto.

I hold onto myself. I push one of my fingers down between my two other fingers, into that smooth place where the fingers come together, and I run my first finger around there and feel it, the curves. Louise comes to me, and how soft she is, and she's let her hair down, how ever' bit of her is soft, and I got my hands around her waist...

Could I blast outa this cell?

Maybe I can steal some soap outa the bath they give me one time a week, rim the walls of the cell, take the grease outa that pork-fat hash and make a fuse out of a strip of my hair and scratch a fingernail, and light her up, and there she blows!!!

No, no...that's all a dream—and I ain't smelling perfume, it's stink!

Nothing will work.

For the first time in my life I don't have no plan.

THIRTY-EIGHT

Weeks pass by into months.

All the alias names I ever used in my life run through my mind, round and round—R.E. Baker and James H. Watson and Will Reed and W.L. Malley and Luther Chriss and Henry Hermann and all the rest of 'em—so many times I almost don't know what my real name is.

It's five months before somebody opens the door to my cell and calls me by my rightful name, "J. Willis Newton."

Lucky for me, it ain't that old son-of-a-bitch Schoemaker. It's one of the top U.S. postal inspectors from Washington D.C., a fella named K.P. Aldrich. He's one of them men where what you notice first and last about 'em is their eyes. Aldrich has what I call "straight eyes." Nothing shifty about 'em.

He brings two chairs into the cell and says he wants to talk.

"I hear you're from Texas, Mister Newton," is the first thing he says to me. "I'm a Texas boy myself."

"Where'bouts?"

"Austin."

"Nice town, Austin."

"Yes it is." Then he cuts the politeness.

First off, he tells me that the laws'd took Schoemaker off the case. Aldrich is the head man, now. Then he gives me information. Like who tipped off the Chicago laws to that apartment on North Washtenaw Avenue where they took Dock to that crook doctor. Damned if it wasn't that doughy-faced Irish gangster with the gimpy leg, that Deany O'Banion! Seems the doctor that treated Dock had ties to O'Banion, and the doctor told O'Banion that Dock was one of the Texas cowboys that'd robbed the Rondout train.

And O'Banion tipped off the laws.

I dunno exactly how I feel when I hear all that. Part of me's hot as a hornet, another part's kinda pumped up. It's kinda like if you was a politician in the capitol of the United States of America and somehow you got President Calvin Coolidge jealous of you. O'Banion was one of the biggest gangsters ever in the history of this country, and there he was, jealous of a bunch of farm boys!

'Course, what I really want to know from Aldrich is about Dock. I'm scared to ask it, but I ask it anyhow. "You ain't said nothing about my brother, Dock, Mister Aldrich."

Aldrich reaches over and puts his hand on my shoulder. He looks me in the eye. "Willis, you country folk have thick hides. Your brother Dock had a tough time of it, but he's mending."

Lemme tell you what: When Aldrich says that, when he says my brother is still alive, it's like something runs right through my body, from my toes to my neck, and unties ever' one of my muscles. Yeah, that's when I find out what I been waiting all these five months to know: Dock's alive.

I feel like I could float up to the moon.

Only life's funny like this: When a man's got a big worry, and that worry winks itself out, whatever other worries he's got tucked up under that big worry puff theirselves up to fill the empty space that's left. Them other worries may not be big as that biggest one, but they sure can feel that way. I want to know about Joe, and if they've got Jess, and how about the other ones?

Aldrich leans back in his chair and smiles slow like he's got a story to tell.

And he does.

"I'm sure you know this, Willis, that your brother Jess is a good bronc-buster but a bad drunk. The key to my business is the same as the key to yours—know your opponent's strengths, know their weaknesses. We tracked Jess down in Villa Acuna, right across the border. Couldn't arrest him, of course, because there aren't any extradition laws. But a couple of our boys start hanging out at one of your brother's favorite tequila bars. Tell him they're rich ranchers, want to buy him a bottle. And then they tell him about a bronc called Cyclone that's supposed to be in a rodeo over on the Texas side. Tell him Cyclone's already throwed forty riders. Nobody can ride him. They bet Jess fifty dollars he can't ride Cyclone either." Aldrich can't help but smile. And it's a straight smile, to go with them straight eyes. You can tell a real smile 'cause the skin around the eyes crinkles. "You think you know the end to this story, Willis?"

I don't know whether to cry, or laugh.

Case No. 65184-D   **Post Office Department**   Chicago Division

OFFICE OF INSPECTOR IN CHARGE
CHICAGO, ILLINOIS

$2,000 REWARD!

The Post Office Department of the United States will pay a reward not exceeding Two Thousand Dollars ($2,000.00) for the arrest and conviction of BRENT GLASSCOCK, alias C. P. Reese, who is wanted for his participation in the hold-up and robbery of Chicago, Milwaukee & St. Paul Train 57, near Rondout, Illinois, the night of June 12, 1924, in violation of Section 197, of the United States Penal Code.

SHOULD THIS OFFENDER BE KILLED WHILE RESISTING LAWFUL ARREST THE SAME REWARD MAY BE PAID AS THOUGH HE HAD BEEN TRIED AND CONVICTED.

Below are the latest pictures and descriptions available of Glasscock and his wife, Avis Glasscock:

(Taken in 1913)

(Taken in 1923)

(Taken in 1918)

(Taken in 1917)

72021

Ans Reese.

(Signature of Woman)

C. P. Reese

(Signature of Man)

DESCRIPTION OF WOMAN: Age, about 31 years; height, 5 feet 9 or 10 inches; weight, 120 pounds; very slender build; eyes, blue gray; hair, light blonde, and bobbed; rather prominent nose; wears large rimmed eye-glasses; complexion very light; neat dresser, sometimes wears "knickers" while traveling by auto; trained nurse and wears a nurse's button.

DESCRIPTION OF MAN: Age, about 40 years; height, 5 feet 10 inches; weight, about 150 pounds; build, medium; hair, dark chestnut, turning gray; eyes, slate blue; neat dresser; nervous temperament; quick movements.

Finger print classification: $\frac{11 \ R \ O \ 19}{26 \ R \ O}$

The known aliases of this man are: Claude Glasscock, Fred Glasscock, John Glasscock, H. Glasscock, John Brent, A. M. Graham, Claude Graham, "Little Mizzou," John Morrison, Claude P. Reese, Claude Staubus, Claude Russell, and Claude White.

The wife has used the above surnames, but has always used "AVIS" as her first name.

Glasscock is an ex-convict and is one of the most notorious bank burglars in the United States, and Canada. He and his wife usually stop at high class furnished apartments or private residences when in a city, and Glasscock, particularly, avoids hotels as far as possible. When traveling, they are said to frequent tourist camps. They have traveled in a Studebaker Special Six touring car, but when last seen had a new Packard Coupe. This car is a Standard Single Six, 1924 Model, with dark blue body, yellow wire wheels, and fender guards in rear, which are connected with nickel-plated bars. Motor No. 40755, and had Illinois License No. 571-302 issued to A. M. Graham.

This man is very fond of hunting and outdoor life. He has stomach trouble and is very careful of his diet.

Glasscock is wanted for many criminal offenses, is considered dangerous and officers and others should be governed accordingly. He is under indictment for the above offense and if located cause his immediate arrest and notify the undersigned by telegraph, government rate collect, or by telephone. If the woman is located, she should not be arrested, but this office should be immediately notified by telegraph or telephone.

A. E. GERMER,
Post Office Inspector in Charge,
CHICAGO, ILLINOIS.

Telephone: Harrison 4700; Local 100.
September 30, 1924.   Chicago P O—Job 9-24—9 27-24 Blue Emergency

I laugh.

Why not?

Then Alridge tells me more. That they've got all the rest of us, too. Glasscock was in a sanitarium in Michigan, getting treated for his stomach troubles, and some little boy that lived nearby recognized him from his "Wanted" poster that was tacked up in the post office. The boy tipped off the laws. It was a gangster moll that turned in Fahy. He'd been messing around with her, and talking too much, and drinking too much. This time, all that "too much" did him in.

Then Aldrich leans forward in his chair.

Way, *way* forward.

"Willis, the insurance companies are real anxious to get their money back, and if we can get it back for them, I think the government will be inclined to make some kind of a deal with all of you. You and your brothers."

"What kind of deal?"

"You don't work with us, it's twenty-five years flat. Maybe a lot more. There's more than one count against you. If they stack 'em up, rest of your life is pretty well eaten up. But I think I can promise you no more than twelve. Maybe less."

"What are the odds it'll be less?"

"Not good. But you go in for twelve, you can be out in four to six. Get a good book to read, you won't notice it."

"Joint boys don't like rats," I say.

"You'll be protected."

I don't say nothing else right off. Aldrich looks and talks like he's a honest man, but I know the laws good enough to never let my guard down all the way. And there's one other problem. I only know where part of the money is. Glasscock's took most of it. If I talk, I gotta get him to talk, too.

"You give me your word you're playing it straight with me, Aldrich?"

"I never say I'm an honest man, Willis, 'cause the ones who have to say it are usually the ones who don't play it. But yes, I am. Fact is, I'm the kind who believes a man ought to tell the truth because a man ought to tell the truth—even if it doesn't get him something."

"But if I talk, it'll get us something."

"It will."

"Gimme some time to think it over."

Aldrich then does something for me I ain't expecting. He says he's arranged it so Louise can visit me. I haven't seen her, or heard from her since the night she brung that $20,000 dollars, and Schoemaker took the money and me to jail. Aldrich says he's fixed it so I can talk to her away from my cell, in a little room where we can sit across the counter from each other. There'll be two guards there.

I don't know what to expect—whether she's even said she'll see me—but when Aldrich tells me she's coming, I'm more excited than I been in a long, long time. Nervous as hell, too. If it looks like they're gonna send me to prison for a long time, maybe she's gonna tell me ever'thing is now over between me and her.

***

She come in a simple white dress. No jewelry.
"Louise...How you been doin', honey?"
She doesn't say nothing. I see a tear creep down her face.
"How's Lewis?" I ask.
"He's okay."
We only got ten minutes to talk. I know I gotta get quick to the point. But she gets there before I do. She sucks in a big breath. She leans towards me on the counter, far as she can get.
"They say there're five counts against you, and they could add up to a hundred and sixty years if you don't make a deal."
I nod, but I think: did Aldrich arrange for Louise to talk to me to get what he wants? And if he gets what he wants, is he gonna do a double-cross?
"He told me that."
"Willis, you might never get out."
"You know, Lou. I got some rules. I don't rat."
Louise looks down. She's scraping the skin around her thumbs. It's red and raw. She looks up again.
"Are you saying it's a matter of honor with you?"
I sneak a peek over at the guards. I don't answer right off.
"Willis, don't fool yourself. There's no honor in any of this."
I remember her saying that. I remember the way she says it, and the way she looks me hard in the eye when she says it. Louise is a good woman. But she hasn't lived my life. I have.
Then I wink at her. And damn if she don't wink back.

287

One of the guards is looking at his watch. There's one more question I gotta ask Louise and I know I gotta do it quick. Even with that wink from her, my heart starts thumping. Hard, hard agin my chest. I feel kinda like how I did at Toronto, the time after that mess with them bank messengers, when I was about to tell Louise that me and the boys had shot a few of 'em.

"Will you wait for me, Lou?"

"Do you think I should?"

"I want you to. There wouldn't be no life left in me if you wasn't there."

"How long do you think I should wait?"

"I can't answer that one, honey."

"I'll wait for you, Willis. But not for a hundred and sixty years."

THIRTY-NINE

The federals give me a front row seat for the trial.

They'd dressed me in a brand-new citizen's suit, a gray worsted, and a good haircut, slick on top. I think I looked sharp.

'Course, they had a armed guard on the left of me, and a armed guard on the right of me.

They looked sharp, too. The handles on their .45s was polished to a shine.

I'll tell you what, that federal courtroom was stuffed with people wanting to watch ever'thing—just stacks of 'em, stacks and stacks of 'em! And there was newspaper men from as far off as New York City, flashing them big camera bulbs that like to blind you, and scribbling on little pads of papers.

Well, hell, the Newton Boys'd pulled off the biggest train robbery in the history of the United States of these Americas, and ever'-body was all worked up over it, and they shoulda been!

Ever' day when I walked in, and even after I set down, the reporters was throwing me questions.

"What were Texans doing in gangster territory?"

"Who was the brains?"

"What about the man who shot your brother?"

"You worried about the death threats?"

If it'd a been up to me, I'da answered ever' one of them questions. But the feds told me not even to look at 'em.

***

What brought about the trial was this: I talked.

Only I talked with honor.

I didn't hurt nobody that didn't deserve it.

I'd told Aldrich if he'd give me his word on that deal, me and my brothers'd spill the beans, tell him what we knowed. Of course, it was Glasscock that knowed where most of the money was. But they offered him a deal, too, and they put me in a room with him, and he'd blabbed his guts out.

He'd led the feds to where he'd buried more'n a million dollars.

There was only one problem left. And it was a helluva problem. Glasscock had already give $500,000 to that fat old louse Murray and that old jug-headed Fahy, and they was still playing like they was innocent. And the federals didn't have much of a sense of humor about all that. They wanted that money back.

So they wanted ever'body else on my team to get up and finger them old boys.

It was gonna be our word agin theirs. And the judge said he wasn't gonna give me and my brothers our sentences 'til the trial was over.

Was it all one, big double-cross?

It's a fact we'd made that deal with Aldrich, but I knowed from past years that life is always throwing surprises at you, and there's just as likely to be bad ones as good ones. And Fahy's lawyer was telling the newspapers that he was gonna "spring a big surprise."

***

Jimmy Murray was setting at one table with his lawyers, but trying to fit somebody that big into a little old gov'ment chair with wood side-arms was like trying to squeeze a black bear into a egg crate. He didn't seem to be sweating no weight off with worry. He looked calm as could be, like all he wanted to do was take a nap.

I didn't like that.

Maybe with them political connections of his, he'd made some kind of a secret deal.

Fahy was setting at another table. He was skinny as Murray was fat, so he fit perfect in his chair. But he was setting bolt upright. He looked as much on edge as Murray was about to go to sleep. And his jug ears was working so hard to hear ever'thing that was going on around him that it looked like they was flapping. He was taking all kinds of notes on a little yellow pad.

I didn't like how he was looking, either. A sneaky desperate man'll say anything to save his skin.

If you was to look at it one way, that trial was like one of them circuses they call "The Greatest Show on Earth." Murray was like a big, old lazy bear about to clomp around the ring, and Fahy was like the jittery little clown about to get shot outa a canon. And us Newtons?

Well, we was Texans.

Fact is, I think the crowd was more curious about us Newton boys than they was about Murray and Fahy. Who the hell was we?

Cowboys? Rubes? Rebel boys?

Ever'body looked like they was more'n ready for the show. If the judge had let 'em bring in peanuts and sodeys, I believe they woulda done it. 'Course, there was one sign this wasn't no circus. Ever' person was getting frisked for hid guns.

Two days before the trial begun, see, that gangster Deany O'Banion—the one that snitched us out—had got hisself murdered. He was in his flower shop, trimming the tips offa some yellow mums, when three men come up to him and acted like they was friends and wanted to shake his hand. His body fell into a case of them pretty, long-stem American Beauty roses.

It wasn't none of my team that'd ordered the hit. We was in the pen. But some of O'Banion's gang thought he'd got rubbed out by somebody connected with us, and they was vowing revenge. The judge was worried that the show might turn bloody. Me and my brothers'd been getting death threats.

***

By rights, I'm the one that shoulda been the biggest witness. I was the one, after all, that'd done most of the plotting with Murray and Fahy, and I was the only one that'd met Fahy face to face.

But the federals said they didn't wanta call me up because I'd strung 'em that line when I first got nabbed, that "Sam Grant" and "Blackie Wilcox" was my partners. And being that the newspapers had printed all that hoo-ey, they said I'd been branded a public liar.

Well, did that burn me up! I had plenty I wanted to say! But all I could do through the rest of the trial was sit there like a muzzled dog.

And hold my breath.

It started out slow and then picked up speed, just like the No. 57 Milwaukee & St Paul Railway train done when it first pulled outa Chicago.

First off, the feds called up railroad people—the train engineers,

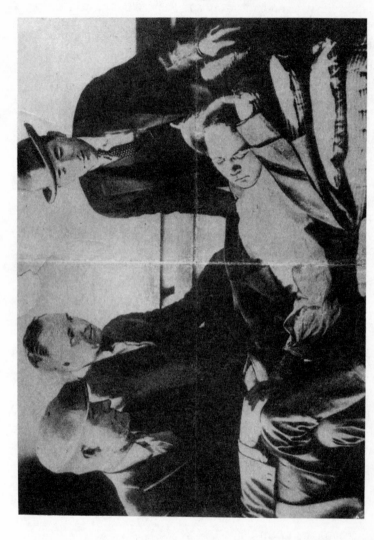

At the courthouse, Dock is on the stretcher. L. to R. Willis, Jess and Joe.

fireman, mail clerks, and such. And it was good to see so many people, all of 'em working people, that was honest. I believe that nearly all of 'em told it the way things really was, just like they seen it.

The railroad fireman—a Mister Ernest J. Dibble—told how Jess'd entertained him with windies and offered him a smoke and complained, "My God, ain't this a helluva way to make a living?"

"I think this was his first experience," that Mister Dibble said. "He just didn't seem like a criminal."

'Course, none of 'em knowed anything about how Murray or Fahy was hooked up with the job. That was up to my boys.

***

Joe was the first of our team to go up. His legs was so long it only took him about four steps to get from his seat to the stand. He was only twenty-two then (the papers called him the "kid" and the "baby"), but he'd filled out a lot—like I said before—and I thought he looked handsome. The federals had give him a nice brown suit and a blue tie.

I hoped to hell Joe would come through.

When the gov'ment lawyer started asking Joe questions, my little brother was polite as he could be, saying "yes sir" and "no sir." And his voice was only a little trembly, and only at the start of it. And he was straight with his testimony at first—that he'd met Murray and that Murray helped plot the job. He said he'd never met Fahy, but he'd heard about him, and that Murray had talked about getting all the inside information from a "postal inspector."

"Is Mister Murray in this courtroom?" the lawyer asked Joe.

"Oh yes, sir. He's that big one over there, that big fella."

Murray'd been dozing off in his chair that whole morning, his jaw dropped down into them two chins of his. But when Joe throwed a finger towards him, that old boy jerked up outa his chair and went to hollering: "I didn't have anything to do with this train thing and I'll bust every bone in anybody's body who says I did!"

I liked that 'cause I knowed the judge wouldn't.

I was right.

The judge was a man named Adam C. Cliffe with black horn-rim glasses. He pulled his glasses down to the tip of his nose and he shot Murray a look that coulda melted steel. "Now look here! You're going to get a square deal in this court, but if anything like this happens again, I won't accept excuses."

Murray's lawyer put his hand on Murray's shoulder and pushed him down. "Oh, your honor, he hasn't a bit of sense. Please excuse him this time."

'Course, all that yapping from Murray meant that his lawyer was gonna have to make us Newtons look like no-count liars, and that's exactly what he done—or tried to do. He couldn't shake Joe on the train details. Joe was airtight on them. But then that dirty lawyer throwed a twist in things.

"It's true, isn't it, Mister Newton, that at first you and your brother Jess disagreed in much of your stories about the dates in the planning of the robbery and such things. But since your arrest, you have met several times and agreed on the statements you are both making before this jury?"

Joe give a smile. "Yes, sir."

Damn! Wrong time to be honest! You could hear some titters and chuckles from the people in the courtroom. I looked over at the jury. A few of 'em raised their eyebrows. Then that defense lawyer started prancing around waving a cut-out story from some newspaper.

"The papers say, Mister Joe Newton, that you have a flapper girlfriend with a 'stunning head of bobbed red hair' who is 'crafty and cunning as a leopard.' They say you've been buying her fancy clothes for a year or so, and last year bought her a brand-new 1923 Studebaker. Is that true?"

Joe give another smile. "Yes, sir."

"Mister Newton, you bought her all these things long before this train robbery. What kind of work were you doing last year that you can buy a woman a car?"

Joe furrowed his brow. "I'm sorry, sir. I can't recall."

"Where did you get that money, Mister Newton?"

"I'm sorry, sir. I can't recall."

"Let me remind you that you're under oath, Mister Newton. Think hard."

"I'm sorry, sir. I can't recall."

That newspaper article had it right, about Joe's red-headed girlfriend. Fact is, Joe'd graduated from them "solid" Woolworth gals to a smooth article named Dorothy. But why in the hell couldn't he have flat-out lied and said he'd got his money from oil, like I always done?

The lawyer looked over at the jury box and smiled: "Isn't it strange, men of the jury, that Mister Joe Newton can remember so many details about the train robbery when he can't even remember what he was doing in nineteen and twenty-three?" He said, "Isn't it hard, men of the jury, to believe anything a man says when he has such a mixed-up memory?"

I seen a few men of the jury nod their heads.

***

If folks in the courtroom tittered when Joe walked off the stand, with them long legs, they tittered five times more when Jess walked on. Jess was all dressed up like a cowboy; a high-crowned white Stetson on his head and high-heel riding boots on his feet and a big, shiny silver Mex'kin belt buckle around his waist. He'd begged the federal lawyers to let him wear that get-up.

He swaggered on the way to the stand, and when he got on it, he set cross-legged and he swayed—real slow—back and fro, back and fro.

People in the courtroom was chuckling.

It didn't take me a second to see what he was doing.

He was drawling ever'thing so slow you could see the lawyers was wanting to reach inside his mouth and pull his words out. He said he'd been a Texas bronc-buster and butcher who'd give up snapping horses and cutting up chuck to mess with guns. And then he told the exact same train-robbing story Joe told—detail for detail. He said Murray was the one that first come up with "some good jobs around Chicago," and that Fahy was the one that'd got us the inside information.

"Can you point out Mister Fahy?" the lawyer asked.

"No sir. I heard all about him, but I never met him."

"How about Mister Murray?"

"Oh yeah. You can't miss him. Big one right there." This time Murray just hurrumphed.

I was wondering what dirty trick Murray's lawyer was gonna pull on the cross-exam. I didn't have long to find out. They'd figured they'd make Jess look like a no-count drunk that couldn't be trusted with nothing—stories *or* money.

"Mister Newton, is it true you took off to Mexico with $35,000 of the train loot?" the defense attorneys asked.

"Yessir, but I'm afraid it's dead and buried now."

"Money can't die, Mister Newton."

"I reckon it's just buried then."

The crowd laughed.

Jess laughed, too, and leaned back in his chair and told his escape story. He told the courtroom how he stopped off at a bootleg joint in San Antone on his way down to Mexico, and how he figured he'd better hide that $35,000. How he went to the bartender and said he was gonna meet a married lady out in the country and could that bartender drive him there for $100? How they took the bartender's old rattle-trap Model T, tied together with baling wire, and drove out into the woods.

"I buried most of the loot under a oak tree," Jess said, swaying back and fro in that witness chair. "I put three knife marks in it. Next day, it come to me I needed to hightail it to Mexico, so I go back to the bar and I says to the bartender: 'Here's another hundred dollars. Take me back where we was last night.' And the bartender says: 'OK, shure, where was that?' Well, my knees go to jelly right under me and I says, 'I got no idea. I was drunk.' And damn if that bartender don't look me straight in the face and says, 'Well, mister, I don't got no idea either. I was drunk too.' "

You could hear people laughing all over again, all over that courtroom. Even the judge give a little smile.

Jess looked out into the crowd. "This ain't a funny story, folks. I really did lose that money. And that's sad, sad, saaaad."

The only one that wasn't snickering was Murray's lawyer. He'd wanted to make Jess look sneaky. Jess just looked like a thick-headed old cowpoke.

I heard a man behind me say to the man next to him: "No wonder these birds got caught, they're not smarter'n that." But his friend said right back: "Don't you be fooled, Harry. It takes a shrewd fellow to pretend to be dumb like that and get away with it in front of all these lawyers."

***

Sucked-in Glasscock was the last one of our team to go up. The dirty, old louse! I could hardly stand to look at him walk to the stand, his hair all slicked back and his cheek twitching. If it wasn't for Glasscock, we'da all been millionaires!

Was he gonna mess things up again?

But before the lawyers went at him, something come down I wasn't expecting. The judge nodded his head over at a coupla of guards, and they put their hands on the ready at their pistols. And in opens the doors to the chambers. And in come two men holding what looks like a hospital stretcher. It's covered with a big white cotton blanket and there are lumps and bumps poking up all over.

The two men set the thing down on a table and one of 'em pulls the sheet offa the thing real slow.

The crowd in the courtroom gasped.

"This look familiar, Mister Glasscock?" the judge asked.

"Yessir."

"What is this?"

"I guess you could say it's part of the root of our evil. Yessir. The root of our evil."

There it was.

All the loot they'd dug up so far. Wide-mouth jugs stuffed with greenbacks. Fruit jars filled with loose diamonds and rubies, all a-glittering. A big white wicker basket overflowing with bonds.

The federal lawyer went over to it.

He pulled out a fist of loose greenbacks, and let 'em flutter down.

He pulled out a fist of bonds, and let 'em flutter down.

He pulled out a fist of diamonds and rubies, and let 'em plunk down.

"What we have here, gentleman of the jury, is one million, two-hundred and forty thousand dollars!" he said.

My eyes hurt.

The root of our evil?

That's what Pa'd called money right after Mister Pike kicked us offa his land back in Rising Star, when I was sixteen.

What would Pa've said if he seen that million dollars?

***

The whole time Glasscock was up there answering questions, my eyes kept flipping from that old boy to all that money.

God.

Glasscock started out alright.

"I've known Murray since 1917," he told the federal lawyer.

"We've broken bread a thousand times. In February of this year, he first suggested mail robbery to me. He said he could get the dope from a good friend. A Mister Frank Fahy."

When the prosecutor asked Glasscock to point out Murray, he done it without a hiccup.

I knowed he'd do that.

But when the federal lawyer asked if Glasscock had ever met Fahy, damn if he didn't say, "Of course."

And then he nodded his head and pointed.

"He's that little jug-headed man right over there."

Fahy near shot outa his chair. "I've never met that man in my life! He's a lying fool!"

Well, Glasscock was lying, alright. But he wasn't no fool. That morning, when the guards was leading us into the courtroom, I'd heard a whisper in my ear. It was Glasscock. "Which one's Fahy?"

"Jug-headed one on the left," I whispered back.

"Gotcha."

I could hardly believe it, how Glasscock jutted his finger out there and pointed plumb at Fahy. If I'da been in the jury, I'da believed they was bosom pals. The only thing was, Glasscock didn't stop there. He kept on going. He started talking about how he'd first met Fahy on a chilly day, setting on a box in a alley behind Jacobsen's Restaurant.

"The first time I met Mister Fahy," Glasscock said, "he flashed a badge at me and said, 'I'm a postal inspector.' I said what we wanted was good dope for robberies. And Fahy said, 'Oh, I can do that all right.' The second time I met him, Fahy told me the registered mail was all in the second car after the engine, and that the clerks had guns, but that they wouldn't shoot them. They didn't know how. Because he was in charge of gun-training."

I near shot out of my chair. That liar! That damn liar!

I was the one that'd planned the job, I was the one that learned all them things, and there Glasscock was setting up there, oily as his oiled hair, acting like he was the leader! But wasn't nothing I could do except keep my mouth shut. Then I looked over at the jury box, and damn if most of them men didn't look like they was buying ever'thing Glasscock said.

Well....

Well....

He was a damn liar. He was a damn good liar.

On the cross exam, the defense lawyers tried to make Glasscock look like a bad liar. But they had a hard time of it. "Why do you keep repeating my questions before answering them?" was about all they could say. "To think up something to say?"

The judge ordered them to take that offa the record.

***

It was the last piece of the trial that had me squirming the most.

Right before them two old louses—Murray and Fahy—went up, the federals put a coupla postal inspectors up on the stand to add a little fuel to their case agin 'em. They told about how they'd trailed Fahy after the robbery and tapped his telephone.

Still, it was pretty much gonna be our word agin Murray's and Fahy's.

Well, Murray grunted and huffed climbing up on that stand, the big strong lights in that courtroom shining off that stay-combed hair of his. And he spun his tale like nobody's business. Since ever'body knowed already he was a booze runner, that's exactly where he took the story.

"Yes, of course, I knew Mister Glasscock, and I'd arranged with him to haul some booze for me the night of June 12th. Mister Dock Newton was shot when he was trying to hijack my shipment. I hear he's a bit off, if you know what I mean. But the night of that holdup, I was visiting a nephew who'd been hit by an automobile. It was the Oak Park hospital, and I was there with my wife."

That liar!

Fahy blowed up to the stand, light-footed, and set with that rod-straight spine. His voice was a little trembly at first, but he kept to his story that he'd been framed, too. He bragged how he'd solved all the big train robberies up around Chicago in them past five years—the Pullman robbery, the Harvey robbery, the Grand Rapids robbery.

"It's the Eastern inspectors back in New York, they're the ones giving me the tumble for this jam. There's more framing on this case than any I've ever worked on," he said. "And why? Those Eastern inspectors wanta cover their hinies. They hire mail handlers without checking them out. It's a cinch for an ex-convict or a criminal to get a station job. And they're the birds who pulled off this Rondout job, some ex-con mail handlers."

Another liar!

But, as it come out, Fahy didn't "spring" no real surprises. I guess the only surprise was that there wasn't no surprises. He'd just been bluffing. And, nope, he couldn't prove one thing he'd said. All he could do was stand on his record. Only problem, so far as we was concerned, was that his record as a inspector was pretty damn good.

FORTY

I slept like a baby that whole night before the verdicts come in.

Why waste a good night's sleep? The rock'd been kicked off the hill, and there wasn't nothing I could do but stand back and watch where it rolled.

The verdicts for Fahy and Murray come in at 1:10 p.m.

They made both of 'em stand up. The judge read Murray's first. He was staring kinda funny at the judge. He had a smile on his face, but I knowed that smile. It was a dog-snarl smile. The jury found him guilty. He got the full 25 years. Fahy fell back into his chair when he heard that. He knowed he was gonna get the same thing. He did.

They practically had to carry him out of the courtroom.

Missus Fahy was standing there screaming: "He didn't have anything to do with that robbery! I'll wait for him!"

Crazy lady.

It was good, and it was bad. It meant the jury'd bought our story. It also meant the jury wasn't happy about the crime. Was Aldrich bluffing us?

The rest of us—me and my brothers and Glasscock—got our sentences next.

Before the judge give 'em to us, they took me and Jess and Joe and Glasscock outside the courtroom for "a breath of fresh air." They said they was waiting for something. They didn't tell us what. We waited for five minutes, then another five minutes, then another five minutes.

And then it come.

It come around the corner way on down the hallway. It was long, white and lumpy.

There was two big men a-carrying it, one of 'em on each end, and the closer them men come to us, the more I could hear they was panting like dogs. Joe looked at me and I looked at Joe, and Jess looked at me and I looked at Jess, and Glasscock looked at me and I glared at Glasscock, and then all of us looked back at what they was bringing.

"Jesus godamight!" I said.

With handcuffs on my arms and chains on my legs, I couldn't move more'n a few inches in any direction. But there wasn't nothing I wanted more in the whole world right then but to run up and throw my arms right on plumb around Dock.

In two minutes, they was right up on us.

When Dock seen us, he moved his head half a inch to the right. And I seen that his eyes lit up. But he wasn't saying nothing. I guess he couldn't say nothing. Still couldn't use his tongue. There was three big cotton pillows under his head and half his face was covered over with thick white cotton bandages.

But I was so happy to see that old boy I coulda shot right up to the moon!

Then I throwed my head back and went to laughing. Laughing like a hyena 'cause it hit me that there was six months of good, hard cussing stuck down in that bull-thick throat of Dock's! And when that old boy did get the use of that tongue back, well, BLOOEY!

Lord have mercy on whatever nurse was standing in the way of that blast!

***

Soon as they carried Dock up, a guard called us back into the chamber and made us stand in a line, right in front of him. Except for Dock. They let him lay.

They'd also let Louise into the sentencing, and she was setting behind us on a hard-back chair. Before the judge started, I turned around and caught her eye. I give her a smile, and she smiled back. But when we did that, my handcuffs felt tighter around my wrists, and my shackles cut into my ankles.

Then the judge begun: "I want to ask that all of you hold back from any show of emotion."

Nobody said nothing. What could we say? We didn't know what kinda emotions we was gonna have.

The judge squinted at each one of us, one by one, over his horn-rim glasses.

He started with Glasscock. "Mister Brentwood Glasscock, you

have prior convictions for assault and bank robbery. The court sentences you to the full twelve years."

Glasscock's head turned red. I guess he thought he'd get just a year or two for giving up all that loot. Crazy man! Don't he know that just because you don't have the money no more, don't mean you ain't wrong for having took it?

I smiled on the inside of me.

The judge turned to Dock. "Mister Dock Newton, the jury is sorry for your condition, but you were an escaped felon at the time of this crime and the court sentences you to twelve years."

Dock's eyes slammed shut.

Poor old Dock! He never did get a break.

The judge turned to Joe. "Mister Joe Newton, you are still a very young man and I suspect were under the influence of your older brothers. You have no prior convictions. I sentence you to three years."

Yeah! I liked that. So did Joe. He smiled and shuffled his legs.

The judge turned to Jess. "Mister Jess Newton, you have no prior convictions except for carrying whiskey in Texas. Your conduct in court has been congenial. Your conduct at the train robbery was congenial. The court sentences you to a year and a day."

Yippy-ti-yi-yo, git along little dogies!

Jess felt the same way. A Texas yell started to jump outa his mouth. He swallowed it. It come out like a hiccup.

I was last.

When the judge looked at me, he frowned. "Mister J. Willis Newton. Mister Newton, I've been a judge for many years, and I'm still not sure if criminals are made or born or both. If I had to pick one, I'd say they're born. But I do know that God has given you some gifts. If you'd have chosen another line of work, you might have become president of Ford Motor Company."

He paused for a second, like he wanted to let that one sink in. *President of the Ford Motor Company?*

Yeah. I mighta been if.... If what?

He banged his gavel. "Twelve years!"

I turned to look at Louise.

She nodded her head.

***

303

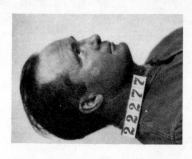

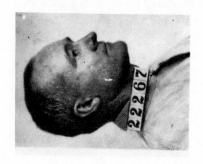
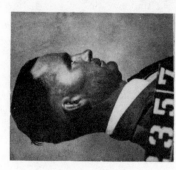

FBI photos of the convicts. L. to R. Top: Willis and Joe Bottom: Dock and Jess

304

Right before they led us away, a young man from the *Chicago Tribune* newspaper come in and asked if us Newtons would pose for a picture for him. He didn't want Glasscock. Just us Newtons. I think Glasscock was a little mad about that. He sucked in his cheeks and stood off to one side.

In all my crook days, I never did want my picture took. Almost ever' picture that ain't a mug shot before I went to the pen, you'd see the side of my face, or, better yet, the back of my head. But this time, I didn't care. "Hell yes, you can take our picture. Just give me a minute."

I motioned one of the guards to comb my hair and straighten my tie.

That picture run on December the tenth, nineteen and twenty-four.

I still got a yellow copy.

Under it they run these words: "WILD WEST BANDITS ON THEIR WAY TO PRISON."

Far as I know, it was the first picture—and the last picture—ever took of the four of us Newton Boys together. Except for poor old Dock, I thought we all looked real sharp.

EPILOGUE

It's now the spring of nineteen and seventy-seven. I never thought I'd live to be eighty-eight. Joe's still alive, too. He's seventy-six. Near ever'body else I've talked about is dead. Like I said way on back, I know some folks think the world'd be better off if I was dead, too. But I don't give a damn what they think.

I live now in Uvalde, that little town in the southwest part of Texas where I seen them singing Baptist orphans more'n sixty years ago, right before I robbed my first train with Red Farley. Uvalde's where Ma and Pa ended up their last days. Dock and Jess, too. Louise is buried here.

I like the weather, and there's good fishing in the Nueces River. And I like to mess with bees. Uvalde's got the best honey in the world, *huajilla*, that comes from them brush country flowers. Also, Mexico's not too far off, where you can get good whiskey at cut rate.

The sheriff here throws me in jail ever' so often, mostly when I drink too much, or one time when I pistol-whipped some old boy. But the sheriff's a nice, easy fella and good company. I call him Kid.

***

Louise died of heart trouble in nineteen and fifty-nine. We was together thirty-nine years before she passed on. Jess died of cancer of the lung in nineteen and sixty. He was seventy-three years old. Dock was eighty-three years old when he died in nineteen and seventy-four. Cancer, too. So me and Joe is the last of the Newton Boys.

***

Ever'body in Uvalde likes Joe. They tell him that what happened so long ago should be forgot. He owns a barbecue stand here and has a little ranch where he runs a few cattle. He's married to a woman named Mildred, a fine church-going woman who holds her head up high, and they have one son.

Me and Joe still got our differences. Even down to how we dress. I still dress like a big-city businessman: good suit, white shirt, necktie, narrow-brim hat (what Joe calls a "dude hat"). And I drive a high-power Cadillac. Joe went back to Western clothes: high-crowned, wide-brim Stetson, checkered shirt, gabardine pants, oiled cowboy boots. And he drives a pickup.

That little brother of mine is still horse-crazy. He rides a pinto cow horse called Old Paint. Except Joe ain't the cowboy he used to be. He's got that arthritis and nowadays he has to stand up on a chair before he can swing a leg over the saddle. Old Paint sometimes pitches when Joe gets on. It ain't real pitching, it's more like rocking. But Joe calls it pitching and he says he'd never have a horse that wouldn't pitch.

***

Somewhere along the way Joe got the idea that him and Old Paint 'r movie stars. So when Hollywood people make picture shows at a Wild West town that's down the road from here, Joe takes Old Paint over there in a trailer and gets a job for him and his horse. In "The Last Command," that picture about the Alamo, Joe played a Mex'kin lancer charging the Texans on Old Paint, and later on he played a Texan in buckskin shooting at hisself. 'Course, he didn't get nothing but extras' pay—scale for hisself and half-scale for Old Paint.

Goddammit, if them movie people had any sense they'd be making a picture show about me. And they'd hire me to play a big part so I could show 'em the way things really was. It burns me up like nobody's business when I hear all the to-do folks make over Bonnie and Clyde, the movie they made about 'em and all that other nonsense, when all them two silly kids ever done was shoot people and rob filling stations and little places like that. Hell, I bet they never had a thousand dollars in their lives!

***

I don't mix much with the people in Uvalde. When I get outa my car to go into a store downtown, some of 'em point at me and tell their kids, "There goes old Willis Newton, that bandit." And some years back, a old Texas lawman who lives in these parts said: "Willis Newton? That man is hard, clean through hard. And I don't think that old crook ever really retired."

How'd he know?

One thing nobody knowed was why I never robbed the bank in Uvalde. I'll let you in on that secret right here: I never robbed no banks in Uvalde because I needed some place to keep my money.

***

A preacher said to me once, "Ain't you at least ashamed for what you done? Don't you realize how many people you hurt?" "Look here, preacher," I said. "Nobody ever give me nothing but hell in my life, and I ain't done nothing I'm ashamed of." Joe says he is. He says the the biggest mistake he ever made in his life was to trade his spurs and chaps to become a bank robber. He'da made a good Baptist. But that's Joe, not me.

Now, there's some things I was *sorry* about. Like when that fool old coward, Frank Holloway, left $200,000 in the vault in Arma, Kansas. He said we had enough. Can you imagine a bank robber, or somebody in business, or anybody you know in this country, saying they got enough?

Why don't the preachers ask the politicians if they're sorry for lying and cheating and spending up ever'body else's money except their own? Why don't they ask the lawyers, the doctors, and the businessmen if they're sorry for skinning people 'ever chance they get?

Lemme tell you what I mean. One evening in Omaha back in nineteen and twenty, I drove my Studebaker up to a car-wash place and asked the colored man there if he'd slick me up. "Yessir," he said, all smiles and politeness. But when he finished he told me the charge would be a dollar. "A dollar?" I said. "They always done it here for fifty cents." "Yessir, you're right," the man said. "But it all starts up there in the White House and ever'body passes it on down. I gits you, so now you go git somebody else and pass it on." I paid the dollar.

What I didn't tell that car-wash man was that I was planning to do just what he said. I was on my way to Illinois to rob a bank.

***

308

As it come out, I only done four years and two months for that Rondout train robbery. I had what they call "good behavior." And when I walked outa the front gate of Leavenworth in nineteen and twenty-nine, Louise was standing right there, waiting for me with a taxi. Godamight! I never seen such a beautiful sight in my life. How come she loved me, and how come she waited for me, I can't say. Some people just love each other, I guess. Their natures match.

***

Some of what I done after Leavenworth was as wild as what I done before, but that ain't part of my story here. Most folks knowed me for the nightclubs I opened up in Tulsa: the Buckhorn Palace, the Music Box, the Bucket of Blood. The papers called me one of the city's "kingpin gamblers." That Prohibition was still on when I started, but even after the Repeal, them crazy Okies voted to keep the state dry. So I sold "imported" whiskey. Imported from Missouri.

My clubs was some of the busiest night spots in Tulsa. Stacks of people come to 'em! Stacks and stacks. Even Bonnie and Clyde showed up one time at my Buckhorn Palace. They'd just shot a sheriff over at Commerce, and they knowed about me through the underground, and they wanted me to hide 'em out. Well, I let 'em stay for a couple of nights in a little house I had out back. Only they wasn't nothing but two silly kids, and I knowed they was bound to get theirselves killed.

***

Altogether, in my life, I was in on eighty bank robberies, twenty before my brothers joined me and sixty afterwards. And I can remember ever' bank we robbed and the dates, and how much we got out of each of them. But robbing banks full-time like that, it was here and it was there...here and there.

'Course, some folks say I never did stop being a robber, even after I moved to Uvalde. And they say I didn't give up all the loot from that big Rondout train robbery. That I'd squirreled some away, and was always leaving town and coming back flush.

But how do they know?

***

I can tell you honest: I liked to pass out money as much as I liked to get it. I liked to help little people I knowed that was down on their luck. And I paid for Louise's boy, Lewis, to go to college. (Me and Lewis are close to this day. Only he lives in California, with his family.)

And I give my brothers Jess and Dock good jobs at good pay hauling whiskey for my Tulsa nightclubs. Except I wasn't always around to tame 'em and they went wild—drinking too much and shooting off guns. The laws called my Music Box "Tulsa's Number One Violence and Crime Hatchery." Jess and Dock just couldn't handle prosperity no more'n they could handle responsibility.

Louise was a diff'rent story. She kept the books for my clubs, and took up money at the door, and was just as much the boss as me. Sometimes, if I was outa town on business, she'd take to drinking and ride taxicabs around town and tip the drivers with her diamond rings. By then, I'd bought her diamonds for near ever' finger. I always had a devil of a time getting them taxi drivers to give me back them rings.

But Louise was true blue—stayed with me in good times, and bad.

Bad times come in nineteen and forty-nine when the competition among the gamblers in Oklahoma was turning into bloody wars, just like it had between them gangsters in Chicago. Somebody blowed up a nightclub near one of mine to bits with nitroglycerin and soon as the owner built it back up, BLOOEY! Somebody blowed it up again! There was folks that said I done both them blows.

One night, when I was standing in my bathroom in my underdrawers, a bullet from a .38 come a-whistling through the window. It ripped into my back, flied through my right lung, and come out my left collar bone.

Soon after I got out of the hospital, me and Louise moved down here to Uvalde. We bought us a big house, and I laid a row of silver dollars in a concrete walk right up to the front door.

***

First time in my life I ever thought about praying was in the year nineteen and fifty-nine when Louise got heart trouble and I thought she might die. I got down on my knees trying to pray. But

L. to R. Willis, Dock and Joe before Dock came out of retirement to attempt to rob the bank at Rowena.

I didn't know how.

***

Goddamn.

***

Poor old Dock!

In nineteen and sixty-eight, when he was seventy-six years old, he got it in his mind to break into a bank in Rowena, Texas. He got a friend to help him, but Dock, like always, showed poor judgment. A burglar alarm went off in the middle of it all, and a sheriff's posse showed up. Well, old Dock wouldn't surrender. For a half hour 'r more he shot it out with the laws. Then a deputy slipped into the back of the bank and black-jacked Dock from behind. By that time the posse had shot the bank full of holes with a tommy gun. A tommy gun agin Dock! The owner of that bank was mad as hell. "They didn't have to make it a battle, like in the movies," he said.

After that sock on the head, Dock's judgment got even worse. After he served eight months in a prison hospital, they sent him to a nursing home and he didn't try to rob no more banks.

There's some people that say I was driving getaway on that Rowena job. That I was setting in the alley in my Cadillac, waiting for Dock and his friend to get done in the bank, and that when all the shooting started, I hightailed it outa there. I woulda been eighty years old at the time. But how do they know?

***

Way I see it, lots of folks would've liked to do what the Newton Boys done—they just didn't have the guts, or they didn't know how. Hell, most folks couldn't rob a kitchen safe.

***

I don't rob banks no more. It's not because I'm too good. It's just because I'm too damn old. But I sure can rob them bee hives. I like that wild honey in the hives along the Nueces River. I'll see a bee taking nectar from a flower and I'll flop to the ground—even at eighty-eight I can get to the ground faster 'n a lot of young folks I know—and I'll skylight him and watch which way he heads for his hive. Most times, them wild bees have their hives in a hole in a old oak or a mesquite tree. If I can't get to where the honey is, I'll take a chain-saw out and just buzz that big old tree down and rob that hive. Some people in Uvalde are sore at me for cutting them trees, but how else could I get that honey?

Another thing I like to do is get drunk and drive my Cadillac down them long country roads around Uvalde. It's 340 horsepower, and I'll hit off helty-skelty, just like the Newton Boys done when we was making a getaway—only faster. Lots of times, I'll see a stream with pecan trees and sycamores and cypresses along the banks. And I'd like to get out and do some fishing. But most times, the ranchers have the gates all locked and that just burns me up. When I was a kid we could prowl 'n hunt ever'where.

Nowadays when I see a gate with a lock on it, I just boil over. I take my .45 thumb-buster out from the glove compartment and shoot the goddamn thing off.

***

Joe's got his pals, who raise hunting dogs, like he does, and at night they take them dogs out into the woods to chase foxes and coons. Most of the time, if I go anywhere, I go by myself.

***

Cotton, cotton, cotton. There's more around Uvalde now than there ever was before. This used to be nothing but cow and sheep-and-goat country. But now with water-pumps and sprinklers you can grow anything anywhere. The land is all plowed now with big gaso-line-powered tractors, six rows at a time! And the cotton is all picked with machines. Just one machine can pick as much cotton as forty people used to. Sometimes if I'm driving past a cotton field, I'll stop and hit down them middles and pick the fluffy, silky white puffs right-left, left-right, right-left. I stuff it in a sack to bring home to neighbor kids who never picked a boll of cotton in their lives. They don't even know what cotton feels like.

Pa? Crazy old Pa! I still can't get him outa my head, even after all these years. Always moving from farm to farm, always hunting for honey ponds and fritter trees. For God's Country. Here and there, here and there. Pa and Ma never lived together again after they split up. But I guess there musta still been something between 'em because later on, the old man moved into a little house only a few blocks from where Ma lived. He'd come over to her house for meals, and in fact, he was waiting on her front porch for supper one night when he keeled over and dropped dead. Had a heart attack.

Ma died two years later of pneumonia.

Joe always said I was too hard on Pa, that he was a good man. But we either planted too early 'r too late. And Pa always looked like he was afraid to nose that plow-point down too deep, for fear the mules'd give out and maybe lay down and die. Before the ground was even busted, much less planted!

By God, them mules sweated when I took a-hold of that plow. I wasn't gonna plow shallow—not even if the mules did drop dead. And I sweated just as much as the mules did. Back in them days, you walked behind a old Georgia stock plow. And there was something about them walking plows that I liked, even if I didn't wanta spend my life following no mule's ass. You had to guide 'em with your hands— and how straight a row you plowed, and how deep or how shallow, said something about what kind of farmer you was. And what kind of a man you was.

***

'Course, you didn't just plow once, and plant your seed, then wait for the cotton. When the plants come up green and strong and pretty— that is, if you had enough rain and at the right time—you chopped them weeds out with hand hoes or cut 'em down with a heel-sweep plow. That heel-sweep plow didn't just cut down the weeds, it piled more dirt on the plants, and from then on you could watch the little green shoots grow up and spread out into big, leafy plants with big, green bolls. And then there come a point when you could say your crop was laid by--that it was far enough along that even weeds could- n't hurt it no more....and you could do other things like mend harness or chop stove wood...until one day, blooey!, them bolls exploded into

Willis in his eighties. He was feisty and unrepentent right up until the day he died

big puffs of white like somebody'd put a shot of nitro inside.

I guess that's the way I feel right now. The crop's been laid by, not even weeds can do it no more harm.

Except there ain't no cotton to pick, and Louise is gone.

***

What'll happen to me after I die, I don't know. I think more about what's gonna happen to this country in the years ahead. Seems like in the years before the first World War, families and neighbors helped each other more. Nowadays, it's ever'body for hisself. Ever'where I look it's snatch and grab, snatch and grab, snatch and grab. Like Ma said, that's why you gotta have laws and the Bible. I remember one of Ma's Bible stories where things got so bad that God destroyed the whole world and had to start things all over again.

Maybe this time God will just let people destroy theirselves.

Whatever happens I won't be alive to see it. Ever'body who's born has only so much time on this Earth. I think my time is just about up. I can tell. For the first time in my life I been feeling tired.

***

Goddamn.

THE STORY AFTER THE STORY
by Claude Stanush

J. "Willis" Newton died in the Northeast Baptist hospital in San Antonio on August 22, 1979. He was ninety years old. It was an irony of fate that his last days were spent in a Baptist institution.

Willis had lived as an outlaw, and he died as one. When I visited him in the hospital in his last weeks, he cussed out the doctors, saying they didn't know what was wrong with him, and asked me if I would buy him a large bottle of mineral oil. When I did, he tipped it over and drank it all down, saying from then on, he was going to be his own doctor. "This'll clean me out," he said.

So far as I know, nobody else visited him in the hospital, not even his brother Joe. I was with him the evening of August 22. When I left, I touched him on his hands, which were crossed on his chest. He didn't say anything, but there was a searching look in his eyes.

He died later that night, alone.

***

After a funeral service at the Methodist church in Uvalde, Willis was buried in the family plot in the Uvalde Cemetery alongside his wife, Louise, and only a few feet away from the graves of Pa and Ma Newton and his brothers Jess and Tull and Dock. There was no eulogy preached at the service. What could the minister say about Willis? He only read lines from the Bible.

> *O give thanks unto the Lord; for He is good: for His mercy*
> *endureth forever.*
> *To Him that by wisdom made the heavens: for His mercy*
> *endureth forever.*
> *To Him which led His people through the wilderness:*
> *for His mercy endureth forever.*

To Him which smote great kings...

I have seen all the works that are done under the sun;
    And, behold, all is vanity;
For that which befalleth the sons of men befalleth
beasts; even one thing befalleth them: as the
    one dieth, so dieth the other; yea, they have all
    one breath;
Then shall the dust return to the earth as it was: and
    the spirit shall return unto God who gave it;
Vanity of vanities, saith the preacher; all is vanity.

AUTHORS' NOTES

ALL HONEST MEN is a biographical novel, firmly rooted in fact, which developed after many years of personal relationships with J. Willis Newton and Joe Newton.

Source material came from taped interviews by Claude Stanush with Willis Newton and Joe Newton at Paisano Ranch near Austin, Texas, in 1973.

Also, from taped interviews by Claude Stanush and David Middleton with Willis Newton and Joe Newton at Trinity University in San Antonio, Texas, in 1974.

Also, from conversations between Claude Stanush and Willis Newton during the years 1973 to 1979, and between Claude Stanush and Joe Newton from 1973 to 1989.

Also, interviews by Michele Stanush with Sheriff Kenneth Kelley of Uvalde, Texas, who knew all four Newton Boys and periodically put them in jail (with the exception of Joe, who had returned to his law-abiding ways).

Also, interviews by Michele Stanush with residents of Tulsa, Oklahoma, who knew Willis and Louise Newton during Willis' nightclub years in the 1930s and '40s.

Also, from police records, newspaper accounts, and historical documents describing the activities of the Newton Boys and their accomplices, many provided by Clark Lee Walker, Keith Fletcher, Michele Stanush, and Ashley Parrish.

Also from interviews with experts to check references to: cotton (Thad Sitton); guns (Pat Stanush); bronc busting (Mark Sharp); trains (Ben Sargent); history of Smackover, Arkansas (Don Lambert); history of Texas prisons (Dr. Robert Pierce); prison hounds (Walker County Sheriff Victor Graham); and the history of Arma, Kansas (Christie Wilson).

We gleaned insight into the era from many books, but want to make special mention of *Booger Red, World Champion Cowboy*, by Charlsie Poe.

On a personal note, we wish to give particular thanks to Rick Pappas for his untiring and invaluable support of the book. And thanks to David Middleton for his help and for the photograph of Willis Newton as an old man.

For critical reading of the text, we thank Barbara Evans Stanush, who gave a poet's insight into the language and flow of the story. (She also cooked mustard greens for Willis.) Alex Nixon, with his unerring eye for drama and depth, provided key suggestions. Great thanks also to Bob Banta, Dr. John Edens, Julie Stanush, Pamela Stanush Edens and Margaret Rambie. And finally, to Janneka Hannay, who, after reading an early draft, urged us to "let the wild ponies loose."